Experimentalist Constitutions

HARVARD EAST ASIAN MONOGRAPH SERIES 472

Experimentalist Constitutions

Subnational Policy Innovations
in China, India, and the United States

Yueduan Wang

Published by the Harvard University Asia Center
Distributed by Harvard University Press
Cambridge (Massachusetts) and London 2024

Published by the Harvard University Asia Center, Cambridge, MA 02138

The Harvard University Asia Center publishes a monograph series and, in coordination with the Fairbank Center for Chinese Studies, the Korea Institute, the Reischauer Institute of Japanese Studies, and other faculties and institutes, administers research projects designed to further scholarly understanding of China, Japan, Korea, Vietnam, and other Asian countries. The Center also sponsors projects addressing multidisciplinary and regional issues in Asia.

The publication of this book receives financial support from the East Asian Legal Studies program at Harvard Law School, the Institute of Public Governance at Peking University, and the Fundamental Research Funds for the Central Universities.

Library of Congress Cataloging-in-Publication Data

Names: Wang, Yueduan, 1987– author.
Title: Experimentalist constitutions : subnational policy innovations in China, India, and the United States / Yueduan Wang.
Description: Cambridge, Massachusetts : Harvard University Asia Center, 2024. | Series: Harvard east Asian monograph series; 472 | Includes bibliographical references and index.
Identifiers: LCCN 2023031954 | ISBN 9780674295896 (hardcover)
Subjects: LCSH: Constitutional law—China. | Constitutional law—India. | Constitutional law—United States. | Subnational governments—China. | Subnational governments—India. | Subnational government—United States. | Decentralization in government—Law and legislation—China. | Decentralization in government—Law and legislation—India. | Decentralization in government—Law and legislation—United States.
Classification: LCC K3165 .W375 2024 | DDC 342/.04—dc23/eng/20230928
LC record available at https://lccn.loc.gov/2023031954

Index by Kate Mertes

♾ Printed on acid-free paper
Printed in the United States of America

To my parents

Contents

Preface

This book is a testament to my love for travel. Although it is not an empirical study like many of my later projects (which seriously blurred the line between academic inquiry and wanderlust), its theme—a cross-national study of subnational innovation—was largely inspired by the diversity of people and wonders across several great civilizations and within each one of them. In particular, the three modern case studies—on civil society policy in China, Hindu nationalism in India, and Obamacare in the United States—were all directly stimulated by my travels within these countries. In fact, I wrote a substantial portion of the book during my many, many flights, partly to pass the unbearably long hours in economy class.

My study of experimentalist constitutions started as a small side project in 2013, three years before I started my academic doctoral program. At the time, I was continually fascinated by the various high-profile political experiments launched by colorful politicians vying for ultimate power—most notably the Chongqing Model and its disgraced sponsor, Bo Xilai.[1] This prompted me to write about how the law and politics of the party-state enabled such endeavors and how this experimentalist mechanism compares to those in democratic settings. By the time I finalized the draft and submitted it as my doctoral dissertation in 2021, however, Chinese politics had changed quite dramatically.

---

1. The Chongqing Model signifies an urban development strategy that was implemented in the Chinese municipality of Chongqing during the tenure of its former Party Secretary, Bo Xilai. It integrated components of state-led capitalism and social welfare initiatives to drive economic growth and enhance living standards, while concurrently strengthening political control and advocating Maoist ideologies.

Following the Xi Jinping administration's sweeping centralization campaign, many subnational experiments ground to a halt, replaced by uniform national directives. Indeed, several of the protagonists in the Chinese case studies have been either arrested on corruption charges or sidelined to political obscurity. What, then, is the point—beyond satisfying curiosity about recent historical events—of studying the process of policy experimentation?

This is where I put on my lawyer hat: Politicians may come and go, but constitutions stay (mostly) the same—even in countries without formally enforceable constitutional law. A core argument of this book is that subnational policy experimentation is produced by the dynamic interaction between partisan/factional politics and a constitutional system. China's factional landscape changed rapidly in the past decade, as it has multiple times during its seventy-plus years of communist rule. On the other hand, China's center-local constitutional structure, guided by Mao Zedong's famed Two Initiatives (两个积极性) principle, has remained surprisingly resilient since the Reform and Opening. Such resilience means that though subnational innovations can be suspended or quarantined (as they were between 1989 and 1992), their reemergence likely requires no more than a change of political wind, and such changes have always been common in China.

* * *

Writing this book has been a most wonderful journey that was only made possible by the many people who traveled alongside me. First and foremost, my family was my greatest support during this long process. Without them, I would not have entered academia at all, much less finished this study. In particular, much of the credit for this book belongs to my parents. Beyond their greatly valuable example as fellow scholars, their unrelenting love and backing encourage me to pursue my passions—including my urge to see and understand more of this big and beautiful world. My grandparents, aunts, uncles, and cousins on both sides of the Pacific have also offered unconditional help and care throughout the years. Though I have spent most of my adult life on foreign soil, my family always makes me feel at home.

I would also like to express my deepest gratitude to my mentors, who had to endure the same troublesome student through two consecutive doctoral programs. As the main supervisors of this project, professors Vicki Jackson and William Alford spent the better part of a decade as my most patient and caring teachers. Their rigorous training and deep insights are the only reason this book ever saw the light of day. I am also thoroughly indebted to professors Elizabeth Perry and Michael Klarman, whose many brilliant reading sessions were continual sources of inspiration as I wrote this manuscript. More importantly, these four have demonstrated to me in the most vivid way possible what it means to be a good researcher and educator—a basic yet exceedingly high bar that I will strive to meet for the rest of my career.

Of course, there are you, my dear friends. You adventured into a desert with me without a functioning GPS, were stranded overnight on an island with me because I forgot to check the ferry schedule, got so intoxicated with me that we barely made it back to the hotel, and offered to stay behind with me in a foreign airport when I lost my passport. Don't get me wrong—I probably could have finished the book without you. But it would not have been a journey worth taking regardless of where it led. I might one day outgrow this book, but it will always remain special to me because I wrote it with you by my side.

Abbreviations

ACA	Patient Protection and Affordable Care Act, the United States
AQMP	Air Quality Management Plan, California, the United States
BJP	Bharatiya Janata Party, India
CAA	Clean Air Act, the United States
CCP	Chinese Communist Party
CPI	Communist Party of India
CPIM	Communist Party of India (Marxist)
EPA	Environmental Protection Agency, the United States
FC	Finance Commission, India
FPL	federal poverty line, the United States
LEV	Low-Emission Vehicle program, California, the United States
MGR	M. G. Ramachandran
NAAQS	National Ambient Air Quality Standards, the United States
NAWSA	National American Woman Suffrage Association
NFIB	National Federation of Independent Business, the United States
NGO	nongovernmental organization
NLEV	National Light Emission Vehicle program, the United States

NPC	National People's Congress, China
NP-NSPE	National Programme for Nutrition Support to Primary Education, India
NWP	National Woman's Party, the United States
NWSA	National Woman Suffrage Association, the United States.
OTC	Ozone Transport Commission, the United States
PC	Planning Commission, India
PIL	public interest litigation
PUCL	People's Union for Civil Liberties, India
RTF	right to food movement, India
SC	Scheduled Castes, India
SCAQMD	South Coast Air Quality Management District, California, the United States
SEZ	Special Economic Zone, China
SIP	state implementation plan, the United States
ST	Scheduled Tribes, India
UPA	United Progressive Alliance, India
VHP	Vishva Hindu Parishad, India
ZEV	zero-emission vehicle

Introduction

> It is one of the happy incidents of the federal system that a
> single courageous State may, if its citizens choose, serve
> as a laboratory; and try novel social and economic experi-
> ments without risk to the rest of the country.
> —Louis Brandeis[1]

China's rise as a global superpower after the Cultural Revolution has
been characterized by adopting ideas and practices often associated with—though not exclusive to—Western democracies, such as
marketization, civil society, and modernized legal systems. In this
regard, the Chinese regime is not that different from various other
twentieth-century communist and/or authoritarian governments,
whose partial subscription to the Western model contributed to their
downfall during the third wave of democratization and the color revolutions. What sets China apart is its ability to turn these potential
agents of regime change into building blocks of the authoritarian state.
This is a process of continuous innovation, through which numerous
unfamiliar ideas and practices are introduced, tested, abandoned, ad-
justed, and assimilated by the party-state. It has resulted in a regime
whose institutions and strategies continuously evolve to meet new

---

1. New State Ice Co. v. Liebmann, 285 U.S. 262 (1932) at 311.

challenges, while its one-party dominance over the country is kept relatively constant. The question is: How does it do it?

The secret—at least part of it—lies in Justice Louis Brandeis's formula of federal laboratories. Like the United States, China has frequently utilized subnational experiments to test new institutions and ideas without endangering the entire regime. This pattern has been directly responsible for some of China's most critical transformations during the past four decades, including its decollectivization of agriculture and introduction of the market mechanism—two reforms directly responsible for the communist country's almost miraculous economic rise. Although most experiments do not become national policies, many nevertheless have resulted in policies that address local needs and provide inspiration for other government jurisdictions.

China's experience seemingly attests to the universal appeal of experimentalism, proving that subnational policy laboratories are not exclusive to established federal democracies, such as the United States, and can work well for developing, authoritarian, and formally unitary states. However, beyond such superficial universality lie many unanswered questions. For example, if China is a genuinely unitary state—as its constitutional law seems to suggest—why do its subnational units have the authority to conduct such bold (sometimes even illegal) experiments? Why would subnational leaders accept the risk of experimentation when no voters pressure them to do so? More generally, do China's policy innovations result purely from ad hoc decision-making by unconstrained and arbitrary autocrats, or do the experiments—like their U.S. counterparts—emerge from institutionalized mechanisms that semiconsistently produce policy innovations?

By answering these questions, the study primarily aims to contribute to two related fields: comparative constitutional law and China studies. Along with the surge in political science scholarship on nondemocratic regimes, there has been a significant increase in studies of authoritarian and semiauthoritarian constitutions since the turn of the century.[2] Scholars note that while authoritarian constitutions are often little more than shams, they can serve important purposes, such as

2. For example, Moustafa, *Struggle for Constitutional Power*; Belge, "Friends of the Court"; Landau, "Abusive Constitutionalism."

facilitating foreign investment, legitimizing nondemocratic rule, coordinating elite politics, and signaling policy priorities.[3] For instance, Tushnet's seminal piece on authoritarian constitutionalism argues that Singapore's constitutional system—including its regular elections, sophisticated judiciary, and draconian libel rules—helps the autocratic regime improve state governance and co-opt its rivals without real risk to its political dominance.[4] However, little attention has been paid to how authoritarian constitutions can be utilized as mechanisms of policy and institutional innovation like their democratic counterparts. This omission is particularly problematic given that many such regimes' survival hinges on their ability to quickly adapt to the constantly changing political, economic, and social landscapes. This study aims to fill this gap by systematically exploring the relationship between an authoritarian constitution—especially its center-local structure—and policy experimentation.

Moreover, despite the increasing scholarly interest in authoritarian constitutions, comparisons between different regime types remain rare. Tamil Moustafa points out that "the once hard-and-fast distinction between democratic and authoritarian polities is increasingly blurred . . . Yet one observes that there is very little cross-fertilization" in comparative constitutional studies.[5] This study answers this call for cross-regime constitutional analysis by comparing the respective advantages and disadvantages of the constitutions of China, India, and the United States in enabling subnational experimentalism. This is done by exploring the evolution and functioning of these three constitutional systems (rather than just their written texts) through a series of case studies. In particular, the study draws a parallel between partisan politics under electoral democracy and factional politics under authoritarianism, enabling a comparison of how key political actors—along with others such as courts and civil society—behave under different center-local constitutional structures.

This analysis also offers a distinct comparative law perspective to the study of China's long experimentalist tradition and more broadly,

---

3. Ginsburg and Simpser, "Introduction."
4. Tushnet, "Authoritarian Constitutionalism."
5. Moustafa, "Law and Courts," 294–95.

provides insights on the relative strengths and pitfalls of the party-state's developmental model. Most earlier works on China's subnational innovations comprise single-country studies that focus on the histor-ical, political, or economic aspects of the phenomenon.[6] This compar-ative law study on the matter thus offers a new take on the constitutional mechanism underlying the experiments, with a special focus on the interplay between the legal/structural and partisan/factional elements. Such a perspective has become increasingly relevant as the party-state has moved toward greater institutionalization in certain spheres under the banner of "law-based governance."[7] In particular, this study pro-vides a framework for analyzing the recent centralization reforms under the reign of Xi Jinping, which have had profound implications for subnational policy experimentation and more generally, for China's developmental model.

Comparison and Case Selection

Before proceeding with the comparative study, it is necessary to understand what China's experimentation is being compared to. What exactly are federal laboratories? Almost a century has passed since Brandeis popularized the term in his famous dissent, and many aspects of contemporary U.S. constitutional politics—including how the federal system functions—would be nearly unrecognizable to his contempo-raries. The federal laboratories have undergone significant changes, which calls for a careful re-examination of the concept. For example, did the federal government's exponential expansion after the New Deal suppress or facilitate the states' ability to generate new policies? How does the intensifying polarization between the Democratic and Repub-lican parties since the 1990s affect the states' incentives (which are roughly split between the two major parties) to innovate and adopt

    6. For example, Heilmann, "Policy-Making through Experimentation"; Montinola, Qian, and Weingast, "Federalism, Chinese Style"; Cai and Treisman, "Did Government Decentralization Cause China's Economic Miracle?"; Tsai and Dean, "Experimentation under Hierarchy"; Teets and Hurst, *Local Governance Innovation*.
    7. Zhang and Ginsburg, "China's Turn toward Law."

others' innovations? Without an up-to-date understanding of such issues, which are critical to the laboratories' operation, it is impossible to draw informed comparisons with other countries.

Besides these changes in the U.S. system, an equally—if not more—significant development is India's establishment of the largest federal democracy. With the end of colonialism in the period during and after World War II, several newly independent countries emerged. Among them, India holds particular promise as a comparison with the United States and China in subnational experimentalism. All three countries have huge landmasses, large populations, and significant diversity among their respective subnational units, thus providing fertile grounds for experimentalism. Like the United States, India has a mostly functioning federal democracy. However, unlike the United States, it faces numerous third-world problems, such as widespread poverty and poor government responsiveness—problems that it often seeks to solve through policy experimentation. Although India and China share many pressing issues typical of developing countries, the two have drastically different forms of government. India is thus a "bridge" between the two divergent superpowers. In the roughest sense, India is simultaneously a developing-country version of the United States and a democratic version of China in the context of experimentalism. Comparing the three thus offers the opportunity to explore the functioning of policy laboratories across varying forms and contexts, which may shed light on the pros and cons of the democratic versus authoritarian models. As such, this study aims to provide both a thick description of experimentalism and limited causal inferences on the subject.[8]

---

8. Ran Hirschl divides comparative legal studies into four categories, including "(1) freestanding, single-country studies mistakenly characterized as comparative . . . (2) comparative reference aimed at self-reflection through analogy, distinction, and contrast; (3) comparative research aimed at generating 'thick' concepts and thinking tools through multi-faceted descriptions; and (4) studies that draw upon controlled comparison and inference-oriented case selection principles in order to assess change, explain dynamics, and make inferences about cause and effect through systematic case selection and analysis of data." This study falls somewhere between the last two categories, though it is more limited in terms of making casual inferences due to the vast differences among the three countries on the subject of experimentalism. Hirschl, "Question of Case Selection," 126.

These objectives are served by selecting appropriate case studies from each country. As stated earlier, the study's general goal is to contrast China's approach to experimentation with the democratic federal laboratories. Both the U.S. and India case studies serve to provide examples of the latter, but their roles are somewhat different. Since the United States is the prototypical example, it is helpful to choose cases that show how the concept has worked and evolved in its original context to provide a baseline for comparison. India, by contrast, is the bridge between the prototypical U.S. model and China's authoritarian model, with the latter being mostly contemporary (since the end of the Cultural Revolution in the 1970s). The chosen U.S. cases, therefore, cover an extended period (from the nineteenth century to the 2010s), as they are used to illustrate the laboratories' historical evolution within the oldest federal system. In contrast, the chosen Indian cases (which span the early 1980s to the 2010s) are from roughly the same era as the Chinese cases (late 1970s to early 2010s), thereby providing a more direct comparison between the democratic and authoritarian models.

Also important was determining what types of experiments to include as case studies. One option was to select the same types of policy innovations—such as economic development or social welfare— for each country, which would make the cases easier to compare. However, this approach would likely mask a critical difference between the democratic and authoritarian experimental models: They tend to produce very different types of experiments. As will be elaborated in later chapters, China's top-down accountability structure gives the central government and factional patrons strong influence over the general agendas of subnational experimentation. This means the focus of subnational experiments in a given period often corresponds to the center's policy priorities, such as economic development in the 1980s and social stability in the 2000s. In contrast, the constant pressure of competitive elections in federal democracies, such as India and the United States, encourages elected officials to closely tailor subnational experiments to the diverse demands of local constituencies and interest groups. Consequently, democratic models produce much more varied—and at times populist—policy innovations, ranging from women's suffrage to clean aid in the United States and from free lunch for schoolchildren to Hindu nationalism in

India. The case selection reflects this contrast between the democratic and authoritarian models, which allows for a more holistic understanding of the different experimentalist approaches and thus facilitates more comprehensive comparisons.

It is also important to clarify the specific criteria used to select experiments for each country. In general, the cases were selected because they were significant subnational policy innovations that successfully addressed an important policy issue shared by other subnational jurisdictions or the nation as a whole. As Brandeis suggested, the purpose of subnational laboratories is to "try novel social and economic experiments without risk to the rest of the country"— meaning that the experimental process should have the potential to generate useful information for other subnational governments and the central government. Therefore, this study only selected experiments that addressed shared policy concerns, allowing analysis of how these innovations spread to other jurisdictions, whether through voluntary peer-to-peer learning, scale-up by the central government, or some combination of the two. The innovations also had to be significant for two reasons. First, as previously mentioned, this study mainly examines a constitutional system's ability to generate and diffuse important and transformative policies, which is crucial to the system's resilience. Second, significant cases usually provide more material for analyzing experimenters' motivations and tracking innovations' diffusions, both of which are crucial to understanding the experimental process.

Federal Laboratories: An American Concept

The concept of federal laboratories was popularized by U.S. Supreme Court Justice Louis Brandeis in his famous dissent in *New State Ice Co. v. Liebmann*.[9] The case concerned the constitutionality of an Oklahoma law requiring ice companies to obtain a license before conducting business. The state's legislature determined that the manufacture, sale, and distribution of ice was a public business that required a license to operate. The majority of the Court struck down the statute, ruling that

9. New State Ice Co. v. Liebmann, 285 U.S. 262 (1932) (Brandeis, J., dissenting).

it is beyond the power of a state, "under the guise of protecting the public, arbitrarily to interfere with private business."[10] In his dissenting opinion, Justice Brandeis voiced his support for Oklahoma's right to experiment with new ways to regulate economic activities, reasoning that

> To stay experimentation in things social and economic is a grave responsibility. Denial of the right to experiment may be fraught with serious consequences to the Nation. It is one of the happy incidents of the federal system that a single courageous State may, if its citizens choose, serve as a laboratory; and try novel social and economic experiments without risk to the rest of the country. This Court has the power to prevent an experiment . . . But in the exercise of this high power, we must be ever on our guard, lest we erect our prejudices into legal principles. If we would guide by the light of reason, we must let our minds be bold.[11]

Since this dissent, the idea of federal laboratories has become a frequently cited virtue of U.S. federalism. For example, in Justice Anthony Kennedy's concurring opinion in *United States v. Lopez*, he cited *New State Ice Co. v. Liebmann* to support his position that Congress exceeded its powers when regulating the carrying of handguns in schools.[12] Kennedy reasoned that because there was no agreement on how best to deter students from carrying guns, "the States may perform their role as laboratories for experimentation to devise various solutions where the best solution is far from clear."[13] A similar rationale—that federalism encourages policy experimentation by the states—has been widely cited by liberal and conservative judges alike in their decisions and dissents.[14] However, the courts rarely endeavor to explore

---

10. *Id.* at 285.

11. *Id.* at 311.

12. United States v. Lopez, 514 U.S. 549 (1995) (Kennedy, J., concurring).

13. *Id.* at 581.

14. See, e.g., Oregon v. Ice, 555 U.S. 160 (2009) at 171 (Ginsburg, J., writing for the Court); Boy Scouts of Am. v. Dale, 530 U.S. 640 (2000) at 664 (Stevens, J., dissenting); Arizona v. Evans, 514 U.S. 1 (1995) at 8 (Rehnquist, C.J., writing for the Court); Chandler v. Florida, 449 U.S. 560 (1981) at 579 (Burger, C.J., writing for the Court); Reeves v. Stake, 447 U.S. 429 (1980) at 441 (Blackmun, J., writing for the Court); Whalen v. Roe, 429 U.S.

the conditions that allow the states to fulfill their experimenter role. Instead, they seem to assume that "experimentalism will automatically emerge from federalist governance and that the locus of experimentalism will be the states."[15]

Scholars, however, have made more serious attempts to identify the exact mechanisms that allow subnational laboratories to flourish. For example, in his pioneering 1969 article, Jack Walker describes a tree-shaped pattern of policy innovation and diffusion in the United States. According to Walker, states like New York, Massachusetts, California, and Michigan are more likely to innovate due to their size, wealth, and level of industrialization; each of these states has a group of proximate follower states that tend to adopt programs only after these pioneers.[16] Andrew Karch finds that this peer-to-peer diffusion is often facilitated by interstate communication mechanisms that provide state legislators with useful information about policy innovations in other states, such as the Council of State Governments and various professional associations.[17] Moreover, Keith Boeckelman finds that many state innovations, especially those concerning redistributive policies, considerably influence federal legislation since states "seek to nationalize policy in areas where state action entails spillovers."[18] However, Susan Rose-Ackerman famously questions whether, as a theoretical matter, U.S. federalism provides sufficient incentive for state governments to conduct policy experiments. According to Rose-Ackerman, because the U.S. federal system does not compensate state policymakers for the valuable information they provide to other actors when they experiment with new policies (i.e., the positive externality problem), states generally conduct fewer experiments than optimal.[19]

589 (1977) at 597 & n.20 (Stevens, J., writing for the Court); San Antonio Indep. Sch. Dist. v. Rodriguez, 411 U.S. 1 (1973) at 49–50 (Powell, J., writing for the Court); Fay v. New York, 332 U.S. 261 (1947) at 296 (Jackson, J., writing for the Court).

15. Wiseman and Owen, "Federal Laboratories of Democracy," 1130.

16. Walker, "Diffusion of Innovations," 892–93.

17. Karch, *Democratic Laboratories*, 105–43.

18. Boeckelman, "Influence of States," 372.

19. Rose-Ackerman, "Risk Taking and Reelection"; see also Strumpf, "Does Government Decentralization Increase Policy Innovation?," 208.

Rose-Ackerman's theoretical account is complicated by the active role of the federal government, especially since the New Deal.[20] For example, Wallace Oates observes that instead of relying entirely on states to come up with new ideas, the federal government may provide general inspiration or frameworks within which states can develop their own programs.[21] As an example, Oates presents the 1977 Amendments to the Clean Air Act, under which states were allowed to design and implement their own systems of "emissions offsets."[22] The amendments led to various emissions trading systems across states, proving the effectiveness of the new mechanism for achieving environmental objectives and ultimately resulting in the national adoption of an emissions trading program.[23] In addition to encouraging state innovation, the federal government sometimes facilitates the spread of such innovations. For example, Susan Welch and Kay Thompson report that the federal government often uses conditional grants to induce states to follow other states' new policies.[24]

In their article "A Constitution of Democratic Experimentalism," Charles Dorf and Michael Sabel go a step further, making an influential proposal that tightly integrates experimentalism with a strong version of cooperative federalism.[25] Democratic experimentalism, as defined in the article, calls for a constitutional arrangement under which "the central government affords broad discretion to local administrative units but measures and assesses their performance in ways designed to induce continuous learning and revision of standards."[26] Under such an arrangement, Congress has the power to "authorize, finance, and, if necessary, withdraw national support for state and local experimentation," with the condition that the local governments receiving such support will stick to the "general purposes as Congress has determined"

---

20. See, e.g., Boyd and Carlson, "Accidents of Federalism"; Lowry, *Dimensions of Federalisms*.

21. Oates, "On the Evolution of Fiscal Federalism," 327–28; see also Karch, *Democratic Laboratories*, 67–103.

22. Oates, "On the Evolution of Fiscal Federalism," 327–28.

23. Oates, "On the Evolution of Fiscal Federalism," 327–28.

24. Welch and Thompson, "Impact of Federal Incentives," 715.

25. See generally Dorf and Sabel, "Constitution of Democratic Experimentalism."

26. Sabel and Simon, "Minimalism and Experimentalism," 53.

and "subject their activities to the corresponding measurement."[27] The federal agencies set and ensure compliance with specific national objectives via best-practice performance standards based on information gathered from the states and other participating actors.[28]

Although these studies provide detailed accounts of the mechanisms of U.S. experimentalism from different perspectives, they raise the question of how the federal laboratories have changed over the decades in response to shifting political, social, and economic landscapes. Such historical perspective is helpful in determining the validity of some key claims about experimentalism, such as Sandra Day O'Connor's assertion that the Supreme Court's protection of "historic spheres of state sovereignty from excessive federal encroachment" is necessary to preserve the states' role as policy laboratories.[29] One aim of this study is to explore how different historical contexts relate to states' functioning as laboratories. The chapter on the United States traces the development of the federal system from its early dualist roots, through the post–New Deal cooperative era, to the contemporary period of "new federalism." In each of these periods, the study examines how the particular political, social, and economic contexts shaped the functioning of federalism and the experimental process. For example, the chapter describes the federal government's increasingly active role in facilitating and diffusing state innovations as part of the centralizing trend of U.S. federalism since the late nineteenth century.

Another key development of the U.S. model—and of democratic experimentalism in general—is the increasing role of political parties in the experimental process. In modern federal democracies, partisan competition often significantly impacts the operation of the federal system, including its experimental function. In his classic work, William Riker argues that political parties are the most important determining factor in the development of federal systems.[30] Larry Kramer similarly identifies political parties as "the principle institution in brokering state/federal relationships . . . by linking the fortunes of officeholders

27. Dorf and Sabel, "Constitution of Democratic Experimentalism," 341.

28. Dorf and Sabel, "Constitution of Democratic Experimentalism," 396.

29. Gonzales v. Raich, 545 U.S. 1 (2005) at 42 (O'Connor, J., dissenting).

30. See Riker, *Federalism: Origin, Operation, Significance*, 129–36.

at state and federal levels, fostering a mutual dependency that protects state institutions by inducing federal lawmakers to take account of (at least some) desires of state officials."[31] More specifically, scholars find that partisan politics are crucial in shaping the incentives of local officials to experiment with innovative policies.[32] Building on Jessica Bulman-Pozen's work on "partisan federalism," the study discusses how the combination of the U.S. Supreme Court's new federalism jurisprudence and intensifying political polarization has contributed to the rise of "laboratories of partisanship" that facilitate state experiments specifically designed to further ideologically charged goals.[33]

Four case studies are presented to demonstrate this evolution: the women's suffrage movement, the unemployment benefit reforms, the Clean Air Act, and the Medicaid expansion. The chapter's approach to U.S. experimentalism helps in evaluating the various judicial and scholarly claims about the federal laboratories from the historical and context-specific points of view. It also lays the groundwork for the comparisons with India and China in later chapters as well as for further research on the historical trends of the federal laboratories.

India: A Developing Twist

One problem with the existing literature on federal laboratories is the intense focus on the U.S. model. It is certainly understandable; the size, diversity, and longevity of the U.S. federal system—not to mention its relatively well-kept and accessible legislative records—make it a prime target for research. However, the focus on a single country prevents the field from making fully informed comparisons among different experimentation models. This deficiency, in turn, has deprived the study of U.S. experimentalism the opportunity to learn from the successes and failures of other similar (or dissimilar) systems. For example, the

31. Kramer, "Understanding Federalism," 1523.

32. See, e.g., Rose-Ackerman, "Risk Taking and Reelection," 614; Manor, "Politics and Experimentation in India," 7.

33. For a more detailed discussion on partisan federalism, see generally Bulman-Pozen, "Partisan Federalism."

debate over whether federal intervention is good for experimentation could be informed by the experiences of countries with different power allocations between the center and subnational units.

To make such comparisons, it is necessary to have a holistic understanding of other countries' experimentation systems as well as the surrounding political, social, and economic contexts. For instance, India is both the world's largest federal system and the largest democracy by population, and it has a constitution that—at least formally—allocates much more power to the central government than the U.S. Constitution does. India also has a remarkable record of subnational policy innovations, such as the world-famous free midday meal for schoolchildren. It thus provides an important case study on how federal laboratories function in developing countries as well as an interesting contrast with the U.S. system. There is a considerable and growing body of scholarship that addresses India's federalism. However, compared to research on the United States, there is little systematic study of how India's constitutional arrangements facilitate or hinder subnational innovations and their diffusion.

One exception is Rajeshwari Deshpande, K. K. Kailash, and Louise Tillin's pioneering 2017 article on Indian states' welfare policy experiments, which describes a pattern of centrally facilitated state policy experiments during the Congress-led United Progressive Alliance (UPA) administration (from 2004 to 2014). As the UPA government "brought issues related to welfare back to the center of politics," many states "introduced substantial innovations to the means by which they implement centrally designed policies" and "introduced new schemes or extended the reach of existing central programs."[34] The authors also observe that "new schemes piloted at the state level have been scaled up to become national policy"[35] and argue that this pattern resulted from the division of constitutional responsibilities. According to the Indian Constitution, the central and state governments share most welfare-related powers, such as social insurance and labor, requiring the two levels of government to cooperate.[36] Such cooperation often

34. Deshpande, Kailash, and Tillin, "States as Laboratories," 89.
35. Deshpande, Kailash, and Tillin, "States as Laboratories," 89.
36. Deshpande, Kailash, and Tillin, "States as Laboratories," 89–90.

takes the form of conditional or unconditional grants from the center to the states, with state governments assuming primary responsibility for designing and implementing welfare programs.[37] Indian states' experimenter role was further expanded when the right-wing National Democratic Alliance led by the Bharatiya Janata Party (BJP) (2014–present) made more grants unconditional, allowing states to broaden the scope of their innovations (though the measure may also destabilize existing welfare programs).[38] The study, however, is limited by the period it examined (post-2004) and—more importantly—its subject matter (welfare policies) and therefore does not offer a comprehensive picture of India's approach to subnational experimentation.

Building on this study and similar work, this book aims to further illuminate the functioning of federal laboratories in the Indian context. The Indian chapter covers the early 1980s through the late 2010s, thus including discussions of several major transitions of Indian federalism: from Congress's one-party domination to political fragmentation and regionalization (late 1980s to early 1990s), then to relatively stable national coalition politics (early 2000s), and finally to BJP's new one-party domination (late 2010s). Each transformation had significant implications for how states approached policy innovation and diffusion. For example, the political and economic decentralization in the late twentieth century substantially boosted Indian states' discretion and resources for undertaking new policy initiatives.[39] The same period also saw an increasingly powerful Supreme Court that more actively regulated center-local relations, sometimes even helping scale state innovations to the national level. This evolution of India's federal laboratories is illustrated by three case studies that encompass different policy areas: the midday meal scheme for schoolchildren (which later became part of the nationwide right to food movement), panchayat raj (a constitutionally mandated grassroots self-government reform), and the BJP's anti-Muslim Hindutva policies. The last case is specifically included to discuss the darker side of experimentalism—which is rare for studies

---

37. Deshpande, Kailash, and Tillin, "States as Laboratories," 91.
38. Deshpande, Kailash, and Tillin, "States as Laboratories," 92.
39. Tillin, "India's Democracy at 70," 70–71.

in this field[40]—in an era of rising global populism and communalism. It is also an instance in which the measurement of policy success is likely to differ based on perspective. While the majority in some states might favor such an "innovation," outside observers might consider it highly divisive or fundamentally antidemocratic. The chapter thus provides a more holistic review of India's take on experimentalism and lays the foundation for contrast with its authoritarian neighbor.

China: Laboratories of Authoritarianism?

China's subnational experimentation has drawn more scholarly attention than India's (though not nearly as much as that in the United States), thanks largely to China's seemingly miraculous economic rise in recent decades. Analyzing China's economic reforms between 1978 and the early 2000s, Sebastian Heilmann points out that China's approach is "not equivalent to freewheeling trial and error or spontaneous policy diffusion."[41] Instead, he identifies an "experimentation-based policy cycle." In the initial stage, subnational governments conduct or encourage discretionary experimentation without legal authorization. When the experiment is endorsed by enough powerful actors in the center, the central government authorizes more regions to pilot similar policies. Finally, after successful pilot programs, the policy is formalized into national regulations or laws.[42] Many believe this cycle of innovation to be one of the most critical components of the "China model," which has resulted in the party-state's economic rise and political adaptability.[43]

Scholars have long debated the origin of China's unique pattern of subnational innovation. For example, some suggest that China's pattern of experimentation was heavily influenced by the country's

40. One exception is Michael Livermore's study on the downside of experimentalism, in which he argues that decentralization can lead to the overproduction of socially harmful information. See generally Livermore, "Perils of Experimentation."

41. Heilmann, "Policy Experimentation in China's Economic Rise," 5.

42. Heilmann, "Policy Experimentation in China's Economic Rise," 9–12.

43. See Heilmann, "From Local Experiments to National Policy," 1; Wang, "Adapting by Learning," 371.

revolutionary past, asserting that a mode of local policy experimentation under central guidance was developed in the communist base
areas before the 1949 founding of the People's Republic of China. According to this theory, Deng Xiaoping later employed this so-called
"point-to-surface technique" in the context of economic modernization,
as this "historically entrenched process . . . allow[ed] policy makers to
move beyond policy deadlock in spite of myriad conflicts over strategy,
ideology, and interests."[44] While it is true that China's revolutionary
legacies have played important roles in legitimizing and facilitating the
experimental process, the theory does not provide a satisfactory expla-
nation for the various ups and downs of the system during the reform
period. For instance, Chen Yun, a revolutionary veteran like Deng, often
tried to restrict the localities' ability to experiment. Indeed, the provinces generated very few meaningful innovations when Chen and his
conservative colleagues gained the political upper hand between 1989
and 1992. Other factors are thus needed to explain the entrenchment (or
lack thereof) of such revolutionary practice.

In this regard, two competing lines of theory are particularly noteworthy: the decentralization theory and the factional competition theory. The former attributes the prevalence of policy entrepreneurship to
China's decentralized power structure—especially with regard to the
economy—since the late 1970s, characterizing China as a relatively decentralized and fragmented authoritarian system in which subnational
governments hold substantial autonomy (mostly de facto, not de jure)
vis-à-vis the central government. This structure gives these governments both the incentive and the capacity to innovate in governing
their own jurisdictions. For example, Gabriella Montinola, Qian
Yingyi, and Barry R. Weingast famously argue that China's post-1978
administrative decentralization led to the creation of "federalism,
Chinese style" or "market-preserving federalism."[45] According to this
theory, China's center-local structure demonstrates several important
federal traits, including that (1) "each government is autonomous

---

44. See generally Heilmann, "Policy-Making through Experimentation."
45. See Montinola, Qian, and Weingast, "Federalism, Chinese Style"; see also
Qian and Weingast, "Federalism as a Commitment."

within its own sphere of authority," (2) "the subnational governments have primary authority over the economy within their jurisdictions," (3) "the national government has the authority to police the common market," and (4) "the allocation of authority and responsibility has an institutionalized degree of durability so that it cannot be altered ... unilaterally."[46]

According to Montinola et al., such federalism results in broad policy innovations by subnational governments because the devolution of power prompts them to tailor policies to their own jurisdictions and forces them to compete with one another by adopting novel policies.[47] Qian Yingyi and Xu Chenggang similarly argue that China's decentralized structure is particularly suitable for institutional evolution because the relative independence of its regions ensures that a failed subnational experiment will not significantly disturb the entire system.[48] The structure thus allows localities to develop a large variety of policy "mutants," which can be emulated by other regions or even adopted by the nation as a whole.[49]

Contrary to the decentralization theory, the factional competition theory suggests that China's extensive experimentation is mainly the result of intraparty political competition under a highly centralized political structure. This theory has two core components. First, it argues that centralization, rather than decentralization, is primarily responsible for the cycle of innovation. Citing the center's power to overrule subnational decisions and to appoint subnational officials, the theory contends that the Chinese regime largely remains "a centralized, unitary system in which power at lower levels derives from grants by the center."[50] Under this theorized structure, many seemingly local experiments are actually coordinated or closely monitored by the central government.[51] The center's extensive power over subnational officials

---

46. Montinola, Qian, and Weingast, "Federalism, Chinese Style," 55.

47. Montinola, Qian, and Weingast, "Federalism, Chinese Style," 58–59.

48. Qian and Xu, "Why China's Economic Reforms Differ," 151.

49. Qian and Xu, "Why China's Economic Reforms Differ," 151.

50. Nathan, "Authoritarian Resilience," 13; see also Cai and Treisman, "Did Government Decentralization Cause China's Economic Miracle?," 508.

51. Cai and Treisman, "Did Government Decentralization Cause China's Economic Miracle?," 516–17.

also enables it to forcefully expand selected innovations to the entire nation.[52] The second component of the argument is that experiments result from political competition between pro- and anti-reform factions. The central patrons of the pro-reform faction (such as Deng Xiaoping), for example, encourage members to experiment with and spread innovative provincial policies that serve to further the faction's political agenda and relative power.[53] If these reforms prove effective in the provinces ruled by faction members, the central patrons then push for national adoption.[54] The factional competition theory thus claims that "the driving force behind reform . . . [is] not pressures from or initiatives of autonomous local officials but competition at the center between rival factions with different ideological predispositions and local connections."[55]

Despite their seemingly irreconcilable differences, the decentralization and factional competition theories both capture certain critical factors underlying China's cycle of policy innovation. However, each also suffers from serious shortcomings that severely undermine its explanatory powers under certain circumstances. The decentralization theory rightfully points out some important structural features that contribute to China's successful economic reforms, such as the subnational governments' extensive authority on economic matters. However, it does not explain the exact mechanisms through which policy innovations initiate and spread. For example, the theory of market-preserving federalism suggests that the Chinese subnational governments enjoy primary authority over their own economies while the central government can only police the common market. If so, however, how is it possible for the central government to scale subnational innovations to nationwide policies (which inevitably involves forcing other localities to change their economic practices)? The

52. See Chung, *Central Control*.

53. See Cai and Treisman, "Did Government Decentralization Cause China's Economic Miracle?," 518; Shih, *Factions and Finance in China*.

54. See Cai and Treisman, "Did Government Decentralization Cause China's Economic Miracle?," 518; Shih, *Factions and Finance in China*.

55. Cai and Treisman, "Did Government Decentralization Cause China's Economic Miracle?," 507.

market-preserving federalism model also fails to explain why sub-national governments (and indeed the central government) are sufficiently incentivized to engage in policy innovation in the first place. In a democratic federation, the combination of elections and partisan politics might, at least theoretically, motivate national and regional politicians to innovate as a way to obtain more votes. Since China lacks such democratic mechanisms, its version of federalism does not automatically generate similar incentives for systematic experimentation. The decentralization theory is thus overly economic and technocratic, failing to appreciate the political and factional aspects of China's unique model of experimentation.[56] As a result, it cannot credibly account for the repeating cycle of regional innovations and national adoptions.

While the factional competition theory remedies some of the decentralization theory's shortcomings, it suffers from others. For instance, its dismissal of China's decentralization as a key institutional factor in the experimentation cycle (and in Chinese politics more generally) directly contradicts historical evidence. While a unified central government can theoretically override subnational governments' experimental policies, exercising such power in practice is difficult for a variety of reasons. Even proponents of the factional competition theory acknowledge that the central government is rarely a monolithic entity. Instead, it is often in a state of factional infighting, which hinders the formation of a unified front against the subnational governments. Moreover, given the country's size and diversity, even when one faction dominates the center, China's decentralized policy-making structure (especially in the economic realm) often makes unilaterally changing local practices a strenuous—if not impossible—task.[57] Thus originates the popular phrase "where there is a policy from above, there is a

---

56. Xu Chenggang's theory of a regionally decentralized authoritarian regime, which is a recent and more sophisticated variation of the decentralization theory, does recognize the centralized nature of China's cadre evaluation system. However, it still lacks an appreciation of the factional aspect of the system, which is critical to explaining the vastly different modes of experimentation across different times. Xu, "Fundamental Institutions of China's Reforms."

57. See Zheng, "Explaining the Sources," 107.

countermeasure from below" (上有政策，下有对策). Indeed, absent such discretion, it would not be plausible for China's subnational governments to conduct or encourage bold and extensive policy innovations, many of which directly violate national laws or even the constitution. The primary flaw of the factional competition theory is thus the opposite of that of the decentralization theory: It excessively downplays the significance of China's institutionalized power devolution.

In addition to these issues, studies of these theories suffer from a relatively narrow focus on economic experiments, especially those from earlier periods (the 1970s–1990s). One problem with this focus is the omission of more political experiments. Although many economic experiments (e.g., decollectivization) are highly controversial when first initiated because they contradict communist orthodoxy, political innovations such as competitive elections present a more direct threat to authoritarian rule. As the regime is likely warier of the risks associated with such innovations, theories about the economic experiment cycle may not apply to these areas.

Focusing on earlier periods also means that studies are not up to date on important changes in recent decades. For example, Cai Hongbin and Daniel Treisman argue that China's experiment cycle is driven by the conflict between "vertically structured, pro- and anti-reform factions."[58] Although these labels are useful for describing the political landscape in the late 1970s and 1980s, China's factional dynamic has since become much more nuanced and complicated. As ideological lines have blurred, factions are no longer simply pro- or anti-reform. Instead, they have vastly different preferences about the direction, magnitude, and implementation of reforms that reflect their different institutional, geographic, and personal connections. To maintain explanatory power, therefore, a theory of China's approach to experimentation must reflect these new circumstances.

The China chapter of this study presents a theoretical framework for the mechanisms behind China's unique government innovation process. This framework aims to address the shortcomings of both the

58. Cai and Treisman, "Did Government Decentralization Cause China's Economic Miracle?," 518.

decentralization theory and the factional competition theory by combining an analysis of China's institutional/constitutional arrangements with that of its intra-elite competition. In other words, it aims to answer the following questions: Is China's center-local structure decentralized, centralized, or both? How does this structure shape the behaviors of different factions when it comes to policy innovations? And conversely, how does the changing factional dynamic affect the system's ability to generate institutional changes? The thesis also includes an analysis of China's political innovations during the twenty-first century, such as those concerning competitive elections and civil society, thereby extending the scope of the experimentation theory across different times and subjects.

In short, the study argues that China's model of experimentalism results from the interaction between its constitutional structure and its often vibrant intraparty political competition. During the studied period, China's center-local[59] relationship was characterized by decentralized policy-making powers and centralized appointment/removal powers. This unique combination resembles a federal system in policy power division but reverses the accountability structure from bottom-up to top-down as well as from electoral to authoritarian. In China, political accountability mainly runs from the party center to local officials, not from voters to the various levels of government. Under this arrangement, decentralized policy powers give subnational leaders significant leeway to conduct bold experiments, while the top-down accountability structure allows the party center to incentivize experimentation by promoting subnational experimenters and selectively spreading successful policy innovations.

Based on this unique structure, political factions within the Chinese Communist Party (CCP) often serve as powerful vehicles for policy innovation. Seeking to leverage policy successes to gain political superiority, some factions encourage members to try new ideas and

59. The word "local" might be confusing in the Chinese context, as most Chinese sources and their official translations use the word "local" (地方) or "local governments" (地方政府) to describe the aggregation of both the subnational governments and governments at the lower levels, rather than the latter alone (e.g., center-local relationship or 央地关系). This book adopts this usage for consistency.

practices in their provinces, hoping that experiments will improve governance in their jurisdictions and prompt national adoption of their innovations, both of which enhance the responsible faction's national political outlook. In this sense, the Chinese system resembles the multiparty competition within federal democracies, which is a key driver of federal laboratories. However, the top-down nature of China's center-local structure makes the entire system susceptible to factional turbulence within the central government.

The chapter on China contains four case studies that illustrate this intriguing dynamic between constitutional structure and factional politics: the decollectivization reform, the Special Economic Zones (SEZ) reform, the township election experiments, and the civil society management policies. These cases cover the period between the start of the Reform and Opening (the late 1970s) and the end of the Hu Jintao era (early 2010s), which largely corresponds to the studied period in India. It omits the Xi Jinping administration due to ongoing uncertainties about its handling of center-local relations, especially with regard to experimentation.

Comparison: Pros and Cons of the Democratic and Authoritarian Experimental Models

Besides providing a systematic overview of the three countries' approaches to experimentation, a main goal of this study is to offer a basis for comparing them. In particular, it strives to contrast the U.S. and Indian federal laboratories with China's laboratories of authoritarianism and to explore their respective advantages and disadvantages with regard to subnational policy innovation and diffusion. Such a comparison will not only facilitate a deeper understanding of the unique characteristics of each model but also contribute to the broader discussion on the intensifying competition (real or imagined) between the system of liberal democracy and the China model.

In a 2009 article, James Manor compares India's experimental model with China's, noting that "the predominant aim of experimentation in China has been to spur economic growth," while India's experiments have focused on other spheres, including deepening democracy, reducing poverty, and protecting the environment.[60] He attributes this difference to the Chinese regime's reliance on economic growth as a main source of legitimacy, while Indian leaders "seek to draw legitimacy from a broader array of sources than do their Chinese counterparts."[61] He also observes that Chinese experiments that are perceived to hold promise "are usually replicated more widely and effectively than are their Indian counterparts" because Indian state leaders "are usually not subordinates of the central leadership."[62] However, Manor's article fails to capture some important aspects of the comparison, such as how China's effectiveness in scaling up innovations has been impacted by the shifting political dynamics among different CCP factions. More generally, his focus on India—an extremely important but less developed federal democracy—does not offer the most convincing account of the contrast between the democratic model of experimentalism and its authoritarian counterpart.

This study represents a more comprehensive and systematic attempt to compare these models. The comparative chapter discusses the three countries' differences in constitutional structures and partisan/factional politics as well as how these differences affect various aspects of subnational experimentation, including incentive, priority, capacity, diffusion, and stability. For example, the chapter starts by analyzing subnational leaders' incentives to experiment. As mentioned earlier, Rose-Ackerman famously argues that "few useful experiments will be carried out in [the federal laboratories]" because federal systems cannot overcome the positive externality problem.[63] This study agrees with other critics of Rose-Ackerman,[64] arguing that the problem is not so severe thanks to the subnational heterogeneity of many federal countries. For instance, socially and economically advanced U.S. states,

60. Manor, "Politics and Experimentation in India," 12.
61. Manor, "Politics and Experimentation in India," 13.
62. Manor, "Politics and Experimentation in India," 19.
63. See Rose-Ackerman, "Risk Taking and Reelection," 594.
64. For example, Strumpf, "Does Government Decentralization Increase Policy Innovation?," 228. For a summary of possible challenges to Ackerman's hypothesis, see Galle and Leahy, "Laboratories of Democracy?," 1346.

such as California and Wisconsin, are often more innovative in areas like welfare and environmental policies.[65] They thus naturally serve as policy experiment hubs for nearby states and the federal government, thereby mitigating the incentive problem. That being said, the chapter also argues that China's top-down authoritarian model represents a more fundamental solution to positive externality because the central government can use its coercive powers over subnational leaders to reward innovative behaviors. The study cautions, however, that such central intervention has its own incentive problem: The central leadership must itself favor experimentation—a criterion that depends heavily upon the political preferences of the faction(s) in power.

Also important is a system's ability to spread innovation across its subnational units. Manor argues that China's top-down system is more effective than the Indian model in diffusing promising innovations,[66] but this claim is too broad, lacking appreciation for China's ever-changing factional dynamic. It is true that Deng Xiaoping's position as paramount leader allowed the reformists to scale up many of their preferred policies with relative ease during the 1980s, including the many critical marketization reforms that kick-started China's economic miracle. The 2000s, however, presented a completely different picture. Many important subnational experiments, including the groundbreaking township elections and new civil society policies, were not nationally scaled despite gaining endorsements from key central politicians. This was largely due to the political gridlock at the time between the two largest factions, the Tuanpai and the Shanghai Gang, whose rivalry and roughly comparable strength made the central government too divided to effectively push for major reforms in such contentious areas. Under this scenario, it is not entirely clear that China's formally unitary system was more effective than its democratic counterparts in scaling up subnational innovations, especially given that many federal systems have gone through significant centralization (e.g., the United States during the New Deal and India under Narendra Modi).

The chapter also discusses the functional stability of the different experimental mechanisms. Under federal systems such as those in the

65. Walker, "The Diffusion of Innovations," 893.
66. Manor, "Politics and Experimentation in India," 19.

United States and India, the various constitutional protections against federal intervention into states' affairs (e.g., the limit set on the U.S. Congress's spending power in *National Federation of Independent Business v. Sebelius*)[67] and the fact that state leaders are elected by local constituents rather than appointed by the center serve as powerful stabilizing factors for subnational experimentalism. This is particularly true under today's polarized political dynamic in many democratic countries, as states ruled by the center's opposition party have strong incentives to resist central policies and develop their own. In contrast, China's top-down political structure means that a provincial leader—whether or not politically aligned with the center's ruling faction—can do very little to resist the center's decisions. This in turn means that the center's factional dynamic is of paramount importance to the operation of the experimental process. As a result, experimentalism in China has undergone drastic swings in the past few decades. For example, due to the 1989 triumph of the conservative faction, China's subnational laboratories went from highly active to almost completely muted in a matter of months and did not become active again until the reformists regained strength in 1992. This contrast highlights the critical role constitutional arrangements play in stabilizing (or destabilizing) subnational experimentalism, especially under the increasingly polarized political environments in many countries.

Besides these general comparisons, the chapter touches upon several more specific constitutional and political issues related to experimentalism, such as the roles of the courts and civil society. For example, it observes that the judiciary's role in shaping a federal system—including the functioning of its federal laboratories—may depend on the degree to which powerful political actors agree with decisions. In other words, court judgments have major impacts only when they gain support from political parties with significant control over the federal or state governments. Compared to their counterparts in federal democracies, the Chinese courts play an even more limited role in this regard, as they traditionally have negligible say on policy matters such as subnational experimentation. The political limits on the judiciary's role in countries such as the United States thus hold an important lesson for China: There

---

67. National Federation of Independent Business v. Sebelius, 567 U.S. 519 (2012).

is little the courts alone can do to substantially alter the course of China's center-local relations, even if they become more powerful. Fundamental changes to China's center-local dynamic, including the stabilization of the laboratories of authoritarianism, will likely require significant adjustments to intraparty competition, such as reforms of the nomenklatura system.

In conclusion, the study examines the implications of the comparative analysis for understanding experimentalism under Xi Jinping's leadership. The recent consolidation of political power has led to a reduction in local autonomy, which has resulted in pessimistic assessments of China's capacity for experimentation. However, it is important to note that this decline in policy innovation is likely to be temporary. The centralizing measures implemented by the Xi administration, such as the anti-corruption campaign and the establishment of central leading groups, have primarily operated at a factional level rather than initiating institutional changes. As a result, their impact on the constitutional structure that has facilitated local experiments for decades has been limited. Therefore, revitalizing experimentalism may simply require a shift in the political landscape—a phenomenon that occurs frequently in China.

CHAPTER ONE

The U.S. Model

This section discusses the evolution of the U.S. model of federalism and experimentalism. It first gives a historical overview of the U.S. federal system—from its dualist roots, through its more cooperative and centralized post–New Deal era, to its so-called new federalism era. As the federal laboratories are largely a function of federalism, the changing center-state dynamic—most notably the expansion of federal power in the early twentieth century—affects how these laboratories function. Other factors, especially the polarization of partisan politics since the late twentieth century, have also significantly impacted the experimental process.

The chapter uses four case studies to illustrate the evolution of U.S. experimentalism: (1) the women's suffrage movement, with its state-led nature and mostly peer-to-peer diffusion pattern, as an example of the "classic" federal laboratories; (2) unemployment benefits, which represent the transition from the classic model to a federally facilitated mode of experimentation; (3) the Clean Air Act, in which the federal government facilitated both the innovation and the diffusion of state experiments and which represents a peak in the federal-centered experimental approach; and (4) the Medicaid expansion, another example of the federally facilitated experimental process, which showcases how the combination of new federalism jurisprudence and partisan polarization has affected the post–New Deal model of experimentation.

U.S. Federalism: The Shifting Basis for the Federal Laboratories

Dual Federalism and Its Gradual Decline in the Pre–New Deal Era

This section tracks the evolution of the U.S. federal system from its dualist roots to its centralization due to a range of political and economic changes between the Civil War and the New Deal. The original text of the U.S. Constitution contemplates a system of dual federalism, with the national government having limited and enumerated powers and the states retaining the rest.[1] Article I, Section 8 of the Constitution lists the powers of Congress, which include, among others, collecting taxes and providing for the "general welfare of the United States" (the Taxing and Spending Clause), regulating international and interstate commerce (the Commerce Clause), and maintaining the military. In addition, Congress can "make all laws which shall be necessary and proper for carrying into execution the foregoing powers, and all other powers vested [in the federal government] by this Constitution" (the Necessary and Proper Clause). Article VI further states that laws made by Congress are "the supreme law of the land," and state judges are bound to enforce them, even if they conflict with state laws. However, the Tenth Amendment confirms the enumerated nature of Congress's powers, stipulating that "the powers not delegated to the United States by the Constitution, nor prohibited by it to the States, are reserved to the States respectively, or to the people." The framers anticipated that this arrangement would leave much regulatory power to the states. Indeed, throughout the antebellum period, the dualist structure allowed state governments to legislate in broad policy areas within their

---

1. Although the traditional interpretation is that such dual federalism represented a highly decentralized structure, Ablavsky points out that dual federalism could also be viewed as a form of centralization, as it subordinated competing claims to authority made by corporations, local institutions, Native nations, and separatist movements in favor of a structure with only two legitimate sovereigns—the Union and the states. See generally Ablavsky, "Empire States." For a more traditional account, see, e.g., Thomas, "Why Federalism Matters."

spheres of authority while limiting Congress to the enumerated powers explicitly listed in the Constitution.[2]

However, dual federalism was threatened from the earliest days by the potentially far-reaching federal power of the Necessary and Proper Clause. The debate revolved around the congressionally chartered Bank of the United States. James Madison argued that chartering banks was not among Congress's enumerated powers and was therefore unconstitutional. Alexander Hamilton, who was responsible for establishing the bank, claimed that the charter was constitutional because the Necessary and Proper Clause allowed Congress to act "if the end be clearly contemplated within any of the specified powers, and if the measure have an obvious relation to that end, and is not forbidden by any particular provision of the Constitution."[3] The issue was taken up by the Supreme Court in 1819. In the Court's unanimous decision in *McCulloch v. Maryland*, Chief Justice John Marshall ruled that the Necessary and Proper Clause—as Hamilton suggested—gave Congress broad implicit powers: "Let the end be legitimate, let it be within the scope of the constitution, and all means which are appropriate, which are plainly adapted to that end, which are not prohibited, but consist with the letter and spirit of the constitution, are constitutional."[4] In practice, however, the decision did not fundamentally alter the dualist nature of the U.S. federal structure during the antebellum era, as Congress "elected to leave dormant many of the powers that the Supreme Court indicated it might properly exercise."[5]

More substantial changes came in the form of the Civil War and subsequent Reconstruction. As the northern and southern states increasingly conflicted over slavery, it became clear that a federal-state power boundary could not be determined in the courthouse—or even through the political process. In 1860 and 1861, eleven southern states announced their secession to form the Confederacy, citing the newly elected President Abraham Lincoln's hostility to slavery as a key

---

2. Scheiber, "American Federalism," 632.
3. Cushman, "Federalism," 188–89.
4. McCulloch v. Maryland, 17 U.S. 316 (1819) at 421.
5. Scheiber, "American Federalism," 632; Cushman, "Federalism."

justification.[6] This led to the Civil War, which caused hundreds of thousands of deaths and ended in 1865 with a complete Union victory and the collapse of the Confederacy. To consolidate the victory, Congress—then controlled by the pro-Union Republican Party—passed the Reconstruction Amendments to the Constitution, which abolished slavery, prohibited states from infringing on certain civil rights, and protected racial minorities' right to vote. In particular, Section 1 of the Fourteenth Amendment provides that "no State shall . . . abridge the privileges or immunities of citizens of the United States; nor shall any State deprive any person of life, liberty, or property, without due process of law; nor deny to any person within its jurisdiction the equal protection of the laws." Section 5 explicitly gives Congress the power to enforce these restrictions on the states. Together, the Reconstruction Amendments were intended to significantly limit states' powers, especially with regard to the rights of former slaves.

However, the intended centralizing effect of these changes was partially negated by subsequent political and judicial developments. Public support for continued supervision over the southern states began to fade in the 1870s, and the anti-Reconstruction Democrats regained power both in the South and on the national stage (the party won the House of Representatives in 1874).[7] The Democrat-controlled southern state legislatures began to pass legislation that clearly contradicted the Reconstruction Amendments, effectively disenfranchising African Americans by depriving them of many civil and political rights. Some of these state "innovations" were upheld by the Supreme Court in a string of notorious decisions, including *Plessy v. Ferguson* (1896),[8]

---

6. For example, Georgia's declaration of causes of secession stated that a key motivating factor for the secession was that "The party of Lincoln, called the Republican party, under its present name and organization, is of recent origin. It is admitted to be an anti-slavery party . . . The prohibition of slavery in the Territories, hostility to it everywhere, the equality of the black and white races, disregard of all constitutional guarantees in its favor, were boldly proclaimed by its leaders and applauded by its followers." "The Declaration of Causes of Seceding States."

7. For a list of conservative takeovers in the South, see "The End of Reconstruction."

8. Plessy v. Ferguson, 163 U.S. 537 (1896).

Williams v. Mississippi (1898),[9] and *Giles v. Harris* (1903).[10] Even where the Court struck down state laws based on constitutional amendments, the southern states "either openly defied or found ways to circumvent the Court's rulings," and these rights "remained governed almost exclusively by state law and local custom."[11] These developments significantly undermined the centralizing effect of the Civil War and the Reconstruction Amendments.[12]

Despite these setbacks, the centralizing trend continued in other fields. For example, Charles McCurdy notes that post–Civil War big business "mobilized substantial financial resources necessary to press the Supreme Court" to dismantle states' legal barriers to a national free market.[13] For instance, I. M. Singer & Company, a manufacturer of consumer sewing machines, successfully persuaded the Court to invalidate a state license tax on out-of-state goods on the grounds that the tax conflicted with Congress's power to regulate interstate commerce.[14] Furthermore, as the U.S. economy became more interconnected, multiplying problems associated with industrialization and urbanization—such as unemployment, work injury, and lack of healthcare—the demand for federal action increased. Congress began to regulate areas traditionally within states' prerogatives, including foods, drugs, and labor relations. One major example is the Pure Food and Drug Act of 1906, which aimed to prevent "the manufacture, sale, or transportation of adulterated or misbranded or poisonous or deleterious foods, drugs or medicines, and liquors."[15] New federal agencies, such as the Federal Trade Commission, were created to handle emerging national issues such as monopolies.[16] Federal and state governments

9. Williams v. Mississippi, 170 U.S. 213 (1898).

10. Giles v. Harris, 189 U.S. 475 (1903).

11. Cushman, "Federalism," 201–2.

12. Scheiber noted that centralization did take place in several other areas between 1861 and 1890, including banking, railroad, and new federal agencies such as the Department of Agriculture. Scheiber, "American Federalism," 637.

13. McCurdy, "American Law," 633.

14. McCurdy, "American Law," 639–41; Welton v. Missouri, 91 U.S. 275 (1876).

15. "Pure Food and Drug Act."

16. Winerman, "The Origins of the FTC."

also began to collaborate through conditional grant schemes, under which the federal government financed programs administered by the states, provided the states followed national guidelines.[17] Although these federal actions were limited in scope, particularly when compared to their New Deal counterparts, they represented a clear trend toward centralizing power and increasing collaboration among different levels of government.

In the early twentieth century, the Supreme Court made some inconsistent attempts to protect the states' exclusive authority from the expanding federal power. During this period, the Court "retained remnants of the doctrine of dual sovereignty" in some cases concerning states' powers.[18] One notable example is *Hammer v. Dagenhart* (1918), in which the Court invalidated a federal law prohibiting the interstate sale of goods manufactured by facilities that employed children on the grounds that goods manufacturing was not commerce and thus fell beyond Congress's authority.[19] In other cases, however, the Court was forced to recognize that many activities traditionally deemed "local" were significantly impacting interstate commerce, thus falling within the enumerated powers of Congress.[20] During the first several decades of the twentieth century, the Court held that Congress could regulate an expanding range of issues, including lottery tickets,[21] adulterated food,[22] and prostitution.[23] These outcomes conflicted with decisions that invalidated national laws on dual federalism grounds, making "the system appear increasingly indeterminate and politically charged."[24]

The effects of the Court's dual federalism doctrines in this period were further complicated by its due process rulings, which often constrained state government power. Williams notes that "what the Court

17. Parrish, "The Great Depression," 741.

18. Peterson, *The Price of Federalism*, 11. See, e.g., Hammer v. Dagenhart, 247 U.S. 251 (1918); Carter v. Carter Coal Company, 298 U.S. 238 (1936).

19. Hammer v. Dagenhart, 247 U.S. 251 (1918).

20. Schapiro and Buzbee, "Unidimensional Federalism," 1211–13.

21. See Lottery Case, 188 U.S. 321 (1903).

22. See Hipolite Egg Co. v. United States, 220 U.S. 45 (1911).

23. See Hoke v. United States, 227 U.S. 308 (1913); see also Cushman, "Rethinking the New Deal Court," 259.

24. Cushman, "Rethinking the New Deal Court," 259.

'gave' to the states . . . it often retracted or limited via its substantive due process decisions."[25] For example, the Court ruled in *Lochner v. New York* (1905)—widely considered a defining case of the period—that New York's limits on working time interfered with the freedom of contract, thereby violating the Due Process Clause of the Fourteenth Amendment.[26] Similarly, in *New State Ice Co. v. Liebmann* (1932), the case in which Brandeis famously coined the term "laboratories of democracy," the majority opinion struck down an Oklahoma statute that required a license to manufacture and sell ice on due process grounds.[27] Brandeis argued in his dissent that the ruling denied the state's right to experiment. Such cases illustrate that the Court's inconsistent attempts to preserve states' exclusive power spheres were often overshadowed by its tendency to rule against government regulations during this period.[28]

Overall, the U.S. federal system gradually lost its dualist character during the period between its founding and the New Deal. The shift was mostly driven by significant political and economic changes, like the Civil War and the integration of the national economy. Although the judiciary made some attempts to preserve the dualist structure through federalism doctrines, the effects were both inconsistent and marginal. This clear trend toward centralization culminated in the dramatic changes during the New Deal, which brought the U.S. federal system into an era of close federal-state cooperation.

Dual federalism and its gradual demise had significant implications for the federal laboratories. In some ways, it is associated with the earlier version of federal laboratories, which largely operated at the state level without federal intervention. The idea was intuitive: the less the national government could impose uniform policies on the states, the more freedom the states would have to experiment with solutions.

25. Williams, "The Commerce Clause," 1897.

26. Lochner v. New York, 198 U.S. 45 (1905).

27. New State Ice Co. v. Liebmann, 285 U.S. 262 (1932).

28. Different theories attribute this inclination to different motivations, such as a desire to protect business interests, constitutional conceptualism, and the principle of neutrality. See, e.g., Horwitz, "Republicanism and Liberalism"; Ackerman, "Constitutional Politics/Constitutional Law"; Siegel, "Lochner Era Jurisprudence"; Cushman, "Some Varieties and Vicissitudes."

Although the contemporary U.S. federal structure long ago deviated from its dualist roots, the idea of linking experimentalism with limited national intervention remains influential. For example, Justice Sandra Day O'Connor argued in 2005 that the Court must "enforce the 'outer limits' of Congress' Commerce Clause authority . . . to protect historic spheres of state sovereignty from excessive federal encroachment," as such spheres are critical to the proper functioning of federal laboratories.[29] However, like dual federalism itself, this version of experimentalism had already reached its limit in the early twentieth century with the emergence of new policy challenges that required national coordination.

Toward Cooperative (or Coercive?) Federalism: The New Deal Era and Aftermath

The Great Depression and the ensuing New Deal brought significant changes to U.S. federalism by vastly accelerating the breakdown of its dualist structure. Since the late nineteenth century, the economy's increasing interconnectedness had been continually expanding federal power as well as prompting piecemeal changes to the Supreme Court's federalism jurisprudence. However, it was the unprecedented economic grievances brought by the Great Depression of 1929 that provoked the urgent need for large-scale national coordination. For example, states were hesitant to enact much-needed but costly welfare schemes, such as unemployment benefits, because doing so would likely leave them at a competitive disadvantage compared to those without such programs.[30] The situation created a popular push for the fast expansion of federal powers. In 1932, Franklin D. Roosevelt won a landslide presidential election on a platform that promised wide-ranging national action to address the depression. After taking office, Roosevelt set his New Deal agenda into motion by establishing new federal agencies and pressing for congressional legislation. Many of these measures, such as providing unemployment benefits and regulating the New York poultry market, fell within the traditional power sphere of the states,

---

29. Gonzales v. Raich, 545 U.S. 1 (2005) at 42–43.
30. Larson and Murray, "The Development of Unemployment Insurance," 185.

putting the federal government on a collision course with the more conservative wing of the Supreme Court, which at the time was still clinging to a dualist understanding of federalism.

In a series of cases decided in 1935 and 1936, the Supreme Court invalidated several key aspects of Roosevelt's New Deal legislation on dual federalism grounds. In *A. L. A. Schechter Poultry Corporation v. United States* (1935), the Court held that Congress exceeded its Commerce Clause power in regulating New York's intrastate poultry market because such intrastate transactions did not directly affect interstate commerce and thus fell outside Congress's prerogatives.[31] Similarly, in *Carter v. Carter Coal Company* (1936), the Court ruled that the Commerce Clause did not give Congress the power to regulate prices, minimum wages, minimum hours, or "fair practices" in the coal mining industry.[32] The Court reasoned that coal mining was not commerce but a part of the local production process, which could only be regulated by the states. Another case, *United States v. Butler* (1936), concerned the constitutionality of using a federal tax on agricultural processing to subsidize farmers who reduced their crops.[33] The decision held that the federal action was not permissible because agricultural production is a matter reserved to the states.[34] Around the same time, several other pieces of New Deal legislation and measures were also struck down by the Court on various constitutional grounds.[35] Together, these decisions made the Supreme Court a primary obstacle to Roosevelt and his New Deal.

The Court's jurisprudence began to shift after Roosevelt's second landslide electoral victory in late 1936, bringing a dramatic end to its dual federalism doctrine.[36] Roosevelt won 523 of the 531 electoral votes

31. A. L. A. Schechter Poultry Corporation v. United States, 295 U.S. 495 (1935).

32. Carter v. Carter Coal Company, 298 U.S. 238 (1936).

33. United States v. Butler, 297 U.S. 1 (1936).

34. However, the Court did make clear in this case that Congress's power to spend is greater and broader than its enumerated powers to regulate the states.

35. See, e.g., Humphrey's Executor v. United States, 295 U.S. 602 (1935); Louisville Joint Stock Land Bank v. Radford, 295 U.S. 555 (1935).

36. Scholars differ on the nature of the Court's jurisprudential shift during the New Deal. Some view the preceding Lochner era as a deviation from the constitutional norms established by the Marshall Court, which were "restored" by the New Deal

and 60.8 percent of the popular vote in this election, giving him and his New Deal an unquestionable mandate. In February 1937, riding the popular wave, Roosevelt revealed his "court-packing plan"—a proposal to add a new Supreme Court justice each time a sitting justice reached age seventy and did not retire within six months. The proposed plan, if passed by Congress, would immediately give Roosevelt the Court majority he needed to overcome most constitutional challenges to his New Deal policies. In a quick turn of events in March 1937, the Court upheld the constitutionality of a New Deal–type state minimum wage law in *West Coast Hotel Co. v. Parrish*.[37] The 5–4 decision accepted that the government could legitimately act to redress bargaining inequities in the workplace, in effect rejecting the contrary majority decision in *Lochner* while making Roosevelt's court-packing plan politically unnecessary.[38] Two "swing" justices voted in favor of the law, an act popularly perceived as a political capitulation to Roosevelt's overwhelming mandate and his court-packing plan. Historians have debated the accuracy of this account, and some have offered alternative explanations for the Court's critical "switch."[39] The justices' motives notwithstanding, the Court became reliably more deferential to the president and his New Deal policies in its subsequent decisions, which resulted in, among many other outcomes, the end of its dual federalism jurisprudence.

One important change was the Court's nearly complete deference to Congress's claims to Commerce Clause powers. In *United States v. Darby Lumber Co.* (1941), a unanimous Court upheld the constitutionality of the federal Fair Labor Standards Act of 1938, which regulated employment issues such as minimum wages, maximum working hours, and child labor.[40] The Court ruled that Congress had the power to impose national standards on employment practices to prevent states

---

shift. Others view the New Deal Court as an unprecedented break from constitutional tradition. See Ackerman, "Constitutional Politics/Constitutional Law," 457–58; Siegel, "Lochner Era Jurisprudence," 2–4; Horwitz, "Republicanism and Liberalism," 61–63.

37. West Coast Hotel Co. v. Parrish, 300 U.S. 379 (1937).

38. Lochner v. New York, 198 U.S. 45 (1905).

39. See Parrish, "The Great Depression," 729–30; Ackerman, "Constitutional Politics/Constitutional Law"; Cushman, "Rethinking the New Deal Court."

40. United States v. Darby Lumber Co., 312 U.S. 100 (1941).

with substandard labor conditions from gaining an unfair competitive advantage in interstate commerce. The Court thus overruled *Hammer v. Dagenhart* (1918), enabling Congress to regulate the manufacturing of goods.[41] A year later, the Court doubled down on the expansion of Congress's Commerce Clause power in the decision of *Wickard v. Filburn* (1942), which concerned the constitutionality of a federal law that limited wheat production by farmers.[42] The Court rejected Filburn's claim that the excess wheat he grew was for private consumption and therefore could not be regulated under the Commerce Clause. It reasoned that if many farmers chose to produce excess wheat for their own consumption, the cumulative action would drive down the price and affect interstate commerce. The Court therefore concluded that the act was a constitutional exercise of the Commerce Clause power, granting Congress the ability to regulate any local activities that might have a cumulative effect on interstate commerce. The Court's new Commerce Clause jurisprudence gave Congress expansive authority to legislate under the clause in the subsequent half-century. Until its decision on *United States v. Lopez* in 1995, the Supreme Court did not invalidate a single federal statute regulating private conduct on the ground that it exceeded Congress's Commerce Clause power.[43]

Another crucial development was the significant expansion of federal grants-in-aid under the Taxing and Spending Clause. Under a typical grant-in-aid scheme, the federal government provides funding and national guidelines for a specific activity, while the state or local governments are responsible for the administration (and often the design) of the activity in their own jurisdictions. The origin of this practice was the Morrill Land-Grant College Act of 1862,[44] under which the federal government granted states land to finance the establishment of colleges.[45] Similar conditional grant schemes became more widely utilized

41. United States v. Darby, 312 U.S. 100, 115–17 (1941), overruling Hammer v. Dagenhart, 247 U.S. 251 (1918).

42. Wickard v. Filburn, 317 U.S. 111 (1942).

43. Despite the expansion of Congress's Commerce Clause powers, states continue to innovate in many areas in which Congress does not normally act. See later discussion in this chapter on this topic.

44. Parrish, "The Great Depression," 740.

45. Pub. L. No. 37–130, codified at 7 U.S.C. ch. 13 § 301 et seq.

under the Woodrow Wilson administration in areas such as education, highways, and agriculture.[46] However, it was not until the Great
Depression that the federal government vastly expanded the breadth
and expenditures of grant-in-aid programs. Shortly after Roosevelt
took office, large-scale federal grant programs were already covering
various important welfare issues, including work relief projects, public
housing, health services, unemployment compensation, and assistance
to the elderly, dependent children, and the disabled.[47]

As with the Commerce Clause, the Supreme Court became more
deferential to Congress's claim of authority under the Taxing and
Spending Clause. In *Steward Machine Co. v. Davis* (1937), the Court was
asked to determine the constitutionality of the new federal unemployment benefit scheme, a critical part of the Social Security Act of 1935.[48]
The scheme imposed a federal payroll tax on most employers but allowed taxpayers to credit up to 90 percent of the tax paid to a federally
approved state unemployment benefits program. In effect, the tax
credit amounted to a grant-in-aid scheme that provided strong financial incentives for states to enact their own unemployment laws. Writing for the five-member majority, Justice Benjamin N. Cardozo held
that the tax credit constituted "temptation" but not "coercion" and was
therefore a valid exercise of the Taxing and Spending Power. The decision did leave open the possibility for federal laws to be deemed invalid
for coercing the states. However, no federal grant-in-aid or its equivalent
was found unconstitutional until *NFIB v. Sebelius* in 2012.[49]

The decades following the New Deal saw further centralization
of policy powers. With the Supreme Court mostly out of their way,
successive federal administrations—particularly those from Harry
Truman to Lyndon Johnson—kept expanding the national government's role in regulating the economy and providing social welfare.

---

46. Parrish, "The Great Depression," 741.
47. Parrish, "The Great Depression," 741; Scheiber, "American Federalism," 646.
48. Steward Machine Co. v. Davis, 301 U.S. 548 (1937).
49. NFIB v. Sebelius, 567 U.S. 519 (2012). In *South Dakota v. Dole*, the Court
established a test for Congress's Spending Clause powers. Although the legislation in
question was not invalidated, the test set forth the groundwork on which future
challenges—including *NFIB v. Sebelius*—could be based. South Dakota v. Dole, 483
U.S. 203 (1987).

These efforts culminated in Johnson's Great Society, a series of major spending programs to address poverty and inequality, including Medicare and Medicaid. As a result, federal involvement in state and local governance expanded at an astonishing rate. From 1950 to 1968, the number of federal grant-in-aid programs increased from 68 to 387, while their cost grew about tenfold.[50]

Another major post–New Deal development was that different branches of the federal government increasingly constrained the states' authority over civil and political rights. *Chicago, Burlington and Quincy Railroad Co. v. City of Chicago* (1897) was the first ruling in which the Supreme Court incorporated individual elements of the Bill of Rights (in this case, the Takings Clause) in its decision against the states through the Due Process Clause of the Fourteenth Amendment.[51] Such incorporations became more frequent in the 1920s, as the Court started citing First Amendment rights, including the freedoms of speech (1925),[52] press (1931),[53] assembly (1937),[54] and exercise of religion (1940).[55] During the chief justiceship of Earl Warren (1953–1969), many other rights were likewise incorporated and applied in decisions against the states, such as the right against unreasonable search and seizure (1961),[56] the right to the Miranda warning (1966),[57] and protection against double jeopardy (1969).[58] Another blow to state autonomy came from the Court's applications of the Equal Protection Clause of the Fourteenth Amendment. In *Brown v. Board of Education* (1954), the Court famously held unconstitutional all state laws establishing racial segregation in public schools on equal protection grounds.[59] The case prompted a fierce backlash from southern states, whose governments

50. Dilger, "Federal Grants to State," 5–10.
51. Chicago, Burlington and Quincy Railroad v. City of Chicago, 166 U.S. 226 (1897).
52. See Gitlow v. New York, 268 U.S. 652 (1925); Stromberg v. California, 283 U.S. 359 (1931).
53. See Near v. Minnesota, 283 U.S. 697 (1931).
54. See DeJonge v. Oregon, 299 U.S. 353 (1937).
55. See Cantwell v. Connecticut, 310 U.S. 296 (1940).
56. See Mapp v. Ohio, 367 U.S. 643 (1961).
57. See Miranda v. Arizona, 384 U.S. 436 (1966).
58. See Benton v. Maryland, 395 U.S. 784 (1969).
59. Brown v. Board of Education, 347 U.S. 483 (1954).

largely resisted enforcing the ruling.[60] In the late 1950s and early 1960s, the civil rights movement successfully turned the national sentiment against southern segregation, prompting Congress to enact the Civil Rights Act of 1964 and the Voting Rights Act of 1965. The federal Executive Branch also began to condition educational grants on compliance with the desegregation standards established in Title VI of the Civil Rights Act.[61] Under this full force of federal power, the southern states finally gave up de jure racial segregation despite wide popular support for the policy among local white voters.[62] In the subsequent decades, more limitations were imposed on the states under the Fourteenth Amendment in areas such as sex discrimination (1971)[63] and abortion (1973).[64] States thus became increasing constrained in formulating their own social policies. From an experimentalism standpoint, these constitutional constraints created a major barrier to regressive but innovative state policies.

Despite the greater federal role, states remained during this period a source of innovation in policy issues that drew less federal interest. Peterson argues that "economic forces in society are forcing each level of the federal system to concentrate on issues within its area of competence," meaning that Congress would focus on redistribution issues while leaving other matters—especially developmental ones—to the states.[65] Indeed, although the Supreme Court no longer blocked Congress's regulation of private conduct during this period,[66] Congress's actions were never all-encompassing. Generally speaking, members of Congress were elected to deal with national matters, and they would "worry about local interests only so far as necessary within a worldview

---

60. See Rosenberg, *The Hollow Hope.*
61. Rosenberg, *The Hollow Hope,* 97–100.
62. See Klarman, "Rethinking the Civil Rights."
63. See Reed v. Reed, 404 U.S. 71 (1971).
64. See Roe v. Wade, 410 U.S. 113 (1973).
65. Peterson, *The Price of Federalism,* 83–84.
66. The Court sometimes shielded state governments themselves from federal regulation, though such protection was not consistent. See National League of Cities v. Usery, 426 U.S. 833 (1976); but see Garcia v. San Antonio Metropolitan Transit Authority, 469 U.S. 528 (1985).

that remains fundamentally nationalistic."[67] As Congress was also constrained by the often cumbersome national political process and its own institutional capacity, it had neither the political will nor the energy to displace the states in all policy areas. State governments, on the other hand, were situated much closer to their constituents, placing them under greater pressure—and giving them greater agility—to respond to the demands of the local population in many policy areas. Consequently, states remained important regulators in areas such as contracts, property, torts, family, corporations, and criminal law—as long as their policies did not conflict with federal laws, regulations, or court precedents. This allowed the states to continue to serve as federal laboratories in these fields, though Congress ultimately decided "the federal equilibrium with respect to such matters."[68]

More importantly, the expansion of federal power during this time opened new space for federally facilitated state experimentation. Although the national government had almost plenary legal authority under the new Commerce Clause and Taxing and Spending Clause jurisprudence, it often could not effectively use this power without the help of state governments. Instead of micromanaging all matters, the federal government frequently found it more productive to allow the states to design and implement programs under federal guidelines and supervision. For example, Dwyer observes that the federal government had delegated considerable authority to the states on environmental regulation because "the federal government needs state bureaucracies (with their technical and administrative resources) and state politicians (with their political and budgetary support) to achieve its environmental goals."[69] Such arrangements enabled the federal government to coordinate problems requiring national attention while avoiding further expansion of the already bulky federal bureaucracy. These programs also allowed the states to tailor specific measures to local needs and conduct policy experiments. The new federal structure thus combined the fiscal and coordination capacity of the national government with the flexibility and innovative potential of the states.

67. Kramer, "Putting the Politics Back," 223.
68. Cushman, "Federalism," 217.
69. Dwyer, "The Practice of Federalism," 1190.

New Federalism: The Rehnquist Court
and Partisan Polarization

Decades of expanding federal legislative and bureaucratic authority accompanied by judicial deference to the national government on issues of federalism had caused unease among those who favored state autonomy. By the late twentieth century, some believed that "so much political power has been relocated to the federal government that, at times, the states could be mistaken for vassals of the federal government."[70] The situation has prompted political backlash from the Republican Party since Richard Nixon's presidency. Ronald Reagan, in particular, was highly critical of the intrusiveness and unmanageability of federal programs, though his effort to roll back the federal government by executive means only "yielded mixed results and modest successes."[71] Reagan made some inroads, however, in influencing the Supreme Court's ideological approach to federalism by nominating justices that favored returning power to the states. His appointees included Justices Sandra O'Connor, William Rehnquist, Antonin Scalia, and Kennedy, who coalesced with George H. W. Bush appointee Clarence Thomas to form the "federalism five."[72] Consequently, unlike the Court's shift on federalism in the early twentieth century, which was largely attributed to changing socioeconomic conditions, the so-called new federalism movement is typically considered a result of the partisan divide and "open ideological struggle on the Court."[73]

The Rehnquist (and later Roberts) Court tried to revive certain elements of dual federalism by setting stricter limits on federal power in favor of the states' spheres of authority. One such limit concerned Congress's ability to require the states to regulate on its behalf. For example, in a series of "anti-commandeering" decisions, the Supreme Court ruled that Congress has no power to compel state legislatures to enact or state executive branches to enforce federal laws. In *New York v. United States* (1992), part of the Low-Level Radioactive Waste Policy

70. Dwyer, "The Practice of Federalism," 1185.
71. Banks and Blakeman, *U.S. Supreme Court and New Federalism*, 75.
72. Banks and Blakeman, *U.S. Supreme Court and New Federalism*, 77.
73. Dwyer, "The Practice of Federalism," 1186.

Amendments Act of 1985 was challenged.[74] The act was meant to incentivize state legislatures to provide for the disposal of the radioactive waste generated within their state borders. The part of the act in question obliged states to "take title" to waste that had not been disposed of before 1996, after which they would become liable for damages caused by such waste. Writing for the majority, Justice O'Connor held that the act unconstitutionally "commandeered" states to act according to Congress's will. She reasoned that while the federal government can exercise direct legislative authority upon individuals on this issue, it cannot compel state legislatures to enact or enforce a federal regulatory program. Similarly, the Court ruled in *Printz v. United States* (1997) that Congress lacks the power to require state executive branches to conduct background checks for firearm sales.[75] The Court further expanded the application of the anti-commandeering doctrine in 2018, holding that Congress lacks the power not only to direct states to enact new laws but also to prohibit states from doing so.[76]

The Court also began to limit Congress's power to regulate private conduct. In *United States v. Lopez* (1995), the Court ruled for the first time since 1937 that Congress had exceeded its Commerce Clause power.[77] The case concerned the constitutionality of the 1990s Gun-Free School Zones Act, which forbade individuals from knowingly carrying a gun near schools. In a 5–4 decision, the Court ruled that Congress's authority under the Commerce Clause did not extend to the carrying of handguns because it was not an economic activity that could substantially affect interstate commerce. In the decision, Chief Justice Rehnquist admitted that the Court's past Commerce Clause rulings had given "great deference to congressional action" but declined to expound.[78] This more limited reading of the Commerce Clause was reaffirmed in *United States v. Morrison* (2000).[79] As in *Lopez*, the Court ruled in this case that parts of the Violence Against Women Act of 1994—which provided civil remedies to victims of gender-based violence—

74. New York v. United States, 505 U.S. 144 (1992).
75. Printz v. United States, 521 U.S. 898 (1997).
76. See Murphy v. National Collegiate Athletic Association, 138 S. Ct. 1461 (2018).
77. United States v. Lopez, 514 U.S. 549 (1995).
78. See United States v. Lopez, 514 U.S. 549 (1995) at 567–68.
79. United States v. Morrison, 529 U.S. 598 (2000).

were unconstitutional because they did not regulate economic activities that affected interstate commerce. According to Rehnquist, restricting application of the Commerce Clause was necessary because the Constitution "requires a distinction between what is truly national and what is truly local."[80]

That being said, on its own, the Rehnquist Court's new federalism jurisprudence had a limited impact on the shape of U.S. federalism. Although some scholars consider the Rehnquist Court's move a "return to dualism" or "return of unidimensionality," they nevertheless caution that the doctrines are little more than "anachronism" that "do little to change the overall shape of federalism in the United States."[81] Some argue that the modest effect of the new federalism decisions may reflect the conservative justices' division on the issue, which rendered them unable to achieve a real "federalism revolution."[82]

More importantly, scholars have pointed out that judges are often susceptible to the concerns and influences of other government branches, making them less likely to seriously challenge Congress's power on behalf of the states.[83] Consequently, the Court's decisions are considered "largely symbolic bows to a federalism myth rather than real limitations on federal power."[84] For example, in *Gonzales v. Raich* (2005), the Court invoked the holding of *Wickard v. Filburn* (1942) to conclude that Congress may criminalize the production and use of homegrown marijuana under the Commerce Clause, even if state law sanctions its medical use.[85] The case is considered a disappointment by proponents of a federalism revival, as it shows "that the Court simply lacks the resolve to take its federalism very far."[86] Perhaps

80. See United States v. Morrison, 529 U.S. 598 (2000) at 599.

81. Schapiro and Buzbee, "Unidimensional Federalism," 1219–24; Schapiro, "From Dualist Federalism," 6–7.

82. See, e.g., Banks and Blakeman, *U.S. Supreme Court and New Federalism*, 98, 299–300; Dinan, "Rehnquist Court's Federalism Decisions," 192.

83. See, e.g., Cross, "Realism about Federalism," 1313–20; Epstein and Knight, *The Choices Justices Make*; Eskridge and Ferejohn, "The Elastic Commerce Clause," 1362; Peterson, "Controlling the Federal Courts," 994.

84. Cross, "Realism about Federalism," 1321; Moulton, "The Quixotic Search," 851.

85. Gonzales v. Raich, 545 U.S. 1 (2005).

86. Young, "Just Blowing Smoke," 2–3.

more importantly, during this period, Congress retained most of its power to induce state action through grants-in-aid. In *South Dakota v. Dole* (1987), for example, the Court affirmed the broad scope of Congress's conditional spending power by upholding the constitutionality of a federal act that withheld some federal highway funding from states that did not maintain a minimum legal drinking age of twenty-one, although it simultaneously set criteria for judging the constitutionality of future conditional spending.[87] Given Congress's far superior fiscal capacities, such grant power can make it nearly impossible for states to resist its demands.

However, the increasing partisan polarization in recent decades has breathed new—if somewhat twisted—life into the Court's new federalism jurisprudence and into U.S. federalism more generally. To be sure, U.S. constitutional politics has always been partisan.[88] For example, Alexander Hamilton's Federalist Party and Thomas Jefferson's Democratic-Republican Party (previously the Anti-Administration Party) were the main forces behind the constitutional controversy over establishing a national bank. What sets contemporary American politics apart is its extreme polarization along partisan lines. The Democratic and Republican Parties "are now more internally unified, and more sharply differentiated from each other, than anytime over the last 100 years."[89]

This polarization and the Court's turn to new federalism have strengthened each other. The polarization has led to what Bulman-Pozen termed "partisan federalism," which refers to a dynamic in which federalism's institutional framework increasingly becomes a main battleground for partisan conflict.[90] As polarization intensifies, the party not in power in Washington becomes more inclined to use its

87. South Dakota v. Dole, 483 U.S. 203 (1987).

88. For an overview on the interaction between federalism and party politics before the recent political polarization, see Finegold, "The United States," 160–78.

89. See Pildes, "Why the Center Does Not Hold," 273; Fleisher and Bond, "The Shrinking Middle in the US Congress"; Abramowitz, *The Disappearing Center.*

90. Bulman-Pozen, "Partisan Federalism"; for a discussion on federalism and party politics before the recent political polarization, see generally Kramer, "Putting the Politics Back."

ruling position in the states to obstruct its archrival's national agendas—
including by arguing that the federal government is exceeding its authority and by resisting federal policies.[91] In such a scenario, the Court's
new federalism doctrines provide new and potent tools for states ruled
by the opposition party in Washington to resist national programs that
conflict with the party's ideological positions. This also means that the
Court's federalism agenda has much stronger political allies, as its doctrines become increasingly likely to be backed and invoked by one of
the two major national parties.

This combination of new federalism jurisprudence and intensifying partisan conflict may have distinct impacts on the functioning of
the U.S.'s federal laboratories. On the one hand, limiting the national
government's power over the states might give states—especially those
governed by the party not in power at the federal level—more space to
experiment with new policies. Indeed, experimentalism has been a key
rationale judges use to justify the new federalism position.[92] On the
other hand, as the case study on the Medicaid expansion demonstrates,
political polarization makes the experimental process less about finding the best policy solutions based on shared objective criteria and
more about devising ways to enhance a particular partisan position.
These dual effects on the federal laboratories are probably best exemplified by the Medicaid expansion saga, which is discussed in the case
studies section.

Case Studies

This section presents the following four case studies, each representing
a major period or transitional phase in the history of the American
federal laboratories: (1) the women's suffrage movement (mid-
nineteenth century to 1920), an example of state-led policy innovation;
(2) unemployment protection legislation (1910s to 1935), which shows the
transition from the state-led approach of the pre–New Deal era to an

91. Bulman-Pozen, "Partisan Federalism," 1096–1108.
92. For example, Gonzales v. Raich, 545 U.S. 1 (2005) at 42–43 (O'Connor, J., dissenting); United States v. Lopez, 514 U.S. 549, 581 (1995) (Kennedy, J., concurring).

experimental process based upon federal-state cooperation; (3) the Clean Air Act (1970 to 2000s), legislation widely viewed as exemplifying the height of the cooperative approach; and (4) the Medicaid expansion (2010 to present), which illustrates how new federalism jurisprudence and political polarization have made the experimental process less centralized and more partisan.

The Women's Suffrage Movement

The U.S. women's suffrage movement is a classic case of state-led policy innovation, as the innovation and diffusion process mostly took a bottom-up (specifically, from states to federal) route. In 1848, the first women's rights convention was organized by Elizabeth Cady Stanton in Seneca Falls, N.Y. The convention passed a historical resolution that demanded women's rights with regard to employment, education, and suffrage. The event has been credited with inspiring similar conversions in other states and, more generally, kick-starting the women's suffrage movement in America.[93] Around the same time, the abolitionist movement also "provided women with a political framework that assisted the development of a feminist movement."[94]

The introduction of the Reconstruction Amendments after the Civil War—which, among other things, established the right of African American men to vote—offered an opportunity for suffragists to press their similar claims at the federal level. With the goal of pursuing a national right to women's suffrage, Stanton and other female leaders of the movement founded the National Woman Suffrage Association (NWSA) in 1869. Virginia Minor, an activist closely associated with the NWSA, attempted to register to vote in Missouri in 1872. When rejected for being a woman, she sued the registrar in state court on the grounds that the Privileges or Immunities Clause of the Fourteenth Amendment guaranteed her—as a citizen—a right to vote. After the Missouri Supreme Court ruled against Minor, she appealed the case to the U.S. Supreme Court. In 1875, the Court unanimously held in *Minor v. Happersett* that the right to vote was not one of the

93. See McMillen, *Seneca Falls*, 98–103; Catt and Shuler, *Woman Suffrage and Politics*, 17; Mead, "The Woman Suffrage Movement," 3.
94. DuBois, *Woman Suffrage and Women's Rights*, 57.

"privileges and immunities of citizens of the United States," thus rejecting Minor's claim.[95] The ruling severely limited the federal government's legal role in promoting women's suffrage absent a constitutional amendment, thereby dealing a serious blow to the NWSA's national strategy.

Another federal-level attempt was made in 1878 when Aaron A. Sargent, a senator from California and an advocate of women's suffrage, introduced to the Senate what would later become the Nineteenth Amendment. The bill was defeated that same year—and each year for the next several decades. Those who opposed the bill often based their arguments on federalism grounds, arguing that enfranchising women through a constitutional amendment would impermissibly allow the federal government to regulate "marriage and the relation between the sexes"—which they deemed an integral component of the states' powers under the federal structure.[96]

The setbacks on the national stage turned the suffragists' attention to the states, and some notable breakthroughs were made in the West during this period. Many western areas that later became states were initially territories whose legislatures possessed the power to determine who could vote. In 1869, Wyoming became the first territory to enfranchise women.[97] This was followed by the neighboring Territory of Utah in 1870.[98] When Wyoming sought statehood in 1890, its leaders insisted on maintaining women's suffrage despite pressure from Congress to repeal the enfranchisement, making it the first state with full women's suffrage.[99] After being temporarily disfranchised in 1887, Utah's women secured their right to vote when Utah was granted statehood in 1896.[100] The movement got another boost when the short-lived Populist Party officially endorsed women's suffrage on the state level, making Colorado

---

95. Minor v. Happersett, 88 U.S. 162 (1875).
96. Siegel, "She the People," 998–1003.
97. Center for American Women and Politics, "Women's Suffrage in the U.S."
98. Center for American Women and Politics, "Women's Suffrage in the U.S."
99. O'Connor, "History of the Women's Suffrage," 662–63.
100. Mead, "The Woman Suffrage Movement," 10–11.

(1893) and Idaho (1896) the first two states to enfranchise women through popular referendums.[101]

During the Progressive Era, state-level suffrage movements gained further ground in the West, though their success in the eastern and southern states was more limited. The movement experienced a period of stagnation around the turn of the century but picked up steam again when a new generation of leaders emerged in the 1900s.[102] The new leadership began to adopt more active campaign tactics, including parades and large public meetings, which elevated the movement's image "to that of legitimate actors in the public sphere" and helped increase support for the cause among the general public.[103] The suffragists successfully capitalized on the West's innovative political environment during the Progressive Era, scoring a series of important state victories, including Washington (1910), California (1911), Oregon (1912), Arizona (1912), Nevada (1914), and Montana (1914). When the Nineteenth Amendment passed in Congress in 1919, thirteen of the sixteen western states had already granted full suffrage to women.[104] By contrast, only two states outside the West—New York (1917) and Michigan (1918)—had fully enfranchised women by that time.[105]

Studies suggest the suffrage movement's relative success in the western states was associated with the distinct combination of favorable factors generally absent in other states, including a progressive political environment, a competitive electoral landscape, and a strong movement presence. Some scholars attribute women's early enfranchisement in these states to the West's egalitarian political culture, early acceptance of women into institutions of higher education, and more widespread endorsement of progressive political parties.[106] Recently,

---

101. Mead, "The Woman Suffrage Movement," 11.

102. Mead, "The Woman Suffrage Movement," 13–14.

103. McCammon, "'Out of the Parlors,'" 791; Finnegan, *Selling Suffrage*.

104. McCammon and Campbell, "Winning the Vote."

105. Many of these non-western states did adopt partial suffrage measures by 1919, such as presidential suffrage, primary suffrage, and municipal suffrage. Teele, "How the West Was Won," 443.

106. Cole, "Wide Field for Usefulness," 292–93; McCammon and Campbell, "Winning the Vote," 67; Flexner, *Century of Struggle*, 88–89, 117.

using suffrage-related data in forty-five states from 1893 to 1920, Teele
has demonstrated that competitive political environments and large
suffrage movements had a substantial positive impact on the enfranchisement of women in a given state.[107] She explains that politicians in
western states tended to have greater incentives to seek new voters than
their eastern and southern counterparts because they generally faced
more competitive races and less established voter preferences.[108] The
stronger presence of the suffrage movement in the West also reinforced
this incentive by providing information about women's voting preferences and the infrastructure for future voter mobilization, both of
which were potentially valuable in future elections.[109]

Peer-to-peer diffusion, especially among neighboring states, also
contributed strongly to the movement's success during this period. An
empirical analysis of state suffrage data by McCammon et al. suggests
that states with higher percentages of neighboring states that fully enfranchised women were more likely to adopt women's suffrage.[110] According to the authors, a law "granting women broader citizenship
rights helped to redefine appropriate gender roles" in a given state,
which "appeared to alter thinking about gender roles by political actors
in neighboring states."[111] In particular, Colorado—the second state to
fully adopt women's suffrage—became a model for other western
states.[112] In fact, it was more of a role model than Wyoming, which
despite its status as the first state to fully enfranchise women, was considered too unique due to its long history of full enfranchisement since
its start as a thinly populated territory.[113] In contrast, Colorado's relatively large population and contentious partisan environment made
its experience highly relevant for other states facing the suffrage issue.
Consequently, it was "commonly invoked in both media accounts and

107. Teele, "How the West Was Won."
108. Teele, "How the West Was Won," 444.
109. Teele, "How the West Was Won," 445–46.
110. McCammon et al., "How Movements Win," 61.
111. McCammon et al., "How Movements Win," 61.
112. McConnaughy, *The Woman Suffrage Movement*, 52–54.
113. McConnaughy, *The Woman Suffrage Movement*, 53.

political debates about the political meaning and implications of woman suffrage over the next score of years."[114]

The suffrage movement's success in the states revived the fight for a federal amendment. In the 1910s, the National American Woman Suffrage Association (NAWSA), then one of the largest voluntary associations in the United States, began to leverage its expanding membership of enfranchised women to lobby for a federal suffrage amendment. In 1913, Alice Paul and Lucy Burn founded the Congressional Union for Woman Suffrage (later the National Woman's Party or NWP), which adopted more aggressive tactics, including actively campaigning against candidates it deemed insufficiently supportive of the cause.[115] Such a show of force in partisan politics compelled Congress to seriously consider a federal suffrage amendment.[116] However, the national movement still faced strong headwinds. Although both the Democratic and Republican Parties endorsed the idea of women's suffrage in principle during the 1916 election, both insisted that the issue should be left to the states rather than addressed through a national amendment.[117]

In 1920, boosted by women's active participation on the home front in World War I, the suffrage movement achieved its biggest objective: the adoption of the Nineteenth Amendment. When the United States entered the Great War in 1917, many women joined the workforce to replace the large number of male workers who had enlisted in the military. In light of this contribution, the NAWSA made the convincing argument that women's sacrifices for the national cause made it illogical to deny them the right to vote.[118] This development decisively changed public opinion in favor of the movement, and President Wilson publicly endorsed the federal suffrage amendment right before it was up for a vote in Congress in 1918. The amendment passed the House with an exact two-thirds majority but failed in the Senate by two votes, with most senators from southern states objecting. Infuriated, both the NAWSA and NWP campaigned against the senators who opposed the

114. McConnaughy, *The Woman Suffrage Movement*, 53.
115. Banaszak, *Why Movements Succeed or Fail*, 11.
116. Flexner, *Century of Struggle*, 262.
117. McConnaughy, *The Woman Suffrage Movement*, 244.
118. Flexner, *Century of Struggle*, 280–81.

measure in the 1918 election. After another failed attempt, the amendment passed both chambers in June 1919. It would take another year of intense lobbying by both suffragist organizations to secure the support of thirty-five of the thirty-six states needed for ratification, again due in large part to strong objections from the South. The Nineteenth Amendment finally became law of the land after Tennessee narrowly ratified it—by only one vote in its lower house—in August 1920.[119] The amendment's adoption legally enfranchised tens of millions of American women, eventually making them a distinct and formidable force in U.S. electoral politics.

The diffusion of women's suffrage in the United States followed a bottom-up pattern that reflected the more dualist federal structure of the time. As illustrated by the *Minor v. Happersett* ruling and later by the states' rights argument surrounding the suffrage amendment, voting eligibility was considered within the states' sphere of power. This dualist structure was a major obstacle to the movement's national strategy throughout the decades leading up to the Nineteenth Amendment. It was therefore unsurprising that the states took the leading role in enfranchising women during most of the movement. Indeed, if not for World War I, the suffragists likely would have required several more years to win over the eastern states needed to successfully push through a national amendment. This pattern of state-led innovation can be seen in many other pre–New Deal policy areas, such as the direct primary, and the minimum wage.[120] It contrasts sharply with some of the post–New Deal cases discussed later in this chapter, in which the federal government played a more proactive role in spreading policy.

Another key factor in this case was electoral democracy. That the U.S. federal system includes two layers of government with separate constituents was critical to the evolution of women's suffrage. After their initial failure at the federal level, the suffragists turned their attention to the subnational level. Since the western states' electorates were much more open to the idea of women's suffrage than the nation as a whole, the activists secured a series of early breakthroughs at a time when most voters in the eastern and southern states were still

119. O'Connor, "History of the Women's Suffrage," 668.
120. Bailey, "West and Radical Legislation," 605.

very much against them. These initial successes helped alter the perception of the role of women, fueling the gradual expansion of women's suffrage to other states. When a critical mass of states had embraced the new idea, popular pressure naturally started to build for its national adoption. In other words, the dual layers of the U.S. democratic system, combined with the diversity of state electorates, enabled certain states (e.g., Colorado) to become natural pioneers due to demands from local voters.[121] As discussed in later chapters, such bottom-up pressure to innovate contrasts sharply with China's top-down model of experimentation.

The case of women's suffrage also illustrates the powerful role nongovernment actors can play in the federal laboratories. Well-organized women's rights associations, which were capable of mobilizing their many members and making strategic alliances with various political forces, were instrumental in the enfranchisement of women in the western states. Similarly, enacting the Nineteenth Amendment in 1920 would have been unthinkable without the organized, persistent, and sometimes militant tactics of the NAWSA and NWP. The freedom of association embedded in the U.S. Constitution is therefore an important source of policy innovation and diffusion. This advantage of a liberal constitutional system is particularly pronounced when innovations benefit groups traditionally underrepresented in—or neglected by—the political process, such as in the case of women's suffrage.

In addition, the difficulty suffragists experienced in enacting the Nineteenth Amendment highlights the onerous process of amending the U.S. Constitution, which strengthens the federal character of the polity, making it harder to scale up state innovations. During the proposal

---

121. It should be noted that federal democracy does not always promote the spread of progressive innovations. For example, Banaszak notes that "The autonomy that federalism imparted to states and cantons created profound variation in the timing of woman suffrage at the local level. It allowed some U.S. states to be trailblazers in the enfranchisement of women, but it had the opposite effect in Switzerland where federalism permitted a few cantons to deny women the vote long after it had become a fait accompli nearly everywhere else in the world." Banaszak, *Why Movements Succeed or Fail*, 20. This also echoes later discussions of this study on how federal democracy might promote or hinder controversial experiments such as policies against religious or ethnic minorities.

and ratification processes, the southern states created significant obstacles to the amendment, making the suffragists' victories close in both cases. Most notably, the South remained stubborn even after national public opinion had turned to favor women's suffrage following women's participation in the war effort. These states' objections were largely rooted in their fear of undoing their disfranchisement of African Americans. One Florida senator said during the debate that the proposed amendment "opens up anew the negro question in all the Southern States" and "is likely to produce another 'reconstruction' conflagration in our Southland."[122] McConnaughy has pointed out that such racial politics made southern politicians "uniquely able to resist" pressure to pass the suffrage amendment.[123] As the case illustrates, the supermajority requirements for amending the U.S. Constitution—especially the need for ratification by three-fourths of the states—make it possible for a small minority of states (often more conservative ones) to prevent changes favored by the rest of the nation. This constitutional obstacle becomes particularly hard to overcome when the states are politically heterogeneous, either on a given subject (e.g., race relations) or more generally (e.g., the geographic partisan polarization in contemporary America).

The national success of the women's suffrage movement also signaled the dawn of a new era in both U.S. federalism and experimentalism. Siegel points out that "when Americans adopted the Nineteenth Amendment, they were . . . intervening in matters of domestic relations that many believed were reserved to state control."[124] The many nationalizing forces that emerged during this period—such as new forms of travel and communication, the national nongovernmental organizations (NGOs), and the war—all contributed to the gradual disintegration of the dualist federal structure and the ultimate triumph of the movement. As illustrated by the next case study, this trend toward a more centralized and interactive system had a profound impact on how the federal laboratories operated.

122. Flexner, *Century of Struggle*, 245.
123. Flexner, *Century of Struggle*, 247.
124. Siegel, "She the People," 953.

The Laboratories in Transition:
The Unemployment Protection Legislation

The development of the U.S. unemployment protection regime, like that of many of its Progressive Era cousins, can be divided into two distinct phases. From its conception in the second decade of the twentieth century until its first bill was signed in 1932, the issue was almost exclusively the states' concern, with Wisconsin serving as the indisputable pioneer of the movement. A watershed moment was Roosevelt's presidential win with a clear electoral mandate in 1933. The new administration quickly took the lead in establishing a national framework that would compel state legislatures to enact unemployment protection laws.[125] The inception of the U.S. unemployment benefit system thus exemplifies two different modes of experimentation under the changing federal structure. Pre-1933 state legislative actions showcase the classic state-initiated experiments and their peer-to-peer diffusions under constitutionally limited national power. Post-1933 events, on the other hand, are early examples of federally facilitated diffusions of policy innovations under the much more cooperative and procenter federal structure of the New Deal era.[126]

From the early days of the pre-1933 phase, Wisconsin produced much of the inspiration for other states. Significant action on unemployment benefits did not emerge in the United States until the depression of 1914–1915. In 1914, a tentative draft on unemployment insurance was presented at a national conference held by the American Association for Labor Legislation.[127] The draft, which was later endorsed by the conference, reflected the thoughts of the "Wisconsin school" on

125. See later discussions in this chapter on the Social Security Act.

126. As discussed earlier in this chapter, the history of federally sponsored state legislations dated back to the Morrill Land-Grant College Act of 1862, under which the federal government granted land to states to finance the establishment of colleges. Similar conditional grant schemes became more widely utilized under the Woodrow Wilson administration in areas such as education, highways, and agriculture, but these earlier examples never reached the scale of the federal sponsorship during and after the New Deal era.

127. Blaustein, *Unemployment Insurance*, 113.

unemployment protection. This school, led by Professor John R. Commons of the University of Wisconsin, emphasized preventing unemployment by making employers bear the cost of unemployment benefits, thus incentivizing them to stabilize employment.[128] However, enthusiasm for this idea waned when the depression ended in 1915.

States rekindled interest in the 1920s, with Wisconsin again leading the way. In 1921, Wisconsin State Senator Henry A. Huber introduced an unemployment insurance bill drafted by Commons that would require employers to bear the full cost of unemployment benefits and to insure their liability for payment with a designated insurance company.[129] Largely due to strong opposition from employers, the bill was defeated by a single vote, but it was reintroduced at each succeeding session until 1929.[130] The Huber bill "was copied during the same period in many other states," including Connecticut, Minnesota, and Pennsylvania.[131] However, due to the economic prosperity of this period and the emphasis on private unemployment benefits, none of these proposals materialized into law.

The outbreak of the Great Depression in 1929, however, significantly increased demand for legislative action on unemployment insurance in the states. In early 1931, two bills—both based on the Huber bill—were introduced in Wisconsin. One of them, the Groves bill, proposed a state fund with individual employer reserve accounts financed solely by the employer as the source of employee unemployment benefits.[132] The Groves bill was signed into law in January 1932, becoming the first unemployment protection legislation in the United States.[133]

128. Amenta et al., "Political Origins of Unemployment Insurance," 150; Blaustein, *Unemployment Insurance*, 113.

129. Blaustein, *Unemployment Insurance*, 114.

130. Brandeis and Raushenbush, "Wisconsin Unemployment Reserves and Compensation Act," 136.

131. Witte, "Development of Unemployment Compensation," 24.

132. Brandeis and Raushenbush, "Wisconsin Unemployment Reserves and Compensation Act," 137.

133. Wis. Stat. § 108.01–26 (2021). In 1931, the State of New York created the Temporary Emergency Relief Administration, which also provided unemployment relief. However, the New York legislation was mainly intended to create new jobs rather than to make direct payments to the unemployed. See Wis. Stat. § 108; Hopkins, "New York State Temporary Emergency Relief Administration."

Around the same time, a report from Ohio emerged as a rival model to the Wisconsin act. In 1932, an Ohio legislative study commission issued a report recommending a new type of unemployment insurance. The commission's leading members "saw themselves as influencing debates across the nation by providing a clear alternative to the Wisconsin plan."[134] The report differed from its Wisconsin counterpart in that it suggested financing unemployment benefits through a state pooled fund rather than through individual employer reserves.[135] Workers who qualified for unemployment benefits would receive them from this common fund, financed through mandatory contributions from employees and employers across the state. This design reflected the idea that the primary objective of unemployment benefits should not be unemployment prevention (as advocated by the Wisconsin school) but alleviating individual financial distress and "lifting the economy out of its doldrums through increased purchasing power."[136] According to this school of thought, it was beyond the capacity of individual employers to either prevent unemployment or guarantee unemployment benefits under circumstances such as the Great Depression, making a more collective approach necessary.

Both the Wisconsin act and the Ohio report became influential across the country, and many state legislatures soon began to introduce bills based on one or the other. In 1931, New York Governor Franklin D. Roosevelt and six other governors created the Interstate Commission on Unemployment Insurance, seeking to coordinate similar actions in other states.[137] The commission issued a report in 1932, recommending state legislation similar to that passed in Wisconsin. Many single-state study commissions appointed during the period also recommended laws based on either the Wisconsin or Ohio model. In 1933 alone, bills resembling Wisconsin's individual employer reserves were introduced in twelve state legislatures, while bills proposing Ohio-like state pooled funds were introduced in sixteen.[138] However, despite

134. Amenta et al., "Political Origins of Unemployment Insurance," 153.

135. For a more detailed description on the Ohio commission's report, see Rubinow, "The Ohio Idea."

136. Baicker et al., "A Distinctive System"; Blaustein, *Unemployment Insurance*.

137. Blaustein, *Unemployment Insurance*, 118–19.

138. Blaustein, *Unemployment Insurance*, 120–21.

the vibrant spread of the idea across state lines, only four more states—California, New Hampshire, New York, and Utah—had enacted unemployment insurance laws before the national Social Security Act was passed in 1935.[139]

This lack of widespread state legislation was due to intense opposition from business and (perhaps related) pre–New Deal federal inaction on the subject. Although sixty-eight bills were introduced in twenty-five states in 1933, none were enacted into law, and the Wisconsin act narrowly avoided being repealed after its effective date had been postponed a year.[140] At this time, the strongest obstacle to state action was pressure from employer groups on the grounds "that passage of legislation in their state would place them at a disadvantage in interstate competition."[141] Coordination at the national level was therefore critical to negate this race-to-the-bottom effect. However, prior to the New Deal, the idea of exclusive state powers was still too strong for the federal government to take action, as there was a good chance that courts would find such legislation to exceed federal power. Indeed, in 1928, the U.S. Senate Committee on Education and Labor held a hearing on unemployment protection, concluding in its official report that there was "no place for Federal interference in such efforts" and that "any public insurance scheme . . . should be left to the State legislatures."[142] Even after the devastating blow of the Great Depression, the Senate Select Committee on Unemployment Insurance concluded in 1931 that while compulsory state legislation might be necessary, a federal unemployment insurance regime would be unconstitutional. However, some Democratic senators (who were in the minority at the time) had already begun to contemplate stronger federal action—a trend that would continue to gather steam in subsequent years.[143]

The landslide wins of Roosevelt and his Democratic allies in the 1932 presidential and congressional elections fundamentally altered the political and constitutional landscape in the United States. It laid the

139. Larson and Murray, "The Development of Unemployment Insurance," 185.
140. Witte, "Development of Unemployment Compensation."
141. Larson and Murray, "The Development of Unemployment Insurance," 185.
142. Blaustein, *Unemployment Insurance*, 123.
143. Blaustein, *Unemployment Insurance*, 124.

political groundwork for the national government to take unprecedented action on unemployment protection and other social issues, including forcing the states to legislate on these matters. In 1934, Senator Robert Wagner and Congressman David Lewis introduced a bill in Congress, officially kick-starting the national legislative process on this issue. The Wagner-Lewis bill imposed a 5 percent payroll tax on employers while allowing them to receive 100 percent credit against the tax for contributing to a state unemployment protection program under state laws. These state laws were required to meet specific criteria, such as a minimum benefit amount and duration, and protection against certain abusive employment terms. Under the bill, state legislation could choose either the Ohio pooled-fund approach or the Wisconsin employer-reserve approach. President Roosevelt initially supported the bill, but soon opted for more comprehensive legislation that incorporated the idea of unemployment benefits.[144]

In a little more than a year, Congress enacted the Social Security Act, thereby unprecedentedly forcing the states to take legislative action on unemployment and several other social issues. In June 1934, the president created the Committee on Economic Security, which was tasked with studying how to build a social insurance regime to mitigate issues such as unemployment and old age.[145] The committee issued its report in January 1935, recommending federal legislation on unemployment insurance to allay the states' fear that state action on the subject would put them at a competitive disadvantage. Like the Wagner-Lewis bill, the report advocated a federal payroll tax on employers and tax credits for insurance contributions made under state unemployment insurance law approved by the federal Social Security Board. The report gave individual states considerable leeway to devise their own unemployment programs, thereby "permitting the states to experiment and adjust their state laws to local economic conditions and characteristics."[146] Indeed, unlike the Wagner-Lewis bill, it did not even stipulate

144. Blaustein, *Unemployment Insurance*, 127.
145. Blaustein, *Unemployment Insurance*, 132–40; Larson and Murray, "The Development of Unemployment Insurance," 186–88.
146. Larson and Murray, "The Development of Unemployment Insurance," 189.

standards for benefit amounts or duration.[147] A bill incorporating these recommendations was sent to Congress along with the president's message that the legislation "should be brought forward with a minimum of delay."[148] The bill passed both chambers with overwhelming margins and was signed into law on August 14, 1935.[149]

Within about two years, all states fell in line, enacting unemployment legislation in response to the Social Security Act, though several did so only after challenges to the act's constitutionality failed. Due to electoral pressure from their residents, most states complied fairly quickly, many calling special legislative sessions to pass the required legislation. By the end of 1936, thirty-six state laws had already been approved by the Social Security Board.[150] However, several of the then forty-eight states held out hope that the judiciary would rule the act unconstitutional. The threat of such a ruling was significant at that point, especially in light of the Supreme Court's recent pattern of ruling against Roosevelt's New Deal legislation. Indeed, the act's use of a tax offset (instead of a national unemployment insurance regime) and its limited state legislation requirements were both partly driven by the desire to avoid unconstitutionality.[151] In May 1937, a 5–4 majority of the Supreme Court ruled that the act did not constitute an attempt to coerce the states to legislate and therefore did not unconstitutionally encroach on the states' prerogatives under the Tenth Amendment.[152] The Court also ruled that the act was a constitutional exercise of federal power to spend for the general welfare.[153] After this ruling, the remaining states immediately passed the required legislation.[154]

---

147. Witte observes that such broad discretion caused the unemployment compensation scheme to differ "so much from state to state that there is a large element of truth in the claim that there is no such things as an American unemployment compensation system." Witte, "Development of Unemployment Compensation."

148. Blaustein, *Unemployment Insurance*, 145.

149. Pub. L. No. 74–271, codified at 42 U.S.C. ch. 7.

150. Blaustein, *Unemployment Insurance*, 159.

151. Larson and Murray, "The Development of Unemployment Insurance," 189.

152. Steward Mach. Co. v. Davis, 301 U.S. 548 (1937).

153. Helvering v. Davis, 301 U.S. 619 (1937).

154. Blaustein, *Unemployment Insurance*, 159.

The establishment of unemployment protection in the United States thus exemplifies the workings of both forms of the federal laboratories. During the pre–New Deal period, the innovation and diffusion of new ideas on unemployment protection occurred primarily at the state level. Wisconsin's—and to a lesser extent, Ohio's—undisputed pioneering roles perfectly illustrate the innovative potential of the federal laboratories. Indeed, Justice Brandeis who popularized the phrase was himself heavily involved in passing the Wisconsin unemployment law. Brandeis began publicly advocating an unemployment insurance scheme as early as 1911 and "devoted much of his public life to seeking its adoption."[155] In 1931, Brandeis provided an outline of his ideas to his daughter and son-in-law, Elizabeth Brandeis and Paul Raushenbush, who were University of Wisconsin professors and leaders of the movement for unemployment insurance legislation. This outline later became an important theoretical basis for the Groves bill that ultimately became a Wisconsin law.[156] Some even claim that the "single courageous State" quote from the *New State Ice* decision (whose oral arguments took place four weeks after the Groves bill was signed into law) "primarily referred, not to Oklahoma's unprecedented 1925 ice statute, but rather to Wisconsin's new unemployment insurance reserves legislation."[157]

However, the states' freedom to choose their own paths proved a double-edged sword in the experimental context. Under a purely state-led experimental system, each state determines how it will learn from its peers, if at all. In the unemployment insurance case, however, this peer-to-peer mode of diffusion had an obvious flaw: States that enacted unemployment legislation would be at a competitive disadvantage compared to those that did not, creating a race-to-the-bottom situation.[158] This is illustrated by the limited successful state legislation prior to the enactment of the Social Security Act despite the strong demand for state action.

155. Murphy, *The Brandeis/Frankfurter Connection*, 94.

156. Paul Raushenbush was one of the two initial drafters of the Wisconsin bill, the other being Harold Groves (who championed the passage of the bill in the State Assembly in 1931). Murphy, *The Brandeis/Frankfurter Connection*, 95.

157. Steiner, "A Progressive Creed," 25.

158. See generally Robertson, "The Bias of American Federalism."

Partly as a response to this deficiency, the New Deal brought the federal laboratories to their "2.0" phase. Instead of leaving decisions entirely to the states, the federal government would occasionally step in to facilitate—sometimes rather forcefully—state innovations and/ or their diffusions. The Social Security Act is an early prototype of this process. The federal government promoted innovations it deemed successful—in this case, the Wisconsin unemployment law[159]—by providing strong financial incentives for other states to follow suit. However, despite this stronger federal involvement, the U.S. system has remained distinctively experimentalist even to this day, as "no national system in the industrialized world cedes to its states, provinces, or cantons as much autonomy to establish tax rates, set benefits, and determine eligibility as does that in the United States."[160] Such autonomy facilitates innovation by permitting states to design their own programs as long as they meet certain minimum requirements, thereby allowing both the federal and state governments to learn from competing models of legislation. This "updated" version of the federal laboratories combined the states' vast innovative potential with the federal government's legislative supremacy and financial resources. As the unemployment case illustrates, the new structure was generally better equipped to handle policies that demand national coordination, such as social welfare and—as the next case study shows—environmental issues.

The Height of Federally Coordinated Experiments: The Clean Air Act

The Clean Air Act (CAA), one of the most influential environmental laws in the world, represents the highpoint of post–New Deal experimentalism in the United States.[161] The CAA famously employs a "cooperative federalism framework," with the federal government setting air quality standards and the states primarily responsible for determining how to achieve these standards and for implementing needed

---

159. Quadagno, "Welfare Capitalism," 640.
160. Baicker et al., "A Distinctive System," 128.
161. Pub. L. No. 88-206, codified at 42 U.S.C. §§ 7401–7671q.

measures.[162] This framework holds the promise of a "multitier regulatory structure that tracks the complexity and diversity of environmental problems," potentially avoiding the externality and internality problems of a single-level approach.[163] For example, a core responsibility of the Environmental Protection Agency (EPA) is setting the National Ambient Air Quality Standards (NAAQS), which set limits on the atmospheric concentration of six air pollutants. If it chooses, a state may submit a state implementation plan (SIP), which lays out how it plans to reduce emission levels from existing pollution sources[164] to become compliant with the NAAQS. SIPs are submitted to the EPA, whose approval is needed to give legal effect to a plan.[165] To obtain such approval, a state's SIP must fulfill a series of requirements under the CAA, including (1) specifying monitoring and enforcement mechanisms; (2) ensuring adequate personnel, funding, and legal authority to carry out the plan; and (3) providing for plan revision in response to new air quality standards, new technologies, etc.[166] If a state declines to submit an SIP or the SIP is rejected by the EPA as inadequate, the state is subject to a federal implementation plan designed and implemented by the EPA.[167] This and other similar responsibility-sharing arrangements under the CAA are praised for achieving the best of both worlds. The federal government's standard-setting power prevents states from racing to the bottom on environmental issues, while the states' broad discretion in implementing the standards encourages policies tailored to local circumstances and innovations that can be adopted by others.[168]

162. Doremus and Hanemann, "Of Babies and Bathwater," 817.

163. See generally Esty, "Revitalizing Environmental Federalism"; Oates, "A Reconsideration of Environmental Federalism."

164. Emission standards for new stationary sources and moving sources (mostly automobiles) are set by the EPA rather than by the states, with the exception that California may set its own moving source standards. Revesz, "Federalism and Interstate Environmental Externalities," 2347.

165. 42 U.S.C. § 7413.

166. 42 U.S.C. § 7410(a).

167. 42 U.S.C. § 7410(c).

168. See, e.g., Dwyer, "Practice of Federalism," 1197–99; Doremus and Hanemann, "Of Babies and Bathwater"; Buzbee, "Contextual Environmental Federalism," 121–26; Engel, "Harnessing the Benefits," 170–72.

One example of such an innovation is California's Air Quality Management Plan (AQMP), which was a source of inspiration for specific provisions of the 1990 amendment to the CAA. To address the serious air pollution issues caused by continuous population and industrial growth in Southern California, the South Coast Air Quality Management District (SCAQMD) enacted the AQMP in 1989 to bring the region into compliance with the CAA's air quality standards.[169] One innovative solution of the AQMP, which included detailed measures for lowering specific pollutants, was a compulsory car-sharing policy for companies. Private firms with more than 100 employees were required to encourage carpools or vanpools through measures such as designating preferential parking spaces for ride-sharers or raising parking fees for those who drive alone.[170] This policy was immediately scaled to the national level through the enactment of the Employee Commute Options in the 1990 CAA Amendments, which made employer-based ride-sharing programs mandatory in areas that met the CAA's definition of "severe ozone nonattainment areas."[171] Such fast-paced national adoption was largely thanks to the extensive role of several SCAQMD officials and lobbyists in advising Congress, as they persuaded the national legislators that California's measures would also improve air quality elsewhere.[172] Similarly, several other AQMP innovations made their way into the 1990 amendments, including provisions that discouraged use of fossil-fuel internal-combustion engines in manufacturing and emphasized cleaner alternative fuels for automobiles.[173]

A much more famous—and arguably the most consequential—example of the CAA's experimental feature is the flexibility of its national automobile emission standards, which facilitated many states' eventual transition to the more stringent California standards. Unlike other parts of the CAA, which generally allow states to set their own standards, the federal automobile emission standards require national uniformity to protect economies of scale in the automobile industry.

169. Lieu, "Regional Impacts," 24.
170. Kamieniecki and Ferrall, "Intergovernmental Relations," 151.
171. 42 U.S.C. § 7511a(d)(1)(B).
172. Kamieniecki and Ferrall, "Intergovernmental Relations," 151.
173. Kamieniecki and Ferrall, "Intergovernmental Relations," 150–51.

Even this preemption, however, leaves open an exception: California (whose automobile emission regulations predated the CAA) adopted more stringent standards by applying for a waiver to the federal standards.[174] Based on this waiver, California adopted in 1990 the Low-Emission Vehicle (LEV) program, which included three main elements: (1) tiers of exhaust emission standards for increasingly stringent categories of low-emission vehicles; (2) requiring auto manufacturers to phase in a progressively cleaner mix of vehicles each year, with the option of credit banking and trading; and (3) requiring that a specified percentage of passenger cars and light-duty trucks be zero-emission vehicles (ZEVs) with no exhaust or evaporative emissions.[175]

The LEV program set a higher bar (that increased progressively in subsequent years) for automobile emissions than the existing federal program. To reduce compliance costs for manufacturers, the program adopted a fleet-based approach: Rather than requiring all vehicles to meet specific emission standards, it required a manufacturer's product line average to meet the standards. This allowed more development time for vehicle types that were difficult to make compliant.[176] The LEV program's "combination of technology-forcing and flexibility" was credited for achieving "near-zero levels of tailpipe emissions from gasoline-fueled vehicles" in California, a feat considered almost impossible in the early 1990s.[177]

Under the CAA structure and with the active help of the EPA, California's model was replicated by many other states. The CAA was amended in 1990 to allow other states to choose the California standards in lieu of the federal standards to meet the NAAQS.[178] Thirteen northeastern states that participated in the Ozone Transport Commission (OTC)—a multistate organization established under the CAA to battle ground-level ozone pollution—expressed interest in switching to the California standards.[179] Of these, Massachusetts, New York, and Maine soon fully adopted them. To accommodate those who did not

174. Revesz, "Federalism and Environmental Regulation," 585.
175. California Air Resources Board, "Low-Emission Vehicle Program."
176. National Research Council, *State and Federal Standards*, 155–56.
177. National Research Council, *State and Federal Standards*, 174–75.
178. 42 U.S.C. § 7507.
179. National Research Council, *State and Federal Standards*, 176.

wish to fully adopt the standards, the EPA brokered an agreement in 1998 between the remaining OTC states and automobile manufacturers, resulting in a third "diluted" option—the National Light Emission Vehicle (NLEV) program—that did not require ZEVs.[180] In subsequent years, more states transitioned to the California standards. As of 2020, twelve states had adopted these more stringent standards, with more states planning to join.[181] These states account for more than 40 percent of U.S. automobile sales, making them a formidable force in regulating emissions and setting industry standards.[182]

It was not a coincidence that California played a leading role in both these CAA-related concerns. The Golden State has been a pioneer in air pollution issues since the 1950s, when it first asked the automobile industry to address the smog problem in Los Angeles.[183] Its standards have since served as models for both federal and state regulators. Lowry notes that several factors contribute to California's continually innovative behavior, including its urgent need for air pollution control due to rapid development, its pro-environmentalist political culture, and its pride at being the nation's leader on the issue.[184] This observation reflects the general tendency for states with higher industrial levels, more educated populations, and more liberal politics to have more environmentally progressive electorates.[185] California's special leadership status again shows that the heterogeneity within the fifty states' electorates can significantly contribute to promoting subnational units' voluntary innovative behaviors.

This model of federal-state collaboration, however, is not without its critics. For example, Buzbee points out that under the cooperative model, many state governments "show enforcement laxity, offering

180. Revesz, "Federalism and Environmental Regulation," 588–91; Jolish, "Negotiating the Smog Away."

181. The existing ones included California, Colorado, Connecticut, Maine, Maryland, Massachusetts, New Jersey, New York, Oregon, Rhode Island, Vermont, and Washington. Nevada also joined in 2020. Vermont Department of Environmental Conservation, "Zero Emission Vehicles."

182. David Shepardson, "Nevada to Join."

183. Lowry, *The Dimensions of Federalism*, 81.

184. Lowry, *The Dimensions of Federalism*, 95–96.

185. Mazur and Welch, "Geography of American Environmentalism."

minimal or nonexistent penalties for regulatory violations," which favors polluters because state governments are more dependent on local employment and taxes than federal agencies.[186] He later notes, however, that "even if most states move in lockstep [with the federal minimum standards] and are inclined to laxity, one state innovator can offer lessons to all."[187] In his influential articles, Revesz uses the example of California's automobile standards to argue that the CAA structure is insufficiently decentralized, as some states with strong preferences for environmental protection (e.g., California and the OTC states) take more significant action than the federal regulators.[188] However, Revesz's argument overlooks the CAA's demonstrated flexibility, which includes authorizing California to have its own standards, allowing other states to follow the California standards, and actively involving the EPA in fostering NLEV adoption in the OTC states.[189]

Overall, the CAA is viewed as an effective model for improving air quality and generally regulating the environment, in no small part thanks to the innovative potential of its cooperative federalism structure. The EPA's own report shows that the 1970 CAA and its 1977 amendment were responsible for the substantial reductions in many major air pollutants between 1970 and 1990, resulting in economic benefits (including benefits to health and agriculture) estimated at $22.2 trillion. The report further estimates that the direct cost of the law—including private compliance and public implementation costs—was around $523 billion, resulting in an extremely high benefit-to-cost ratio of 42.[190] Another report estimated that the 1990 CAA amendment increased the law's annual cost by about $65 billion in 2020 while adding another

186. Buzbee, "Clean Air Act Dynamism," 41–42; Buzbee, "Contextual Environmental Federalism," 121.

187. Buzbee, "Clean Air Act Dynamism," 45.

188. Revesz, "Federalism and Environmental Regulation," 585–93; Revesz, "Rehabilitating Interstate Competition"; see also Adler, "Jurisdictional Mismatch," 169–70.

189. However, the Trump administration's decision to seek an end to California's waiver to keep its own standards (though the decision was later reversed by the Joseph Biden administration) boosted Revesz's argument that the CAA and other environmental legal regimes are overly centralized. Abramsky, "California Is Fighting Trump."

190. EPA, "The Benefits and Costs of the Clean Air Act 1970 to 1990."

$2 trillion in benefits in the same year.[191] Various third-party studies confirm that the CAA and its amendments have played a major role in improving air quality in the United States.[192] A large portion of these impressive achievements can be attributed to national programs inspired by prior state innovations, such as energy efficiency standards for consumer appliances, acid rain provisions, cap-and-trade mechanisms, regulation of mercury emissions from power plants, and the California automobile emission standards.[193]

The CAA is therefore rightly considered a high point for post-New Deal experimentalism. Dorf and Sabel argue that the CAA established "joint federal/state responsibility that functions largely according to the principles of democratic experimentalism" by combining centralized financing and coordination with decentralized policy-making to produce a continuous cycle of innovations.[194] To make this combination work, the center must have substantial power over subnational units, including the ability to use its superior financial power to encourage (and sometimes coerce) states to innovate or to adopt others' innovations. In addition, the federal government must take a more experimentalist—or at least a somewhat hands-off—approach rather than micromanaging the implementation of its policy frameworks to ensure that state innovations are not preempted by the national government. In the case of the CAA, both prerequisites seem to be present. Dwyer observed that "although it has as much legal authority as it needs, the federal government cannot implement its air pollution program without the substantial resources, expertise, information, and political support of state and local officials."[195] As a result, although the CAA makes the federal government ultimately responsible for the nation's air quality, Congress and the EPA delegate to the states substantial policy-making powers and give them resources to develop relevant

191. EPA, "The Benefits and Costs of the Clean Air Act from 1990 to 2020."

192. See, e.g., Chay and Greenstone, "Air Quality, Infant Mortality"; Greenstone, "Impacts of Environmental Regulations"; but see List, Millimet, and McHone, "The Unintended Disincentive."

193. Engel, "Harnessing the Benefits," 170–71; Oates, "On the Evolution of Fiscal Federalism," 327–28; but see Boeckelman, "Influence of States," 370.

194. Dorf and Sabel, "Constitution of Democratic Experimentalism," 434.

195. Dwyer, "The Practice of Federalism," 1224.

capacities, thereby enabling them to develop innovative approaches that can be replicated elsewhere.[196] The CAA thus "giv[es] life to Brandeis's description of the states as laboratories of experimentation in public policy."[197]

The CAA also provides an interesting example of the role of the judiciary in the federal laboratories. In a series of cases in the 1970s, lower federal courts invalidated the EPA's requirement that states implement various measures mandated by the CAA (e.g., vehicle emission testing programs). Though this happened long before the *New York* and *Printz* decisions, a few circuit courts noted that the requirement amounted to unconstitutional commandeering.[198] These decisions limited the EPA's ability to force the states to comply, leaving it with less direct methods, such as threatening a federal takeover of environmental policies and reducing federal grants. Some have even questioned whether the CAA will survive after the *NFIB v. Sebelius* decision.[199]

On the other hand, courts can play a role in enforcing the CAA. The CAA includes the famous citizen suit provisions, which allow individual citizens and activist groups to bring lawsuits to enforce the CAA against private polluters and government agencies.[200] Citizen suits can constrain the states in two ways. First, some circuit courts allow citizens or groups to directly sue the states for administrative or regulatory failures in enforcing the CAA (though some circuits refuse).[201] Second, citizens can sue the EPA to take action against the states,[202] and states may also sue the EPA to force it to take certain actions.[203] However, since the EPA and Congress have many powerful administrative and legislative tools (such as withholding funds)[204] to

196. Ryan, "Federalism and the Tug of War," 581–82.

197. Dwyer, "The Practice of Federalism," 1223.

198. For example, District of Columbia v. Train, 521 F.2d 971 (D.C. Cir. 1).

199. Adler and Stewart, "Is the Clean Air Act Unconstitutional?'"

200. 42 U.S.C § 7604.

201. Sivaram, "Why Citizen Suits."

202. Adler and Stewart, "Is the Clean Air Act Unconstitutional?"

203. Massachusetts v. Environmental Protection Agency, 549 U.S. 497 (2007).

204. The EPA often makes threats to the states about withholding their funds (e.g., the EPA threatened to withhold highway funds from states for air quality violations 855 times from 1990 to 1997), but actual imposition of such sanctions is relatively rare (e.g., 14 times from 1990 to 1997). "Highway Fund Sanctions."

coerce the states, the courts' role in enforcing the CAA against the states may be limited.

More recently, the CAA and its cooperative federalism structure have taken a partisan turn, particularly on the issue of climate change. During the George W. Bush administration, Democrat-ruled states began to enact legislation regulating greenhouse gas emissions—an area the Republican federal administration failed to address. Most notably, California attempted to add greenhouse gases to its automobile emission standards under the special authority granted to it by the CAA.[205] The move had great environmental and industrial significance because, as discussed previously, many states (mostly Democratic) had opted to follow California's standards rather than the looser federal ones. However, California's application for a waiver (which was necessary for its standards to take effect) was denied in 2007 by the Bush administration, which objected to adding greenhouse gases as a regulated pollutant.[206] A few years later, the Barack Obama administration not only reversed this denial but extended California's standards to the entire nation from 2012 onward.[207] In 2019, the Donald Trump administration revoked California's waiver, despite potentially disastrous climate and economic consequences (though this decision was later reversed by the Joseph Biden administration).[208] These conflicting responses reflect how federalism has increasingly become an arena for the intensifying fight between the two major political parties, a theme that is explored in more detail in the next case study.

Laboratories in a Polarized Time: The Medicaid Expansion

This case study of the Medicaid expansion under the Patient Protection and Affordable Care Act (ACA) highlights how the partisan polarization in recent decades has changed the federal laboratories—and U.S. federalism more generally. Medicaid is a classic cooperative federalism

205. Meyer, "Why Trump Wants to Revoke California's Clean-Air Waiver."
206. Carlson, "Iterative Federalism," 1098–99.
207. Carlson, "Iterative Federalism," 1127–28.
208. Mahajan, "Trump Revoking California Emissions Waiver."

program that provides health insurance coverage to people with insufficient resources, and the states play a prominent and innovative role in its implementation. It was created under the Social Security Amendment of 1965, which authorizes the federal government to provide matching funds to states for providing healthcare to residents who meet certain eligibility requirements. As in the CAA's cooperative federalism structure, the federal government only establishes minimum requirements for Medicaid programs, while participating states enjoy broad powers to design and administer their own programs, including establishing eligibility standards and benefit coverage.[209] In addition, states can apply for an "innovation" waiver under Section 1115 of the Social Security Act, which allows the Secretary of Health and Human Services to waive federal requirements for state Medicaid programs if the state initiative is determined to be an "experimental, pilot, or demonstration project" that "is likely to assist in promoting the objectives of the program."[210] Using this waiver, states can alter Medicaid eligibility requirements and benefits beyond their already broad discretion. For decades, states have been using these waivers to experiment with new delivery methods and cost-sharing structures as well as to expand healthcare coverage to more people.[211]

Although Medicaid's cooperative federalism structure offers obvious experimentalist benefits similar to those of the CAA, it has raised major inequality issues related to interstate discrepancies in healthcare insurance coverage. Because each state designed its own Medicaid program, eligibility requirements and participation vary wildly from state to state, causing great disparities in healthcare coverage. For example, nearly 50 percent of the nonelderly adult population in Florida, Nevada, New Mexico, and Texas experienced a period without health insurance between 2009 and 2012, but only about 20 percent did so in Massachusetts and Vermont.[212] The divergence can be largely attributed to ideological differences. According to one study, states with higher percentages of self-described liberals had significantly higher Medicaid

209. Clark, "Safeguarding Federalism," 552–53.
210. 42 U.S.C. § 1315.
211. Kaiser Commission on Key Facts, "Five Key Questions."
212. Graves and Swartz, "Understanding State Variation," 1832.

participation rates than more conservative states.[213] Lying at the heart of the liberal-conservative divide on Medicaid is "the deservingness question"—whether healthy, single adults deserve subsidized health insurance. While liberals generally favor universal healthcare coverage, many conservatives believe that Medicaid programs should only be extended to "the truly deserving poor" and not to able-bodied working people.[214]

One of the ACA's main objectives was to address interstate inequality, especially the embarrassingly high uninsured rates in some parts of the country, by expanding the Medicaid program in a top-down, uniform fashion.[215] The ACA took its cue from a similar 2006 law enacted by the Massachusetts legislature.[216] Among other things, the Massachusetts law significantly expanded healthcare coverage by lowering eligibility standards for subsidized health insurance coverage and Medicaid.[217] The reform was a great success in expanding healthcare coverage, as the uninsured rate for lower-income adults in the state decreased from 24 percent in 2006 to less than 8 percent in 2008.[218] The ACA included a similar Medicaid expansion provision, which required states that received federal Medicaid funding (that is, all states) to expand their Medicaid programs by January 1, 2014, to cover all individuals under age sixty-five with an income less than 138 percent of the federal poverty line (FPL).[219] The federal government would bear the full cost of the expansion until 2016, after which its share would gradually decrease to a minimum of 90 percent in 2020.[220] This requirement, if implemented, would substantially lower eligibility requirements in many states, especially those with a more conservative populace. Since the ACA made the expansion a mandatory part of the Medicaid program, states refusing to implement the expansion would risk losing

213. Sommers et al., "Reasons for the Wide Variation," 913–14.
214. Grogan, Singer, and Jones, "Rhetoric and Reform."
215. Pub. L. No. 111–48, 124 Stat. 119 (2010); DeParle, "The Affordable Care Act."
216. Roy, "How Mitt Romney's Health-Care Experts Helped Design Obamacare."
217. McDonough et al., "The Third Wave," 423–26.
218. Doonan and Tull, "Health Care Reform," 72.
219. 42 U.S.C. § 1396a(a)(10)(A)(i)(VIII).
220. 42 U.S.C. § 1396d(y)(1).

part or even all of their federal Medicaid funding.[221] Given these strong financial incentives, Congress expected that all states would continue to participate in Medicaid and that the expansion would result in insuring an additional 15.9 million people by 2019.[222]

However, the constitutionality of the Medicaid expansion was challenged in *NFIB v. Sebelius* (2012) on federalism grounds.[223] In its opinion, the Court reasoned that the legitimacy of Spending Clause legislation depends on whether a state voluntarily and knowingly accepts the terms of a given program. The Court ruled that federal power does not include threatening to terminate other grants as a means to pressure states to accept a Spending Clause program. The opinion also took issue with the fact that states refusing the expansion could theoretically lose all Medicaid funding (which could amount to 10 percent of a state's total budget), arguing that the financial inducement was so great that it effectively coerced states to participate. This view—that the Medicaid expansion violated the principle that spending power cannot be used to coerce states into enacting legislation or participating in a federal program—was supported by seven justices (John Roberts, Scalia, Kennedy, Thomas, Stephen Breyer, Samuel Alito, and Elena Kagan). In the end, the Court held that states must be given the right to opt out of the expansion without losing their preexisting Medicaid funding. This case holds great significance for federalism jurisprudence, as it was the first time the Court enforced limits on spending power since *United States v. Butler* (1936).[224]

That being said, the case should have had limited consequences because it did not change the extreme generosity of the ACA's Medicaid expansion offer to the states. The package offered by Congress, in which the federal government would foot 90 to 100 percent of the expansion bill, should have been financially irresistible to the states. This is especially true because state governments could actually save money in this

221. 42 U.S.C. § 1396c.

222. Clark, "Safeguarding Federalism," 555.

223. NFIB v. Sebelius, 567 U.S. 519 (2012).

224. In *South Dakota v. Dole,* the Court established a test for Congress's Spending Clause powers, which laid the groundwork on which *NFIB v. Sebelius* was based. However, unlike NFIB, the Court upheld the legislation in question in Dole. South Dakota v. Dole, 483 U.S. 203 (1987).

scenario. Most obviously, states would spend less on uncompensated care as uninsured rates go down. More importantly, states would benefit from their low share of the expansion cost (0 to 10 percent), as their pre-ACA share was 25 to 50 percent. States could also save money by (1) eliminating spending on separate health-related programs previously funded by the state but covered by the expanded Medicaid program, such as mental health services and substance use disorder programs; and (2) moving some groups covered under pre-ACA Medicaid to the expansion population, which had a higher federal matching rate.[225] For example, one study found that such offsets saved Montana $25.2 million in the 2017 financial year, and its share of the expansion cost for the same period was only $24.5 million—meaning that the state "profited" $700,000 from the expansion.[226] This study further estimated that even if the state share reached the 10 percent maximum, the net cost after the offsets would still amount to only about 1 percent of the state budget.[227] In other words, the ACA's generous matching offer made the Medicaid expansion fiscally hard to resist even without the threat of rescinding pre-ACA Medicaid funding. Indeed, there was no evidence that the federal government ever considered removing pre-ACA funding to punish nonparticipating states.[228]

In practice, however, the Supreme Court's decision substantially affected adoption of the Medicaid expansion in many states and by extension, the health and lives of millions of people. As enacted, the ACA would have resulted in a mandatory expansion of Medicaid eligibility in all fifty states and the District of Columbia by January 1, 2014. After the ruling made the expansion optional, however, only twenty-four states and the District of Columbia chose to implement it at that time.[229] Although more states later expanded or planned to expand in subsequent years,[230] ten states had still not adopted the expansion by

225. Hayes et al., "The Fiscal Case."
226. Hayes et al., "The Fiscal Case."
227. Hayes et al., "The Fiscal Case."
228. Clark, "Safeguarding Federalism," 604.
229. Mitchell and Bencic, "Overview of the ACA."
230. The states that joined later than January 1, 2014, include Michigan (2014), New Hampshire (2014), Pennsylvania (2015), Indiana (2015), Alaska (2015), Montana

mid-2023.[231] The consequences of these delays and refusals have been significant. As of January 2019, the median Medicaid eligibility limit in states that had not expanded the program was only 38 percent of FPL for parents in a family of three ($9,447)—a much higher bar compared to the 138 percent FPL for an individual ($14,580) that the Medicaid expansion required in the same year.[232] In addition, childless adults remained completely ineligible in most nonexpansion states.[233] Since the ACA only provides individuals with incomes above 100 percent FPL with subsidized insurance options (because it envisioned those below the FPL would be covered by Medicaid after the expansion), 2.3 million adults in the nonexpansion states fell into a "coverage gap," having incomes above their states' limits for Medicaid but below the federal limit for subsidized insurance in 2019.[234] The COVID-19 pandemic further revealed the effect of nonexpansion on the low-income population. Between February and May 2020, 42.5 percent of newly laid-off workers in the thirteen nonexpansion states became uninsured; the rate in expansion states was about half this (22.6 percent).[235]

These hold-out states' refusal to expand can mostly be explained by their ideological and partisan inclinations. As mentioned previously, prior to the expansion, states with more conservative populations tended to design their Medicaid programs in ways that covered only "the truly deserving poor." The deservingness issue reemerged in these states during debates on the Medicaid expansion, and for the same ideological reason, these states were more inclined to resist the expansion. The ten states still refusing the expansion by mid-2023 were Alabama, Florida, Georgia, Kansas, Mississippi, South Dakota, Tennessee, Texas, Wisconsin,[236] and Wyoming. Unsurprisingly, these states have

---

(2016), Louisiana (2016), Virginia (2019), Maine (2019), Idaho (2020), Utah (2020), Nebraska (2020), Oklahoma (2021), and Missouri (2021).

231. Kaiser Family Foundation, "Status of State Medicaid Expansion."
232. Garfield, Orgera, and Damico, "The Coverage Gap."
233. Garfield, Orgera, and Damico, "The Coverage Gap."
234. Garfield, Orgera, and Damico, "The Coverage Gap."
235. Dorn, "The COVID-19 Pandemic."
236. Wisconsin is somewhat exceptional in this group, as its Medicaid program covers adults up to 100 percent of the FPL, meaning that there is no coverage gap in the state. Kaiser Family Foundation, "Status of State Medicaid Expansion."

similar political trends: Their electoral colleges all voted for the Republican nominee in the 2016 presidential election and have had at least one state legislature chamber controlled by the Republican Party since *NFIB v. Sebelius* was decided. Although some politicians in these states tried to frame their decision as motivated by fiscal prudence rather than conservative ideology and partisanship,[237] the previous analysis on the generosity of the expansion funding and its offset effects substantially weakens this argument.

The partisan nature of the opposition to Medicaid expansion was on full display when several states expanded their programs by using the Section 1115 waiver to creatively circumscribe ideological objections. Seven states have used Section 1115 to modify their Medicaid expansions between 2014 and 2020: Arkansas, Indiana, Iowa, Michigan, Montana, New Hampshire, and Pennsylvania.[238] As all these states had strong Republican opposition to the expansion in their legislatures, the waivers were used to innovate the expansions in ways that would allow reformers to distinguish their programs from the standardized Medicaid expansion. For example, Indiana used the waiver to create a complex expansion structure that includes premiums for all newly insured individuals, regardless of income,[239] and severe consequences for failure to pay premiums on time. The purpose was to ensure that newly eligible individuals must work to become paying healthcare consumers, making them members of the "working poor" rather than people receiving handouts—thus satisfying the "deservingness" test of conservatives in the state.[240] Other waiver states devised similar ideology-driven innovations, including voluntary work incentives and private insurance options, to distinguish themselves from the ACA's expansion approach.[241] Gogan, Singer, and Jones have nicely summarized these strategies:

237. Leonard, "Opposing Medicaid Expansion."

238. Commonwealth Fund, "Status of Medicaid Expansion."

239. Standard federal rules do not allow charging premiums for adults under a certain poverty level.

240. Grogan, Singer, and Jones, "Rhetoric and Reform," 265–66.

241. Grogan, Singer, and Jones, "Rhetoric and Reform," 257–58.

Essentially, proponents [of Medicaid expansion] in these seven states have convinced a conservative legislature that their reform is sufficiently innovative and different that they are *not* doing a Medicaid expansion as called for in the ACA and *not* building on the traditional Medicaid program, which conservatives view as faulty and dysfunctional.[242]

One major takeaway from the Medicaid expansion saga is that political polarization can augment the significance of the Supreme Court's federalism jurisprudence. As mentioned previously, although the Court's decision on spending power in *NFIB v. Sebelius* is doctrinally significant, it should have had limited real-world effect because the ACA's expansion offer was simply too good for states to reject—even without the threat of losing pre-ACA Medicaid funding. The lucrativeness of the offer reflects the fundamental power imbalance between the federal and state governments in the post–New Deal world. The national government's resource advantage has grown so vast that state governments often cannot function properly without federal help, even in areas where states have the authority to act without federal intervention. However, *NFIB v. Sebelius* turned out to be quite impactful. Because it allowed states to opt out of the expansion, more than half of the states chose not to expand on the original start date, and ten were still holding out in 2023, leaving millions uninsured who would otherwise have been covered. As rejecting the expansion offer made little fiscal sense, the states' decisions to resist expansion can only be adequately explained by their conservative ideological and partisan positions on healthcare issues.

More specifically, political polarization in the United States has transformed the federal laboratories, making the experimental process less technocratic and more ideological. On the surface, the various Medicaid expansion experiments in states that utilized the Section 1115 waiver—such as premium charges, voluntary work incentives, and private options—were examples of the cooperative federalism structure embedded in the pre-ACA Medicaid structure. Indeed, states have been using similar waivers to innovate their Medicaid programs for decades, most famously Massachusetts in its 2006 health reform (which became

242. Grogan, Singer, and Jones, "Rhetoric and Reform," 248.

a major source of inspiration for the ACA).[243] However, the expansion experiments in the seven waiver states were less about changing health-care coverage—which had largely been determined by the ACA's coverage requirement and generous funding—and more about framing the reforms in ways that would satisfy conservatives in their legislatures. They were thus different in nature from the classic policy experiments under cooperative federalism, such as the diffusion of the California automobile emission standards, which was primarily driven by a utilitarian and technocratic desire to improve specific policy outcomes. To be sure, all policy outcomes are, to some extent, subjective. For example, the average Massachusetts voter has always been more likely to assign higher policy priority to clean air than the average Texas voter. However, as ideological and partisan polarization intensifies, state innovations and their diffusions have become less about maximizing a widely accepted policy objective and more about supporting or resisting a position distinctly associated with a particular party.

This shift toward partisanship, although not against federalism in principle, conflicts somewhat with the idea of federal laboratories. As illustrated by state resistance and innovation during the Medicaid expansion, partisan polarization and federalism reinforce each other: Federalism provides the critical institutional infrastructure for partisan conflict, while partisanship gives states the incentive to resist the expansion of federal policy powers. However, the federal laboratories are not only about states acting differently from the national government but—as the word laboratory suggests—about finding better policies in a quasi-scientific or at least somewhat objective fashion. Indeed, Brandeis himself was not merely advocating for the states' right to experiment in his famous dissent in *Liebmann*. Rather, he was envisioning a scientifically based policy-making process that could be achieved through extensive experimentation by the states.[244] Of course, a policy can never be as scientific as natural science experiments, as

---

243. Long, Stockley, and Nordahl, "Coverage, Access, and Affordability," 304.

244. Tarr argues that Brandeis's depiction of "laboratories of democracy . . . has little to do with federalism and in fact rests on an understanding of public policy inimical to federal diversity," and "reflects his hope for scientifically based public policy." Tarr, "Laboratories of Democracy." But see Rosen, *Louis D. Brandeis: American Prophet*, 112.

people (and more often, parties) almost never completely agree on what constitutes a successful experiment due to different ideologies and interests. However, shared objectives—such as economic growth or clean air—can help facilitate shared measurements of success, making the policy innovation process more like a real experiment aimed at an objective and well-defined goal. Partisan polarization is inherently in tension with this idea, as it increasingly deprives the polity of shared objective measures for policy success in many contentious but critical areas, such as healthcare, climate change, and race relations. In these areas, state policy experimentation becomes more about finding the best way to enhance a particular partisan or ideological agenda. Under such circumstances, it might be more accurate to characterize the states as "laboratories of partisanship" rather than as laboratories of democracy.

Conclusion

The four case studies illustrate how the U.S. federal laboratories have transformed over the years, often in response to changes in the federal structure. The early version of the laboratories, exemplified by the successful spread of women's suffrage, was mostly based on a system in which the states enjoyed exclusive discretion in certain policy spheres. However, as demonstrated by the employment protection case, the emergence of new social and economic problems requiring national attention intensified the call for increased overlapping and concurrent jurisdiction, including more federal involvement in the experimental process. This gradual evolution, which extended from the late nineteenth century until the mid-twentieth century, resulted in a new and more centralized version of the federal laboratories, one in which the federal government played a critical role in facilitating both the initiation and spread of state innovations. This model of experimentation reached its height with the implementation of the CAA, which established a cooperative structure that allows state innovations to thrive and diffuse under the federal government's generous funding and broad policy framework. More recently, the Supreme Court's new federalism jurisprudence has set the stage for revitalizing the power division between the federal and state governments, though this development alone is unlikely to seriously undermine the cooperative dynamic between federal and state governments in the experimental process.

Another recurring theme in these case studies is how electoral politics shape the functioning of the laboratories. Particularly noteworthy is the dual-layered nature of U.S. democracy. That the federal and state governments are separately elected and thus accountable to different electorates means that states are often better situated to make policies in a bolder—though not necessarily superior—fashion. For example, during the women's suffrage movement, after failing to push their demands at the national level, the suffragists soon found support in the more progressive western states, which embraced the idea more quickly than the rest of the nation. These initial successes gradually led to the adoption in other states and laid the popular foundation for enacting the Nineteenth Amendment, which imposed women's suffrage on the states (many in the South) that refused to follow the trend. However, such policy-making boldness can also have controversial effects. The partisan polarization in recent decades, especially when combined with new federalism jurisprudence, has given the states more freedom to deviate from federal policies while making the experimental process more partisan and ideology-driven. Such dual effects are demonstrated by the constitutional challenge to the Medicaid expansion, which resulted in many Republican states rejecting the expansion despite the highly lucrative federal offer and the human toll of nonexpansion.

Besides the federal structure and partisan politics, other factors have helped shape the U.S. approach to experimentalism. In particular, the judiciary has demonstrated that it can play an important role in defining the constitutional boundaries between the state and federal governments, which has major implications for how the federal laboratories function. In at least three of the four case studies (women's suffrage, unemployment protection, and Medicaid expansion), the Supreme Court's decisions affected the trajectories of the experimental process to some degree. However, due to the judiciary's institutional limits, court doctrines have systemic impacts on the federal system only when they gain political support from other major actors, such as political parties. Another component of the U.S. approach is its vibrant civil society. In the women's suffrage example, the state innovations and their diffusions would be unthinkable without NGOs like NAWSA and NWP, which were instrumental in lobbying and compelling the state and federal governments to adopt the reforms. Both the judiciary and civil society are distinguishing factors that set the federal laboratories apart from their authoritarian counterparts and likely have contributed to these laboratories' long-term stability and creativity.

CHAPTER TWO

The India Model

This chapter discusses the Indian model of experimentalism, which has many unique features compared to both its U.S. and Chinese counterparts. It starts with an overview of Indian federalism, whose highly pro-union structure underwent a major reinvigoration of the state governments in India's federal system in the late twentieth century due to India's economic decentralization and political fragmentation. This created a less centralized federal structure with significant experimental potential, as the reinvigorated Indian federalism gave the states more autonomy and resources to try new policies while the pro-union character of the Constitution enabled the center to facilitate subnational experiments. The chapter then explores various features of the Indian model through three case studies: (1) the panchayati raj experiment, in which the states designed and implemented their own grassroots self-governance systems under the center's broad framework; (2) the midday meal scheme, an example of how India's powerful Supreme Court served to spread state socioeconomic innovations; and (3) the 2002 Gujarat riots and the Hindu nationalist policies of the BJP, which demonstrate how India's changing partisan landscape affected innovative state communal policies and their diffusion. The third case study deviates from experimentalism literature's usual focus on benign innovations to explore the dynamics of controversial policy innovations that intend to harm or suppress certain sectors of society.

Indian Federalism: An Overview

A country's federal structure, like its constitution, is a living organism that evolves along with changing political, economic, and social circumstances. In this sense, federalism in the United States and India are almost diametrically opposed in the direction of their evolution. The U.S. federal government started with limited and enumerated powers but has since amassed enormous authority, overshadowing the states in many important policy areas. In contrast, the texts of the Indian Constitution give the central government significant power to rein in the states, to the point that many scholars question whether India is truly a federal system. However, the political fragmentation and economic liberalization in recent decades have made the Indian states more autonomous and powerful, a process some refer to as the "federalization" of the Indian Constitution.[1]

When designing its constitution, India was in dire need of a strong central government that could unify the country and launch ambitious development programs. The newly independent India consisted of many former British provinces with diverse cultural and linguistic heritages as well as hundreds of former princely states that had been semi-autonomous for centuries (some of which were annexed through force or threat of force after Indian Independence). In addition, the bloody partition from Pakistan not only reminded the founders of the possible cost of future secessions but also created a likely enemy, prompting the need for a national government strong enough to manage conflict. Moreover, to deal with India's extreme poverty and what was perceived as social backwardness, the country's founders—particularly Jawaharlal Nehru and B. R. Ambedkar—adopted a mixed economy with many government-controlled public sectors and aggressive social justice programs (such as reservations for lower castes). Universal and coordinated implementation of these policies required a strong central government that could command vast resources and rein in diverse regional interests and traditions. The modernist founders thus considered a centralized constitutional structure necessary to end

---

1. Arora et al., *Indian Federalism*, 111; Saxena and Singh, "Role of the Federal Judiciary," 64.

India's pervasive poverty and dismantle "the structures of influence that pervaded India's provincial villages and feudal havens."

The Indian Constitution largely reflects this demand for centralization. The drafters chose the term "union" to highlight that though "the country . . . may be divided into different States for convenience of administration . . . its people [are] a single people living under a single imperium derived from a single source."[2] Consequently, the provisions of the Indian Constitution do little to stress the sovereignty and autonomy of the states. Rather, they tend to emphasize the interdependence between the union and state governments, especially the dependence of the states on the union. Several aspects of the constitutional design clearly demonstrate this tendency:

a. The union government can create, abolish, divide, or combine states through the approval of a simple majority in Parliament, without consent from the states involved.[3]

b. The union government can suspend a state government and impose direct central rule (i.e., the President's Rule) if a state government is unable to function according to the Constitution.[4]

c. India's Supreme Court has the power to issue directions, orders, and writs, which are applicable against both the union and state governments, to enforce the so-called fundamental rights.[5]

The Indian Constitution also divides specific legislative powers between the union and states in a way that highlights the former's dominant policy-making role. The allocation of legislative powers is specified in the Seventh Schedule of the Constitution, which contains three lists: the Union, State, and Concurrent Lists. The Union List includes

---

2. "Constituent Assembly of India," 7.48.248.

3. Constitution of India, Articles 2 and 3. By contrast, the U.S. Constitution forbids the division of the territory of a state to create a new state without the existing state's consent. U.S. Const. Art. IV, § 3.

4. Constitution of India, Article 356. There is no clearly comparable provision in the U.S. Constitution.

5. Constitution of India, Article 32. The U.S. Constitution likewise gives the judiciary the jurisdiction to decide all cases arising under the Constitution. U.S. Const. Art. III, § 2.

matters affecting the entire country, such as the military, foreign policy, and railways. The State List includes issues deemed more local in nature, such as local government, public health, and police. The Concurrent List contains powers that concern both levels of government, such as social security, labor disputes, and economic planning. Both the union and state legislatures can enact laws on the issues listed in the Concurrent List. Union laws typically prevail over state laws on the same issue, though the union government can opt to allow certain state laws to prevail in their own jurisdictions. Article 248 stipulates that any residual powers not included in the three lists remain with the union government.

Moreover, Article 282 of the Constitution explicitly gives the union government the power to make conditional grants to the states concerning matters on the State List. This means the union, like the U.S. federal government, can often bypass the limitations set by the Seventh Schedule by inducing states' voluntary compliance through central funding.[6] The scope of such power was affirmed by the Supreme Court in *Bhim Singh v. Union of India*, in which the Court ruled that "no restriction can be placed on the scope and width of [Article 282] by reference to other Articles or provisions in the Constitution as the said Article is not subject to any other Article in the Constitution."[7] This has resulted in "the effective dominance of the Union government over state governments in terms of legislative powers."[8]

The Indian Constitution and subsequent political developments have also given the union fiscal superiority over the states. The Constitution assigns the union large, easy-to-collect revenue sources, such as income tax, corporate tax, and customs duty, causing substantial vertical imbalances between the two levels of government, as states are forced to rely heavily on payment transfers from the center. To resolve this imbalance, the Constitution provides for the non-political Finance Commission (FC), which is appointed by the president every five years

---

6. For discussions of the transfers made under Article 282, see Singh, "Fiscal Federalism," 536–38; Verma and Iyer, "NK Singh"; Rajashekara, "The Nature of Indian Federalism," 251.

7. Bhim Singh v. Union of India, 5 SCC 538 (2010) at 56.

8. Tillin, *Indian Federalism*; Singh, "The Federal Scheme," 454–55.

and makes semibinding recommendations to the union government on transfer payments to the states.[9] The Nehru administration also established the separate Planning Commission (PC) in 1950 to determine grants and loans to the states for implementing development plans, which can amount to more than a third of total center-state transfers.[10] Unlike the FC, which is an independent body, the PC—while it existed—was a part of the union government and reported directly to the prime minister. The PC's fiscal decisions were thus inherently discretionary and political, further strengthening the states' dependence on the union.[11] Moreover, the Constitution forbids states from borrowing money without the center's consent if they are indebted to the center.[12] Since almost every state is indebted to the center, this provision gives the center significant control over the states' borrowing practices.[13]

Finally, the Indian Constitution makes it relatively easy for the union government to play its ultimate "trump card"—constitutional amendments—against the states. Unlike constitutional amendments in the United States, which require ratification by three-fourths of the state legislatures (or ratifying conventions), constitutional amendments in India need votes only from the majority of the total membership of each house and the majority of not less than two-thirds of those present and voting in each house. Even for provisions that directly affect state powers (such as the Seventh Schedule), amendments enacted by Parliament require ratification by only half of the state legislatures—a comparatively low bar since the ruling party or coalition in the center often has a strong presence in the state assemblies.[14] One prominent example is the Forty-Second Amendment Act of 1976, which moved five subjects from the State to the Concurrent List,

9. Rudolph and Rudolph, "The Old and New Federalism," 155.

10. The PC was replaced by the less powerful NITI Aayog (National Institution for Transforming India) in 2014 under the Modi administration. Singh, "Fiscal Federalism," 524–25.

11. Parikh and Weingast, "Comparative Theory of Federalism," 1607–8; Majeed, "India: A Model," 509–10.

12. Constitution of India, Article 293 (3).

13. Singh, "Fiscal Federalism," 6.

14. Constitution of India, Article 368.

including important issues such as education and the administration of justice.[15]

In sum, at least on its face, the Indian Constitution is highly pro-union. Its provisions not only allow the center to determine policies on most important matters but also enable the union to further diminish the already limited state prerogatives by means such as transfer payments, President's Rule, and constitutional amendments. It is therefore unsurprising that Wheare famously described India's constitutional structure as "quasi-federal."[16] Other similar characterizations include "federal with a strong unitary or pro-center bias," "federal in structure but unitary in spirit," and "federal in normal times but with possibilities of being converted into a purely unitary [polity] during [an emergency]."[17] Consequently, union-state relations are determined by how the central government utilizes its constitutional powers, which in turn mostly depends on party politics in the Parliament. As the partisan dynamic in the center has fluctuated considerably since India's independence, so has its center-local constitutional relationship.

Between independence and the mid-1980s, the union-centric character of the Indian Constitution was further strengthened by the dominance of the Congress Party at the union level and the extensive power of the PC (discussed below) over the states' economies. During Nehru's premiership (1947–1964), the Congress Party held an unquestionable majority in both the Parliament and most state assemblies, allowing him to coordinate center-local issues through intraparty negotiations. In addition, in 1950, Nehru established the powerful PC (an institution never mentioned in the Constitution), which was tasked with setting the national and state five-year plans and suggesting the disbursement of discretionary grants to the states. This combination of political and economic control allowed Nehru to rein in the states without frequently resorting to the center's coercive constitutional powers.

15. The act was passed by supermajorities in both houses of Indian Parliament and ratified by more than half of the state legislatures. The Constitution (Forty-Second Amendment) Act, 1976.

16. Wheare, *Federal Government*, 27; Manor, "India Defies the Odds," 21. But see Khosla, *The Indian Constitution*, 46.

17. Kashyap, "Intergovernmental Relations Revisited," 22.

The situation started to change under the rule of Indira Gandhi
(1966–1977 and 1980–1984), during which the Congress Party lost its majority in many state assemblies. As the state government increasingly
resisted central authority, Gandhi began to abuse the Constitution's
emergency mechanism by routinely imposing President's Rule on states
governed by opposing parties.[18] She also centralized power within the
Congress Party, to the point where all Congress state chief ministers
were effectively nominated by her.[19] Such political centralization—
especially the frequent imposition of President's Rule—shortened state
governments' time horizons, discouraging them from undertaking
transformative reforms.[20] Gandhi's apparent abuse of power also
caused severe political backlash (including the Congress Party's first-
ever loss in a national general election in 1977), which laid the groundwork for the decline of India's one-party dominance.

The power balance began to shift significantly toward the states
due to rapid political regionalization in the 1980s and 1990s.[21] In the 1989
general election, neither the Congress Party nor its two main rivals (the
center-right Janata Dal and right-wing BJP) obtained a majority in the
lower house of Parliament (Lok Sabha)—a historical first in India. Although Congress remained the largest party, the Janata Dal was able
to form a coalition government with the support of the BJP and several
state-based parties. The election marked the end of Congress dominance in the center and the rise of regional parties on the national
stage—indeed, no single party was able to obtain a majority on its own
between 1989 and 2014.[22] This led to a period of political turmoil in the
center, as governments were frequently brought down because their
coalition partners withdrew support in the middle of their term.

Around the turn of the century, India entered an era of stable coalition politics. The union government was led by the BJP's National
Democratic Alliance from 1998 to 2004 and by Congress's UPA from

18. Ray and Kincaid, "Politics, Economic Development," 151–52.
19. Malik, "Indira Gandhi," 149.
20. Weiner, "The Regionalization of Indian Politics," 347, 360–61.
21. On India's political regionalization and decentralization in the late twentieth
century, see generally Sinha, "The Changing Political Economy"; Tillin, "India's
Democracy at 70," 70–71; Brass, "National Power and Local Politics," 91.
22. Tillin, "India's Democracy at 70," 70.

2004 to 2014. In both cases, the largest national party's seats fell far short of an outright majority and had to rely heavily on state-based regional parties as coalition partners. Vote counts from the general elections during this period suggest the growing importance of the regions: The combined vote share of regional parties grew from 22 percent in 1989 to more than 45 percent in 2014. Consequently, many regional parties gained important cabinet positions and participated in making major national policies.

Another factor that contributed to the states' growing power and autonomy is the liberalization of the Indian economy, which increased the states' fiscal capacities. As mentioned previously, Nehru's and Gandhi's grips on the states were partly achieved through national economic planning and the expansive use of federal grants. In particular, the PC had become a powerful institution overseeing a command economy and a tool for central control. Decades of poor economic growth and the 1991 economic crisis prompted the Indian government to change course toward a more market-driven model.[23] In this process, the union gave up significant power over industrial planning and public investment,[24] reducing its economic leverage against the states, which began to rely more on private investment and less on central industrial licenses and grants as sources of growth and revenue. Furthermore, as the Indian economy started to boom in the 2000s, the states' revenues also grew markedly, allowing state politicians to launch many popular policy initiatives. On average, Indian states' share of total tax revenue increased from about 45 percent during the thirty years following Independence to about 55 percent after the economic liberalization.[25] This contributed to increasing the power of the state chief ministers at a time when the union government's power was declining.[26]

23. Shastri and Wilson, "Economic Crisis, Momentary Autonomy."

24. Many of these reforms, including the deregulation of industries and trade, were accomplished through parliamentary legislations and government policy changes, not constitutional amendments. Sinha, "The Changing Political Economy," 29–30; Mohanty, "Decision Making Process"; Thakur, "The Politics of India's Economic Liberalisation Agenda," 212–15.

25. Panda, Dasgupta, and Joe, "Resource Sharing," 20.

26. Manor, "India's States," 11.

In addition, the Indian judiciary became more active in protecting the states from union encroachments. For the first few decades after Independence, the Supreme Court largely adopted the position that the union government's use of President's Rule was outside the scope of judicial review.[27] This position was partially reversed in *S.R. Bommai v. Union of India* (1994), in which the Supreme Court placed significant constraints on the exercise of this emergency power.[28] The Court held that the union's power to proclaim the President's Rule is not absolute and that the judiciary has the power to revive a dissolved state assembly if the proclamation is issued in bad faith or on extraneous or irrelevant grounds. The decision, combined with the shift toward political regionalization, significantly reduced the arbitrary dismissal of state governments (the recent imposition of President's Rule on Kashmir is one exception), thereby weakening one of the most potent constitutional tools of central control over the states. The Court also became more inclined to rule in favor of the states when adjudicating the legislative competencies of the union and state legislatures.[29]

Despite these general trends toward reinvigorated state power, the union retained considerable power over the states. For example, despite their growing tax revenues, state governments needed transfer payments from the center to make ends meet, especially after the center-left UPA government initiated a new round of large-scale, centrally sponsored schemes in the 2000s.[30] The union also maintained its leadership role in furthering democratic governance and social and economic rights, which form the basis of various prominent union policies, laws, court cases, and constitutional amendments. Furthermore, despite the general decline of other union branches during this period, the Supreme Court's power and prestige grew rapidly as a result of the new public interest litigation (PIL) system and its popular rights jurisprudence, making it a powerful centralizing force on policy matters

27. Arora, "Autonomy and States' Rights," 52.

28. 3 SC 1. For a more complete discussion on the case, see Jacobsohn, *The Wheel of Law*, 129–38.

29. Saxena and Singh, "Role of the Federal Judiciary," 56–58.

30. For a discussion on centrally sponsored schemes and their influence on contemporary Indian federalism, see Rudolph and Rudolph, "The Old and New Federalism," 157.

related to political or socioeconomic rights—such as in the right to food cases discussed later in the chapter.[31]

Perhaps most importantly, though some heavily pro-union provisions of the Constitution became less frequently invoked due to political regionalization in the states and coalition politics in the center, they could become active again in response to partisan dynamic changes. Indeed, this occurred when India's federal system took a centralizing turn in the past few years due to the emerging political dominance of Narendra Modi and the BJP. In the 2014 general election, the BJP (with Modi as its candidate for prime minister) won a majority (282 of 543) of the Lok Sabha seats on its own—something no single party had achieved since 1989. Its archrival, the incumbent Congress Party, won only forty-four. Since then, the BJP has gone on to defeat the Congress Party and some regional parties in a series of state assembly elections, often similarly without the need to form coalitions.[32] Modi and the BJP solidified their political dominance when they swept the 2019 general election with a larger majority of 303 Lok Sabha seats, leaving the Congress Party with only fifty-two. These landslide victories can be primarily attributed to political realignment around Hindu nationalism and identity, which led to the formation of an ethnopolitical majority vote bank for the BJP.[33] These victories have effectively ended—for now—India's decades-long trend of political fragmentation and regionalization, which had been a cornerstone of state government reinvigoration. It is therefore unsurprising that the union government has become more assertive in forcing its policies onto the states, such as in the case of the Citizenship Amendment Act and the abolishment of Jammu's and Kashmir's special constitutional status.

That being said, it is unlikely that the Indian federal system will completely revert to its Congress-dominated days. As India's economic liberalization deepens, the center no longer holds the same kind of

31. See generally Moog, "Activism on the Indian Supreme Court"; Mate, "Rise of Judicial Governance."

32. As of March 2020, the BJP held a simple majority in twelve state legislative assemblies, including Arunachal Pradesh, Assam, Goa, Gujarat, Himachal Pradesh, Karnataka, Madhya Pradesh, Manipur, Tripura, Uttar Pradesh, and Uttarakhand.

33. Heath, "Communal Realignment and Support"; Chhibber and Verma, "Rise of the Second Dominant Party System," 138–45.

economic sway over the states that it did before the 1990s. Indeed, Modi has dismantled the PC, an act that further weakened the center's economic control over the states.[34] Equally important is the strong presence of many regional parties in state assembly elections. Although regional parties have become less relevant in national politics due to the BJP's electoral hegemony, they continue to play a key—or even dominant—role in many state governments.[35] Yamini Aiyar and Neelanjan Sircar argue that this continued relevance of regional parties in the states is due to the BJP's ideological majoritarian narrative, which is antithetical to regional aspirations and identities.[36] One should therefore expect states to continue playing an active role in the functioning of India's federal system, including by serving as laboratories of new policies.

In sum, India's combination of decentralized and centralized features has generally made it a fertile ground for experimentation over the past several decades. The political and economic decentralization since the late 1980s has granted state politicians more autonomy, resources, and incentives to become policy entrepreneurs, while the pro-union character of the Constitution and the country's centralized fiscal structure has enabled the union to serve as a facilitator of subnational experiments. This resulted in a series of state-led welfare policies in the 2000s, many of which the center attempted to scale up. Examples include the National Health Insurance Programme, which was inspired by Andhra Pradesh's insurance scheme; the National Rural Health Mission, which similarly followed previous state schemes; and the National Food Security Act's food assistance program, which was built upon reforms in Tamil Nadu and other states.[37] However, the decentralization of power has also made it difficult for the center to effectively encourage and spread policy innovations and has sometimes even fueled populist politics, resulting in mass communal violence. It is still too early to tell how the BJP's new electoral advantage will systematically affect federalism and experimentalism in India, though in

34. Punj, "Planning Commission's Disbandment."
35. "India Election Updates 2020."
36. Aiyar and Sircar, "Understanding the Decline," 219.
37. Tillin, Deshpande, and Kailash, "Introduction," 10.

response to this change, many BJP-ruled states have already begun to devise "innovative" policies that exploit communal sentiments for political gains. These different aspects of India's model of experimentation will be explored in the following case studies.

Case Studies

This section contains three case studies, each designed to illustrate how one or more features of Indian federalism have affected the country's experimental process since the decentralization process began in the 1980s. They include (1) the panchayati raj reform, which demonstrates how states used their vast discretion to establish their own unique village assembly systems after a mandate by the union government's Seventy-Third Constitutional Amendment; (2) the midday meal scheme, an example of how the increasingly powerful Supreme Court stepped in to help spread a major state innovation after the weakened union executive failed to do so; and (3) the Gujarat riots and the BJP's Hindu nationalist policies, which demonstrate how India's shifting party dynamic altered the federal system's ability to produce and spread anti-minority innovations.

Panchayati Raj

Long before its revitalization in the late 1980s, panchayati (which refers to self-governing village assemblies) was already an important political and constitutional term in India. Before the British Raj, Indian villages "possessed an organized institutional framework that looked after the civic, administrative, and political needs of the community, and was endowed with the necessary powers and resources to perform [these] various tasks."[38] After the long decay of these self-governing structures under colonial rule, Mohandas Gandhi made panchayati a core component of his political ideal. He imagined independent India as a highly decentralized polity consisting largely of self-governed and self-reliant villages. Rejecting a centralized parliamentary democracy as

38. Dwyer at al., "Panchayati Raj."

the pursuit of "English rule without the Englishman," Gandhi argued that an independent India should be based on the nation's premodern roots of village self-rule.[39] During the drafting of the Indian Constitution, this vision was dismissed by the modernizing forces within the Congress Party, especially Nehru and Ambedkar. The modernizers preferred a more centralized constitutional structure, which they deemed necessary for India's economic and social transformation. As a compromise between the modernizers and the Gandhians, the Constitution included the following in its Directive Principles:

> The State shall take steps to organise village panchayats and endow them with such powers and authority as may be necessary to enable them to function as units of self-government.

In the 1950s, a short-lived attempt was made to establish panchayats to help implement the union government's rural development programs. The first was inaugurated by Nehru himself in Rajasthan in 1957, and the system soon spread to other states. However, the union government soon found that panchayat leaders "were primarily interested in retaining and accumulating power and in distributing patronage" and were ineffective in promoting central programs.[40] As the union withdrew its support, the panchayati institutions began to decline in the 1960s due to "the absence of regular elections ... perfunctory audit ... [and state and local officials'] allergy to sharing authority with those nascent institutions."[41] An attempt to revive panchayati raj also failed because the state governments were unwilling to decentralize power to the panchayat level.[42]

It was not until the 1980s that the union government finally took decisive action to fulfill its constitutional obligation to establish nationwide panchayati raj. Like the panchayati reform of the 1950s, the attempt was motivated by the desire to effectively carry out various government

39. Khosla, *India's Founding Moment*, 75–80.
40. Mathur, *Panchayati Raj*, 20.
41. Pillai and Kumar, *Panchayati Raj Experience*.
42. Mathur, *Panchayati Raj*, 30–32.

schemes, which had been overburdened by the corrupt and ineffective local bureaucracies tasked with implementing them.[43] Panchayats were expected to accurately identify the schemes' intended beneficiaries and bring more accountability to their implementation. Since the early 1980s, successive Congress administrations had set up special committees to recommend ways to reform the panchayat institutions. In 1986, the committee under L. M. Singhvi recommended vesting panchayati raj with constitutional status to compel the states to endow it with political and economic resources.

In 1989, Prime Minister Rajiv Gandhi's government officially endorsed the idea, and in 1992, the Seventy-Third Amendment to the Constitution passed the union Parliament.[44] Among other things, this amendment provides the following:

a. A three-tiered panchayat system established in every state at the village, intermediate, and district levels (except for states with two million or fewer people, which need only two levels).

b. Direct elections for all panchayati seats at the village and intermediate levels.

c. Five-year terms for all panchayat officials and mandatory elections before the term expires.

d. Reservation of no less than one-third of panchayati seats and chairperson offices for women (states may opt to reserve more).

e. Reservation of panchayati seats and chairperson offices for the Scheduled Castes (SCs) and Scheduled Tribes (STs) in proportion to their populations, with no less than one-third for SC and ST women.

f. Devolution of power from states to the panchayats, including the power to decide various local matters and to implement many state- or union-funded development schemes.

g. An independent finance commission for each state that reviews the financial positions of the state's panchayats and recommends how much revenue panchayats should receive.

43. Khosla, *The Indian Constitution*, 72.

44. For legislative history on the Seventy-Third Amendment, see Sarma and Chakravarty, *Integrating the Third Tier*, 37–39.

At least on their face, these provisions represent a significant step toward local self-governance and participatory democracy, as institutional arrangements such as mandatory direct elections every five years and independent financial commissions could mitigate past failures in maintaining regular elections and sufficient financial resources. The progressive reservation policies for SCs, STs, and women also hold great promise for advancing democratic values and social justice. However, the actual effects of these constitutional designs largely depend on their implementation, which the amendment mostly delegates to the states.

The Seventy-Third Amendment requires all states to make or amend panchayati raj laws to conform to these provisions. These obligations are particularly "commandeering" of the states for two obvious reasons. First, the amendment effectively forces state governments to share their already limited constitutional prerogatives and financial resources with the new institutions, as the potential functions of the panchayats (listed in the Eleventh Schedule of the Constitution) largely overlap with the Seventh Schedule State List. Second, deliberation on the amendment only "reflected the decision of the national elites and policy makers" and had little input from the state level.[45] This commandeering made some sense, however, as history had proved—and would prove again—that state elites object to sharing their power with panchayats. Therefore, in the absence of a bottom-up revolution, forceful and somewhat unilateral union action was probably necessary (though far from sufficient) to establish meaningful local self-governance institutions on a national scale.

That being said, with the exception of the abovementioned provisions, the Seventy-Third Amendment gives the states broad discretion in designing their own panchayati systems. For example, a state assembly is authorized to design its election process and reservation policies, as long as it duly observes these requirements. Most significantly, the amendment gives state legislatures much leeway in specifying how much power and financial resources to vest in their panchayats. On delegating power to the panchayats, the amendment vaguely stipulates that:

45. Mathur, *Panchayati Raj*, xxiv.

The Legislature of a State *may*, by law, endow the Panchayats with such powers and authority as may be necessary to enable them to function as institutions of self-government . . . with respect to: a) the preparation of plans for economic development and social justice; b) the implementation of schemes for economic development and social justice as may be entrusted to them including those in relation to the matters listed in the Eleventh Schedule.[46]

Similarly, the amendment provides only a rough framework for the devolution of fiscal resources from the states to the panchayats:

The Legislature of a State *may*, by law, a) authorise a Panchayat to levy, collect and appropriate such taxes, duties, tolls and fees . . . b) assign to a Panchayat such taxes, duties, tolls and fees levied and collected by the State Government . . . c) provide for making such grants-in-aid to the Panchayats.[47]

The Seventy-Third Amendment is thus an interesting combination of a few union-imposed mandatory requirements and broad state discretion in shaping their own panchayat systems. This is a double-edged sword. On the one hand, such freedom allows the states to tailor panchayat laws to their specific circumstances, including their local self-governance histories and experiences. Perhaps more importantly, it provides them with an unprecedented opportunity to be federal laboratories by trying out innovative ways to enhance democratic participation at the grassroots level. On the other hand, the setbacks of previous panchayat projects are a reminder that states might drag their feet, as they are generally unenthusiastic about sharing their power and financial resources with independent local institutions.

46. Emphasis added. The Eleventh Schedule, which lists the functions that can be delegated by the states to the panchayats, was added as part of the Seventy-Third Amendment. It includes issues such as agriculture, drinking water, roads, poverty alleviation, education, health and sanitation, women and child development, and social welfare. Most of them can also be found at the State and Concurrent Lists in the Seventh Schedule.

47. Emphasis added.

In practice, some of the key commandeering features of the Seventy-Third Amendment have brought unquestionably positive changes to India's democratic system. One such change is the nationwide establishment of panchayat institutions and regularized elections at the grassroots level. Before the amendment was enacted, the representatives closest to the voters were state assembly members. By 2005, however, there were 227,698 panchayats at the village level, 5,906 at the intermediate level, and 476 at the district level.[48] With few exceptions, elections for seats in these panchayats have been held every five years.[49] This means that the pool of constitutionally protected elected representatives has increased about 500-fold, thereby bringing the government considerably closer to its people.[50]

Moreover, the Seventy-Third Amendment's mandatory reservation requirements have greatly contributed to the political and social empowerment of women, SCs, and STs. States have mostly followed the amendment's requirements, with some setting an even higher 50 percent quota for women. A 2013 dataset shows that among India's 2.9 million elected panchayat representatives, 46.7 percent were women, 19.4 percent were from SCs, and 11.7 percent were from STs.[51] Various studies note that reserving panchayati positions for these groups, who have long been excluded from local politics, contributes to their unprecedented political presence.[52] Such empowerment has, in turn, benefited public goods provision for these vulnerable groups. One study shows that both female and SC panchayati officials tend to push for investment in the welfare of women and SC constituents, thus generating a virtuous circle.[53] Given that women, SCs, and STs in India number close to a billion, the inclusion of these groups in the political process alone likely qualifies panchayati raj as one of the most impactful social and political policies.

48. Sodhi and Ramanujam, "Panchayati Raj System."

49. Mathur, *Panchayati Raj*, 46.

50. Chaudhuri, "What Difference Does a Constitutional Amendment Make?," 169.

51. Nadkarni, Sivanna, and Suresh, *Decentralised Democracy in India*, 224.

52. See, e.g., Sharma, *Panchayati Raj and Reservation Policy*; Chattopadhyay and Duflo, "Impact of Reservation"; Tiwari, *Panchayati Raj and Women Empowerment*.

53. Chattopadhyay and Duflo, "Impact of Reservation."

However, the states' broad discretion in designing their own panchayati raj has yielded mixed results. On the one hand, most states have done a relatively poor job of transferring functions and resources to the panchayats. As mentioned above, the Seventy-Third Amendment stipulates that state legislatures *may* transfer functions and revenue to the panchayats, and the Eleventh Schedule lists twenty-nine areas over which panchayats can legitimately be responsible. In reality, however, the list of state panchayati powers largely follows the Eleventh Schedule without modification and without specifying how such functions will be transferred to—or carried out by—the panchayats.[54] Therefore, much local governance power, including administering certain key poverty-alleviation schemes, remains firmly in the hands of state bureaucracies.[55] Moreover, state governments usually retain considerable control over the panchayats, such as through making laws that override panchayats' autonomy and withholding approval for panchayat activities.[56]

The same holds true for the transfer of key financial and personnel resources to the panchayats. Although the Seventy-Third Amendment mandates that states authorize panchayats to collect taxes, most states refuse to transfer more buoyant taxes, such as the excise tax.[57] Panchayats are thus left with taxes that are difficult to collect due to strong resistance from the local population, such as taxes on buildings and other property.[58] Consequently, panchayats generally have limited fiscal autonomy and are highly dependent upon central or state grants earmarked for specific purposes. On the personnel front, most states have neither provided adequate training to panchayat members nor systematically transferred jurisdiction over local government functionaries to the panchayats. As a result, panchayats (especially at the village level) generally lack the expertise and experience to administer local affairs, making them susceptible to exploitation by bureaucracies.[59]

Some states' unwillingness to cede functions and resources to the panchayats is hardly surprising. India is considered a "patronage

54. Nadkarni, Sivanna, and Suresh, *Decentralised Democracy in India*, 192.
55. "Report of the Task Force"; Manor, "Politics and Experimentation in India."
56. Nadkarni, Sivanna, and Suresh, *Decentralised Democracy in India*, 193.
57. "Report of the Task Force."
58. Nadkarni, Sivanna, and Suresh, *Decentralised Democracy in India*, 200–201.
59. Nadkarni, Sivanna, and Suresh, *Decentralised Democracy in India*, 194.

democracy," a country where the state distributes substantial resources in an extensive, inefficient, and discretionary fashion.[60] Among the three levels of government (i.e., union, state, and panchayat), the state governments traditionally have the greatest discretion in distributing such benefits, as the Constitution gives them primary responsibility for most policies that affect people's daily lives.[61] Furthermore, elected state officials can often indirectly influence the distribution process through their power over the bureaucrats responsible for implementing welfare policies.[62] Such power gives these politicians the opportunity to attract votes by intervening on behalf of their constituents.[63] Ceding functions and resources—many of which are closely associated with patronage politics—to the panchayats would thus diminish elected state officials' ability to score political points for future elections. The lackluster implementation of the Seventy-Third Amendment is therefore politically understandable.

On the other hand, several states have utilized the broad discretion afforded them by the Seventy-Third Amendment to advance local self-rule in highly innovative ways. One example is the ambitious Gram Swaraj reform in Madhya Pradesh, which was passed by the state legislature in 2001. The reform aimed to transfer most powers of the village panchayats to the gram sabhas (meetings of all village residents who may vote in panchayat elections). A gram sabha quorum is 20 percent of its members, of which at least one-third must be women; SCs and STs must also be included in proportion to their populations in the village.[64] The amended act empowers a gram sabha and the committees it has elected to assume much of a village panchayat's decision-making power, such as the power to identify beneficiaries of government programs.[65] It also gives a gram sabha the power to supervise the panchayat's functioning and audit its finances.[66] The reform has thus made

60. Das and Maiorano, "Post-Clientelistic Initiatives"; Bussell, *Clients and Constituents*, 7.

61. Chandra, *Why Ethnic Parties Succeed*, 131–32.

62. Bussell, *Clients and Constituents*, 150–55.

63. Bussell, *Clients and Constituents*, 166.

64. Sisodia, *Experiment of Direct Democracy*, 36–37.

65. Gupta, "Gram Sabha," 209–10.

66. Manor, "Democratic Decentralisation," 68.

gram sabhas—not panchayats—the center of local self-governance, effectively moving villages from a system of representative democracy to one of direct democracy. Empirical studies find that the reform has indeed transferred significant power to the gram sabhas, which regularly hold meetings.[67] However, participation by villagers—especially women—remains rather low, often allowing local elites to capture these gatherings.[68] Despite this deficiency, most observers recognize the unprecedented nature of Madhya Pradesh's reform and its value as "a school of experimentation and institutionalization of democratic decentralization."[69]

It is generally agreed, however, that the most influential experiment in panchayati raj was the one initiated in Kerala, which was largely a product of the state's tradition of progressive policy entrepreneurship. Following its first electoral victory in Kerala in 1957, the Communist Party of India (CPI)—and its successor CPI (Marxist) or CPIM—remained at the forefront of progressive policy innovations that ranged from land reforms to public health projects, eventually creating the world-famous Kerala model of development.[70] By the late twentieth century, however, the CPIM's policy initiatives were frequently frustrated by the state's political stalemate, with both the CPIM and its rival coalition commanding around 45 percent of electoral support and "the electoral fortunes swinging in favour of one front or the other depending upon chance factors or realignments among some of the minor parties."[71] At this point, the party concluded that decentralizing powers to the panchayats would help overcome the stalemate because "greater autonomy for the local bodies would create better mobilization prospects for radical forces within their localized pockets of influence"—a conclusion that made the party one of the staunchest supporters of panchayati raj.[72] Indeed, Kerala was initially like the many other states that responded to the Seventy-Third Amendment in a lackluster fashion. In 1994, its state government, led by a center-left

67. Gupta, "Gram Sabha," 213; Sisodia, *Experiment of Direct Democracy*, 183–88.
68. Sisodia, *Experiment of Direct Democracy*, 183–88; Gupta, "Gram Sabha," 213.
69. Gupta, "Gram Sabha," 213; Manor, "Democratic Decentralisation," 66.
70. Parayil, "The 'Kerala Model.'"
71. Isaac and Franke, *Local Democracy and Development*, 37.
72. Isaac and Franke, *Local Democracy and Development*, 35.

coalition, introduced a bill that gave very limited authority to the pan-chayats. It was not until the CPIM took power in 1996 that the real devolution of power began.[73]

Indeed, the CPIM's ambitious plan, the People's Campaign for Decentralized Planning, was almost a complete overhaul of the state's governing structure. Through legislation, the campaign empowered the panchayats to design and implement a full range of local develop-ment policies, especially local development schemes.[74] Most notably, the state legislature devolved 35 to 40 percent of development plan expenditures to the panchayats.[75] Unlike other states' panchayats, which mostly serve to implement state governments' decisions, Kerala's pan-chayats are empowered to plan how to use these funds.[76] As a result, the village panchayats' discretionary budgets more than quadrupled within a single year, from 1 billion rupees in 1996–1997 to 4.2 billion rupees in 1997–1998.[77] Indeed, a 2000 World Bank report indicates that Kerala was the most fiscally decentralized state in India and second only to the country of Columbia within the entire developing world.[78]

In addition, oversight of several state government service-providing functionaries, such as those working in agriculture, primary education, and children's health, were transferred to the panchayats.[79] The leaders of the panchayati raj thus gained the power to supervise and impose certain punishments on these officials.[80] The state government also established a massive training program, which provided admin-istrative training to more than 100,000 panchayat personnel each year.[81] Taken together, these aspects of the campaign—in a span of just a few years—transformed Kerala's panchayats into power centers of local self-governance with substantial fiscal and personnel capacities. Kerala's extraordinarily bold experiments in decentralizing power to

73. Franke, "Local Planning."
74. Heller, Harilal, and Chaudhuri, "Building Local Democracy," 631.
75. Heller, Harilal, and Chaudhuri, "Building Local Democracy," 630–31.
76. World Bank, "Overview of Rural Decentralization," II: 108.
77. Heller, Harilal, and Chaudhuri, "Building Local Democracy," 631.
78. World Bank, "Overview of Rural Decentralization," I: 27.
79. World Bank, "Overview of Rural Decentralization," II: 109.
80. Venugopal and Yilmaz, "Decentralization in Kerala," 322.
81. Chaudhuri, "What Difference Does a Constitutional Amendment Make?," 191.

the panchayats are closely associated with its distinct history of left-leaning party politics. The CPIM had been a key force in state elections for many decades, often leading the state government under a progressive agenda—including genuinely decentralized governance.[82] Studies have shown that this unusual progressive tradition was the major driving force behind the initiation and persistence of Kerala's panchayat innovations.[83]

In addition to enabling institutionalized self-government, Kerala's panchayat experiment has had a significant developmental impact. Heller, Harilal, and Chaudhuri's empirical study shows that local service delivery and development improved in almost every aspect as a result of the campaign.[84] This effect was particularly pronounced in redistribution-related areas, such as road building, housing for the poor, and child welfare. The study also finds that the campaign had a disproportionally large impact on socially and economically disadvantaged groups, such as women and members of the SCs and STs.[85] More recently, Kerala's model of panchayati raj proved itself again during the COVID-19 outbreak. During the early phase of the pandemic, Kerala was widely perceived as the state that best contained the outbreak, despite being one of the first with confirmed cases.[86] Many point out that a key component of Kerala's successful response is its highly active and well-resourced panchayati institutions. The local panchayats not only kept people informed of the disease and firmly enforced the lockdown but also assisted those struggling with food or money and called those in self-isolation twice a day to monitor their symptoms and needs.[87] Kerala panchayats performed these emergency roles effectively

82. Venugopal and Yilmaz, "Decentralization in Kerala," 319–21.

83. Heller, Harilal, and Chaudhuri, "Building Local Democracy," 633–35; Venugopal and Yilmaz, "Decentralization in Kerala," 319–21.

84. Heller, Harilal, and Chaudhuri, "Building Local Democracy," 632–33.

85. Heller, Harilal, and Chaudhuri, "Building Local Democracy," 635.

86. Hollingsworth and Suri, "India Coronavirus." Kerala experienced a surge in cases after the nationwide lockdown was lifted by the union government, but still maintained one of the lowest test positive rates and fatality rates in the country. *DW News*, "Tackling Coronavirus Pandemic."

87. Varghese, "Why Has Kerala Been so Successful in Tackling Coronavirus?"; Raghunandan, "Responding to COVID-19"; Manor, "COVID-19 and a Valuable Lesson."

and with relative ease, as they had already accumulated many years of experience in running the local health and welfare systems.[88]

The panchayati raj experiment thus showcases some of the key pro-experiment features of Indian federalism. Although the practice of panchayati raj has strong local roots, the union government—not the state governments—initiated this round of panchayat experiments. Although local governance has always been part of the Seventh Schedule's State List, the relatively low bar for constitutional amendments makes it easy for the union to overpower the states. This allowed the union to effectively commandeer the states to establish panchayati institutions that meet specific mandatory requirements, such as regular elections and reservations for marginalized groups. At the same time, India's vast size and diversity, coupled with its decentralization in recent decades, compelled the union to delegate most authority over the reform's design and implementation to the states. Such discretion gave rise to major subnational experiments, including Madhya Pradesh's Gram Swaraj and Kerala's People's Campaign for Decentralized Planning. These innovations, in turn, may inspire further national reforms, as illustrated by the union government's recent plan to issue a national guideline on participatory planning based on the Kerala model.[89]

However, the lackluster performance of most states in enabling the panchayati institutions also demonstrates the shortcomings of India's experimental model. The states' vast discretion means the success of the panchayat reform depends heavily on the political will of individual states' ruling parties or coalitions. This, in turn, means that the reform's outcome will be uneven across state lines and that innovations like those in Madhya Pradesh and Kerala are unlikely to be replicated by other states that do not share their particular political circumstances.[90] This case study thus seems to suggest that more union interference—in the form of executive or judicial enforcement of the Seventy-Third Amendment—may be necessary to promote local democratic decision-making in some states.[91] However, as later discussion

---

88. Varghese, "Why Has Kerala Been so Successful in Tackling Coronavirus?"
89. Muringatheri, "Other States to Emulate Kerala."
90. Mathur, *Panchayati Raj*, 41–43.
91. Brahmanandam, "Review of the 73rd Constitutional Amendment."

on India's recent minority policies shows, one should not be confident that the central government will always champion causes commonly perceived as in the vanguard.[92]

The Midday Meal Scheme and the Right to Food

The midday meal scheme, which eventually became an important component of the right to food movement, is another example of India's distinct version of experimentalism. India had been struggling with a low literacy rate since Independence. In 1981, for example, only about 40 percent of its citizens could read and write.[93] This low literacy rate was in large part due to India's low primary school enrollment and high dropout rate, both of which could be attributed to the extreme poverty of many Indian households. The problem was worsened by the traditional gender roles accepted in many parts of India, which made girls even less likely than boys to attend school. To combat this problem and to address the prevalent childhood malnutrition, several localities had been experimenting with free midday meals for decades.[94] However, none of these early programs made significant progress in achieving their stated objectives due to a lack of financial and administrative resources.[95]

The breakthrough came in the form of a politically and economically bold experiment in Tamil Nadu, a populous state in the southernmost part of India. In 1982, the state government, under the popular movie-star-turned-chief-minister M. G. Ramachandran (MGR), launched the Chief Minister's Nutritious Noon-Meals Programme. Unlike similar previous schemes, MGR's program not only provided its beneficiaries with nutritious foods but also significantly expanded

92. In the U.S. context, Althouse similarly questions "whether to trust Congress to choose the vanguard policy and impose it on the entire country—to take the risk Justice Brandeis wanted to avoid." Althouse, "Vanguard States, Laggard States," 1824.

93. UNESCO Institute for Statistics, "Literacy Rate, Adult Total."

94. Swaminathan, "Tamil Nadu's Midday Meal Scheme," 4811–12.

95. Swaminathan, "Tamil Nadu's Midday Meal Scheme," 4812; Ramachandran, "Mid-Day Meals."

eligibility.[96] At its launch, the program provided lunch to a whopping 6.5 million schoolchildren, who received about 400 calories of nutritious food (including vegetables, eggs, and cereals) per meal.[97] Eventually, other vulnerable groups, including preschool children, widows, and the elderly, were also covered by the program.[98]

The initiation of the midday meal scheme could be largely attributed to the populist and pro-welfare strategies of the main political parties in Tamil Nadu. MGR himself explained his rationale for launching the program:

> This scheme is an outcome of my experience of extreme starvation at an age when I knew only to cry when I was hungry. But for the munificence of a woman next door, who offered a bowl of rice gruel to my mother and us, [sic] when we were starving for three days, [sic] and saved us from the cruel hand of death, we would have left this world long ago. Such merciful women, having great faith in me, elected me as chief minister of Tamil Nadu. To wipe the tears of these women I have taken up this project.[99]

Despite their altruistic tone, the chief minister's words revealed a key motivation behind the midday meal scheme: that the politically mobilized rural poor had put great electoral pressure on subnational politicians to outdo one another in providing social welfare. Since the 1960s, India had witnessed a steady increase in political participation among the lower classes; Tamil Nadu was no exception. Singh notes that MGR's ADMK (Anna Dravida Munnetra Kazhagam) Party gained a political advantage over its archrival DMK (Dravida Munnetra Kazhagam) by "reach[ing] out to the most marginalized communities, for example, women and people from the lowest socioeconomic strata who had been at the margins of DMK mobilization."[100] Consequently, both parties

---

96. Swaminathan, "Tamil Nadu's Midday Meal Scheme," 4812.
97. Ramachandran, "Mid-Day Meals"; Maneesh, "Mid Day Meals."
98. Ramachandran, "Mid-Day Meals."
99. Pandian, *The Image Trap*, 1917.
100. Singh, *How Solidarity Works for Welfare*, 128.

started to initiate innovative social policies to present themselves as "the real friend of the poor."[101] The Chief Minister's Nutritious Noon-Meals Programme was only one among many such innovations, though it was certainly the most famous—and most expensive—example of the state's popularity-driven welfare programs.

Given the nutritious content of the provided foods and the program's wide eligibility, it came at a high financial cost for the predominantly poor state with a large budget deficit. The state government had to commit around 10 percent of its budget to keep it running. This amount exceeded the planned annual investment in agriculture as well as the combined planned annual investment in education, urban development, drinking water, and sewerage.[102] Such significant investment in a program that was unlikely to yield any immediate economic benefit was highly controversial given that Tamil Nadu—like the rest of India—was suffering from poor investment in its economy. As it took a large part of Tamil Nadu's budget that could have been used for development projects in agriculture or infrastructure, the midday meal program arguably hurt the state's immediate economic prospects. Indeed, the program was opposed by World Bank nutritionists and economists, who regarded its opportunity costs to be exceedingly high.[103]

MGR nevertheless remained determined to carry on. To fund the expensive meals, he used all the money he could find, including that in the state contingency fund, one day's salary from each government employee, and one month's salary from each ruling party state legislator.[104] MGR also personally chaired a government committee comprising senior state officials to oversee the scheme's implementation and overcome any political and administrative hurdles. Consequently, despite serious financial and logistical challenges, Tamil Nadu's midday meal scheme was quickly implemented throughout the state, achieving many of its stated goals. Reports indicate that by the end of 1982, school

101. Forrester, "Factions and Filmstars," 290.
102. Harriss, "Meals and Noon Meals," 402.
103. Harriss, "Meals and Noon Meals," 402.
104. Chawla, "MGR's Midday Nutritious Meal Scheme."

enrollment had increased by 70 percent and dropouts had decreased by 90 percent.[105]

The midday meal scheme was a huge political triumph for MGR. The immediate and highly visible effect of the program, coupled with MGR's efforts to brand it as his personal project, brought him immense popularity among the common people. According to a news report, the people at the feeding centers always reminded the children that the food was a gift from MGR himself:

> At one such centre, the wailing children were asked: "Who is giving you this sappadda (food)?" Chorused the children in reply: "MGR is giving us this sappadda."[106]

The policy paid off politically for MGR in the 1984 state assembly election, as it "greatly endeared [MGR's party] to the people."[107] MGR's party won 195 of the 234 seats, a victory that can be partially attributed to the popularity of his pro-poor policies.[108] It was, therefore, no surprise that MGR's political opponents viewed the scheme as a shrewd populist move to promote his own political image at the cost of the state's financial and economic health. A Rajya Sabha opposition member commented that "MGR is grossly exploiting the state's machinery and finances to project his own image by distributing alms [and] to divert the people's attention from their hardships."[109] However, there was little they could do but watch MGR's popularity and fame grow as he continued to promote and expand the midday meal program.

The success—at least from a political perspective—of Tamil Nadu's midday meal scheme prompted similar programs in other states and eventually at the national level. Gujarat and Kerala were the earliest to follow suit, introducing their own midday meal programs in the

---

105. Chawla, "MGR's Midday Nutritious Meal Scheme."
106. Chawla, "MGR's Midday Nutritious Meal Scheme."
107. Venkatramani, "AIADMK Govt in Tamil Nadu."
108. Other significant factors included MGR's own illness at the time of the election and the assassination of his ally, Congress leader Indira Gandhi. Venkatramani, "MGR Banks on Surge."
109. Chawla, "MGR's Midday Nutritious Meal Scheme."

mid-1980s.[110] By the early 1990s, about half of India's states had implemented some form of the program.[111] In 1995, the union government launched the National Programme for Nutrition Support to Primary Education (NP-NSPE), thereby scaling Tamil Nadu's innovation to the national level.[112] The NP-NSPE, which was a Centrally Sponsored Scheme (a form of conditional grant), called for cooked midday meals to be introduced in all government and government-aided primary schools within two years. The states would implement the program, and the cost would be shared between the two levels of government. The union would supply 100 grams of grains per child per day and subsidize grain transportation. The states would bear the costs of vegetables, oil, fuel, cook wages, and the provision of cooking facilities in schools. During the two-year intervening period, states were allowed to distribute monthly grain rations to the families of enrolled children in lieu of providing cooked meals in the schools.[113]

Few states, however, made the transition from grain rations to cooked meals as the NP-NSPE mandated. States that had established schemes prior to 1995—such as Tamil Nadu, Gujarat, and Kerala—continued to offer cooked meals in schools, but most states that lacked programs prior to 1995 had still not transitioned to cooked meals six years after the NP-NSPE launch.[114] By 2001, schoolchildren in these states were still receiving only three kilograms of raw wheat or rice grains per month, the distribution of which "was sporadic and of low

110. Kattumuri, "Food Security"; Jayaraman and Simroth, "The Impact of School Lunches."

111. Press Information Bureau, "Mid Day Meal."

112. For more information on the original 1995 NP-NSPE, see Ministry of Human Resource Development, "National Programme of Nutritional Support," 1–2. James Manor observes that "Parties in other states—and at the national level—which eventually adopted variations on this experiment, found it comparatively easy to do so for two reasons. Ramachandran always maintained rather courtly relations with leaders of all parties outside his state. And he posed no threat to those parties' prospects in other states because his appeal was largely anchored in his charismatic appeal among fans of the Tamil cinema—who lived overwhelmingly in his home state." In Manor, "Politics and Experimentation in India."

113. Ministry of Human Resource Development, "National Programme of Nutritional Support," 1–2.

114. Drèze, "Future of Mid-Day Meals," 4673.

quality," and "conditional attendance requirements went unen-
forced."[115] Such inconsistency in program implementation across state
lines was not unique to the NP-NSPE. In the late 1990s, India was
characterized by "significant variation at the state level in access to
subsidized food . . . depending upon how subsidies [were] targeted, how
food [was] stored and delivered, and how aware poor people [were] of
their entitlements."[116]

Responding to the ineffectiveness of many states' food programs,
India's civil society mobilized around the demand for a constitutional
right to food (RTF), including the right to a midday meal. The key
players in the RTF movement were NGOs such as the People's Union
for Civil Liberties (PUCL) and the Human Rights Law Network,[117]
many of which had extensive experience in social and legal mobilization on matters such as the right to information and employment.
These shared experiences gave them the necessary organizational and
legal expertise to launch the RTF movement and made it easy for them
to work jointly. For example, in 2000, 300 NGOs participated in a
meeting aimed at highlighting the continuous drought-related hunger
in the state of Rajasthan.[118] The RTF movement had been triggered
by a particularly severe drought that hit Rajasthan and several other
northern states in 2001, causing a significant number of starvation
deaths in the region.[119] In April 2001, the PUCL filed a PIL case in the
Supreme Court, claiming that the starvation took place "while . . . the
stocks of food grains in the country are more than the capacity of
storage facilities."[120] It also pointed out that the states could well afford
to expand their existing food schemes—including the midday meal
programs—to alleviate the widespread hunger in their jurisdictions.
The plaintiff argued that Article 21 of the Constitution, which guarantees the fundamental right to "life with human dignity," requires the
government to provide food to its people under certain circumstances
such as a drought. Based on this reading, the PUCL petitioned the

---

115. Jayaraman and Simroth, "The Impact of School Lunches."
116. Hertel, "A New Route to Norms Evolution," 611.
117. Hertel, "A New Route to Norms Evolution," 612.
118. Srinivasan and Narayanan, "Food Policy and Social Movements," 248–49.
119. Srinivasan and Narayanan, "Food Policy and Social Movements," 248–49.
120. Jayaraman and Simroth, "The Impact of School Lunches."

Supreme Court to order the release of grain stocks to famine-hit areas and to enforce various food schemes.

In the landmark case *PUCL v. India*, the Supreme Court of India famously established a constitutional right to food, which includes a legal entitlement to cooked midday meals for schoolchildren.[121] The Court ruled that the right to food was necessary to uphold Article 21 of the Constitution of India. Pursuant to such a right, the Court required all state governments to provide, among other things, cooked meals instead of grain rations under the midday meal schemes.[122] The Court's approach was forceful and hands-on: It not only kept the litigation open to retain oversight on relevant government policies but also issued fifty interim orders over the years detailing how the schemes should operate.[123] It specifically issued two mandatory Court orders on midday meals, one in 2001 and another in 2004. The first demanded that state governments provide every child in public primary schools with a prepared midday meal with a minimum nutritive content of 300 calories and eight to twelve grams of protein on each school day for a minimum of 200 days per year.[124] The second order extended the scope of the scheme to include more children and required the central government to provide financial assistance for cooking, transportation, management, and midday meals during summer vacations in drought-affected areas.[125] The ruling and the subsequent orders effectively turned the midday meal scheme from a loosely followed union government policy into a judicially enforceable entitlement, thereby putting significant legal and public pressure on both the union and state governments to ramp up their efforts to implement the scheme.[126]

121. PUCL v. Union of India and others (Writ Petition [Civil] No. 196 of 2001).

122. Other requirements included implementing the Famine Code, allocating more grain for the work scheme, selling grain to families below the poverty line at the set price, and issuing ration cards for free grain to all individuals without means of support.

123. Abeyratne, "Enforcing Socioeconomic Rights," 35–36.

124. PUCL v. Union of India and others (November 28, 2001, interim order).

125. Chutani, "School Lunch Program in India," 151–52.

126. Ministry of Human Resource Development, "National Programme of Nutritional Support," 3; Birchfield and Corsi, "Between Starvation and Globalization," 723–26.

The Supreme Court's ruling and subsequent orders on the midday meal program were implemented by both levels of government in a relatively timely and thorough fashion. To comply with the Court's orders, the union government revised the NP-NSPE in 2004, raising the meal's nutritional standards and subsidizing states to cover the costs of cooking, management, and meal provision during vacations in drought-affected regions.[127] The state governments likewise moved to comply with the Court's orders fairly quickly. According to a study that assessed the fulfillment of the new requirements in thirteen states, two fully implemented the requirements in 2002, five in 2003, four in 2004, and two in 2005.[128] This speed contrasts sharply with the states' lackluster response to the union government's NP-NSPE, reflecting another significant shift in India's constitutional structure. Despite the union government's declining influence over the states since the late 1980s, the Supreme Court's power and prestige had grown considerably over the same period.[129] In the midday meal case, the judiciary served as a counter-influence to the decentralization occurring during this period, as state administrations could ill afford to be accused of disobeying a clear order by the immensely popular high court—even if they could refuse to implement a union scheme on the same issue with little consequence.

Studies show that the expanded midday meal program had immediate and profound effects on the nutritional status of millions of children and their enrollment in schools across the country. Afridi discovered that the expanded program reduced the gap between the recommended dietary allowance and the average daily intake of a primary school student by up to 30 percent for calories, up to 10 percent for iron, and almost 100 percent for protein.[130] Singh, Park, and Dercon found that the Andhra Pradesh program (introduced in 2003) completely negated the effects of the severe drought on the nutrition of the state's children. For example, the midday meal program was

127. Press Information Bureau, "Mid Day Meal."
128. Jayaraman and Simroth, "The Impact of School Lunches."
129. See generally Mate, "Rise of Judicial Governance"; Moog, "Activism on the Indian Supreme Court"; Mehta, "The Indian Supreme Court"; Sen, "India's Democracy at 70."
130. Afridi, "Child Welfare Programs," 162.

responsible for 0.77 standard deviations in height gain (the approximate distance between the twenty-fifth and fiftieth percentiles) for an average sixty-five-month-old boy whose household suffered from the drought.[131] Using data from more than 420,000 schools observed between 2002 and 2004, Jayaraman and Simroth concluded that the expanded meal program was responsible for a statistically significant 13 percent increase in primary school enrollment.[132] Afridi found that this positive effect of the expansion was particularly pronounced for girls, who traditionally had lower attendance rates than boys.[133]

One notable takeaway from the case is the populist nature of Tamil Nadu's midday meal experiment. MGR launched the scheme with full knowledge that its high cost would take key resources from other development projects and thus hinder short- and even mid-term economic growth, especially given the state's poor financial situation. This deliberate act of prioritization reflects Tamil Nadu's nature as a "competitive populist" regime, in which "competing political parties project welfare policies to appeal to the public."[134] This version of populism was especially important in the Indian context, as successive administrations since Independence had strived to make the democratic process inclusive of the rural poor, who composed the vast majority of the nation's population. The increasing inclusiveness resulted in these groups using their votes to reward welfare projects like the midday meal scheme, even when their opportunity costs were high. Such popular capture of the experimental process offers an interesting contrast with authoritarian regimes, which are typically not influenced by electoral concerns but often still care deeply about their long-term popularity with the people.

However, the most striking feature of the midday meal story is probably the exceptionally important role of the Indian judiciary. It was the Indian Supreme Court—rather than the union Cabinet or Parliament—that cemented the project's national expansion by recognizing a constitutional right to food. This is somewhat similar to the

131. Singh, Park, and Dercon, "School Meals," 276–78.
132. Jayaraman and Simroth, "The Impact of School Lunches."
133. Afridi, "The Impact of School Meals."
134. Tillin, Deshpande, and Kailash, "Introduction," 17.

Fourteenth Amendment jurisprudence in the United States, under which the Supreme Court recognized many fundamental rights and imposed them on the states. In essence, both the Indian and the U.S. rights cases represent ways through which national governments impose their will onto states, greatly expanding federal power at the expense of state autonomy. However, two things set the role of India's apex court apart from that of the U.S. Supreme Court. First, the Indian Supreme Court, beyond its vibrant civil and political rights jurisprudence, demonstrated its willingness to recognize expansive socioeconomic rights—in this case, a right to food. This broader scope means more expansive federal power over the states, as it equips the Court to effectively oversee many welfare-related issues that were originally governed exclusively by the states. In other words, the Indian Supreme Court can expand welfare programs across the states—much like the U.S. Supreme Court expanded same-sex marriage—making it a powerful instrument for spreading successful state innovations.

Second, and more importantly, the Indian Supreme Court's growing power and prestige—especially relative to the declining influence of other union branches in the RTF movement—placed it in a unique position to scale up state experiments. As illustrated by the initial failures of the NP-NSPE, the regionalization of party politics since the late 1980s had severely weakened the central government's ability to press the states into implementing its preferred policies. The Supreme Court, on the other hand, had gained immense national popularity since the 1980s thanks to its civil rights jurisprudence and increased accessibility through the PIL system.[135] Consequently, the Court became "arguably the most powerful court among democratic polities,"[136] placing it in a powerful position to scale up certain rights-related innovations. The states' rapid compliance with the order in *PUCL v. India* indicates that state politicians were cautious about disobeying the Court's orders, though they had been ignoring similar requirements from the NP-NSPE for years.

135. Mehta, "The Indian Supreme Court," 246–47.
136. Mate, "Rise of Judicial Governance," 170.

The "Laboratory of Hindutva": Hindu Nationalism in Gujarat

The final case study on India concerns a darker subnational experiment: using communal conflict—including deadly violence—to achieve electoral gains. India is not alone in engaging in such experimentation. A better-known U.S. example is the southern states' resistance to the Supreme Court's landmark civil rights case *Brown v. Board of Education*.[137] The case, which ruled racial segregation in public schools unconstitutional, was highly unpopular among many white voters in the south, who rewarded state politicians who openly defied the Court's ruling. The pattern was illustrated by the landslide 1958 reelection of Arkansas Governor Orval Faubus, who notoriously ordered the Arkansas National Guard to prevent black students from attending Little Rock Central High School.[138] By the same token, southern state legislatures' "creativity in finding ways to avoid the law was seemingly inexhaustible."[139] Reed Sarratt identified four types of laws that southern state legislatures enacted during this period: pupil placement,[140] school closing, tuition grants,[141] and anti-NAACP (The National Association for the Advancement of Colored People) legislation.[142] When making these laws, the legislatures often borrowed ideas from similar laws in other states,[143] and in this process, some states, such as Virginia, became a "showplace for segregation devices."[144] In these cases, the federal laboratories became a powerful tool to generate and spread policies that were in serious tension with liberal democratic values.

India offers one of the most recent and consequential examples of using subnational experimentalism to generate populist and anti-

---

137. Brown v. Board of Education, 347 U.S. 483 (1954).

138. Rosenberg, *The Hollow Hope*, 78.

139. Rosenberg, *The Hollow Hope*, 79.

140. These laws gave local school boards the power to determine students' school assignments, effectively making it harder for black students to attend white schools.

141. These grants were mainly intended to allow white students to attend segregated private schools.

142. Sarratt, *The Ordeal of Desegregation*, 28–38.

143. For example, Sarratt, *The Ordeal of Desegregation*, 32–33.

144. Rosenberg, *The Hollow Hope*, 79.

minority policies. Hindutva—the ideology that promotes the hege-
mony of Hindus and the Hindu way of life—rapidly grew after the
Congress Party's defeat in the 1977 general election. In 1992, a Hindu
mob mobilized by the BJP demolished the Babri Masjid mosque in
Ayodhya, claiming it sat on the site of the Hindu god Ram's birthplace.
The resulting riot cost more than a thousand lives, most of whom were
Muslims. The Ayodhya incident, along with the general upsurge of
Hindutva ideology, paved the way for the much bloodier Gujarat
riots—and, ultimately, the rise of Modi as the dominant force in Indian
politics.[145]

The Gujarat riots of 2002 were an unmitigated humanitarian
disaster largely facilitated by entities associated with the state's government and the ruling BJP. On February 27, 2002, a train of Hindu pilgrims
returning from Ayodhya stopped in Godhra, a town in Gujarat. During
the stop, a coach car caught fire, resulting in fifty-nine deaths. Without
investigating, the state government, then led by Chief Minister Modi,
immediately placed the blame on Muslims.[146] The next day, the government displayed the remains of all fifty-nine victims in the railway
station in Ahmedabad (the largest city in Gujarat) and endorsed a state-
wide strike organized by radical right-wing group Vishva Hindu Pari-
shad (VHP). This led to communal riots in many cities and rural areas
throughout the state, resulting in 495 deaths in just three days. The violence against Muslims continued for months, costing more than a
thousand lives in total. Studies have found that the ruling BJP deliberately ordered the state's civil servants and police force to ignore the
riots,[147] and some BJP officials were even actively involved in instigating
mob violence.[148] Indeed, Modi himself justified the riots by saying that
the violence against Muslims was "an equal and opposite reaction" to
the Godhra train burning.[149] Consequently, the Modi government was

145. Dhattiwala and Biggs, "Political Logic of Ethnic Violence," 486.
146. There is still no definitive conclusion about how the fire started. Dhattiwala
and Biggs, "Political Logic of Ethnic Violence," 486.
147. Spodek, "In the Hindutva Laboratory," 357; Shamdasani, "The Gujarat Riots,"
547.
148. Berenschot, "The Spatial Distribution of Riots," 223.
149. Dhattiwala and Biggs, "Political Logic of Ethnic Violence," 486–87.

widely condemned by domestic and international media for being complicit in one of the worst pogroms in India's history.[150]

Ironically, rather than dealing a blow to his political career, Modi's incendiary and deadly approach during the riots vastly improved his electoral outlook in Gujarat. The BJP's position in the state had been precarious prior to the Godhra incident. It had lost a string of national and local elections, indicating that it was likely to lose the impending state election,[151] but the riots changed this outlook. Immediately after the violence, Modi called a new election in Gujarat and "represented himself as Gujarat's bulwark against Muslim violence and terror," an apparent attempt to capitalize on the communal sentiment of the Hindu population.[152] The strategy worked well for the party: In the December election, the BJP won 127 of the 182 assembly seats (up from 117 in the 1998 election). Indeed, the party's electoral success was most salient in the regions hit hardest by the riots.[153]

Later studies confirmed that the violence against Muslims was deliberately and strategically facilitated. For example, Dhattiwala and Biggs found that during the 2002 riots, the BJP did not actively instigate violence in areas where it had little hope to win in the upcoming election or already had enough support to win. The killing of Muslims was most prevalent in battleground electoral districts (i.e., where the BJP had previously won around 33–36 percent of the vote), indicating that the party intentionally fanned anti-Muslim violence in these areas to attract more voters in the coming election.[154]

From the perspective of experimentalism, there was a real risk that Modi's model of inciting communal sentiment for electoral gain might be repeated—by him or by right-wing politicians in other states or even nationally. After all, Gujarat was often referred to as the "Hindutva laboratory" by both the media and the leaders of the Hindu nationalist movement.[155] Since Modi's experiment appeared to work extraordinarily

---

150. Mishra, "The Gujarat Massacre"; Ghassem-Fachandi, *Pogrom in Gujarat.*
151. Spodek, "In the Hindutva Laboratory," 361.
152. Spodek, "In the Hindutva Laboratory," 365.
153. Spodek, "In the Hindutva Laboratory," 366.
154. Dhattiwala and Biggs, "The Political Logic of Ethnic Violence," 504; Berenschot, "The Spatial Distribution of Riots."
155. Spodek, "In the Hindutva Laboratory"; Sud, "The 'Laboratory of Hindutva.'"

well for him in the 2002 election, one might expect the strategy to be repeated by other BJP candidates. Indeed, after Modi's 2002 win, the VHP's leader declared the success of the "Gujarat experiment" and announced the intent to "make a laboratory of the whole country," saying, "Gujarat has become the graveyard of secular ideology and we will extend it to Delhi via Jaipur."[156]

However, this fear did not materialize in the decade following the 2002 riots, largely thanks to the BJP's reliance at the time on coalition politics in both the states and the center. In his seminal work *Votes and Violence*, Wilkinson uses empirical evidence to convincingly demonstrate that the 2002 riots were an exceptional case based on Gujarat's atypical electoral circumstances. According to Wilkinson, Gujarat was the only state in 2002 with both a low level of party fragmentation (the Congress and BJP had obtained 80 percent of the votes in the previous election) and a ruling party (the BJP) that did not rely on minority votes at all.[157] This gave Modi a free hand to use anti-Muslim violence to advance his electoral goals. However, in most other states—as well as in the Lok Sabha—partisan dynamics were highly fractured and competitive, making minorities (especially Muslims) pivotal swing voters for many political parties. Since BJP leaders elsewhere could not win elections on their own, they were forced to accommodate the needs of Muslim voters—especially their security needs—to maintain a ruling coalition with smaller parties that relied on minority voters.[158]

In fact, Modi himself soon shifted from the extreme Hindutva position to broaden his political base and prepare to enter national politics. Immediately after securing the 2002 Gujarat election, Modi switched gears, placing the government's emphasis on economic development. Such action surprised and marginalized the Hindu nationalist groups that helped elect him through the riots, effectively denying his old comrades "their share of space in a polity that is rightly or wrongly termed the laboratory of Hindutva."[159] This "betrayal" was so complete that the angry VHP launched a Hindu nationalist campaign against

156. *Hindustan Times*, "Gujarat Experiment."
157. Wilkinson, *Votes and Violence*, 155–56.
158. Wilkinson, *Votes and Violence*, 144.
159. Bhattacharya, "After Heated Speeches."

Modi and even supported a rebel BJP leader running against him in the 2007 state election.[160] Modi's new direction succeeded, as the nation increasingly associated him with Gujarat's fast growth rate and not the bloody 2002 riots. Capitalizing on this positive image, Modi mostly avoided Hindu nationalist rhetoric during his 2014 national campaign, instead focusing on issues such as growth, infrastructure, and corruption. The strategy helped Modi achieve a one-sided victory: The BJP independently secured a simple majority in the Lok Sabha—the first single-party majority in the chamber since 1989—and more than doubled its share of Muslim votes from the 2009 election (from 4 percent to 9 percent of all Muslim votes).[161] At this point, it seemed that Gujarat was not the laboratory of Hindutva but a mere stepping-stone for Modi's personal ambitions.

The rise of the BJP as the dominant party in India, however, began to undermine the electoral calculation behind Modi's moderated stance toward communal matters. Wilkinson's prediction that the BJP would limit its use of Hindu-Muslim conflict for electoral gain was premised upon the partisan fragmentation in most state legislative assemblies as well as in the Lok Sabha, but this is no longer the case. After the 2014 election, the BJP discovered that it could not only independently obtain a majority in the center but also win an increasing number of state elections without coalition partners. For example, in 2017 alone, the BJP won a simple majority in four of the seven state legislative assembly elections held that year. Scholars suggest various reasons for this dramatic shift in the electoral landscape, some pointing to factors such as Modi's personal charisma and the BJP's organizational advantages.[162] However, many agree that the more fundamental cause was the recent political realignment around the Hindu identity, through which traditional intra-Hindu cleavages like language, region, religion, and caste took a back seat to more general identity.[163] This led to a consolidated Hindu vote bank for the BJP, which rendered Muslim

160. Bhattacharya, "After Heated Speeches."

161. *Economic Times*, "Muslim Vote."

162. Chhibber and Verma, "Rise of the Second Dominant Party," 134–37.

163. Heath, "Communal Realignment"; Chhibber and Verma, "Rise of the Second Dominant Party System," 138–45.

votes increasingly irrelevant for the party because 80 percent of the Indian population identifies as Hindu.

This significant change in the electoral landscape, coupled with India's lackluster economic performance during Modi's first term as prime minister, drove Modi and the BJP to adopt a strategy reminiscent of the one they used in Gujarat in 2002. India had experienced considerable economic difficulty in the years leading to the 2019 general election, including a high rate of unemployment, a liquidity crisis, and a consumption slowdown. Modi, therefore, shifted the focus of his campaign from economic issues to security and communal matters, especially the threat posed by Muslims inside and outside the country. In many states, the campaign centered on issues such as the threat of "infiltrators" and "outsiders" from Pakistan (a thinly veiled reference to Indian Muslims), a pledge to abolish the special constitutional status of Jammu and Kashmir (the only Muslim-majority state), and the promise of a citizenship act that would make Muslim refugees who fled from persecution ineligible for Indian citizenship.[164]

The communal rhetoric of the campaign perfectly matched the needs of the consolidating Hindu voting bloc, resulting in a surge of vote shares from almost all Hindu castes and communities, including SCs, STs, and Other Backward Classes—none of whom were traditional supporters of the BJP.[165] It was thus unsurprising that the election was characterized by some observers as "a victory of Modi's tried and tested anti-Muslim plank that replicated the Gujarat model nationally."[166] This plank was also increasingly adopted by BJP leaders in subnational politics, most notably by the chief minister of Uttar Pradesh and notorious Hindutva firebrand Yogi Adityanath.[167]

In addition to learning from Modi's 2002 tactics, BJP-ruled states began to devise their own Hindutva "innovations." One example is the changing of primary school textbooks by the BJP government in Rajasthan. After defeating the Congress Party in the 2013 state election,

---

164. Shashidhar, "The Great Branding Campaign"; *India Today*, "BJP Manifesto 2019"; Ayyub, "I've Reported on Modi."

165. Sardesai, "The Religious Divide," 163.

166. Sardesai, "The Religious Divide," 162.

167. *Economic Times*, "Yogi Adityanath Drives BJP."

the BJP state government appointed a committee tasked with drafting new textbooks that embodied Hindutva principles. Introduced in 2016, the new textbooks had deleted almost all mention of minority identities (including Christian and Muslim) and aimed to carefully guide students to "view their country and community from the 'Hindu majoritarian perspective.'"[168] For example, the textbooks include content that glorifies cow-protection and excludes Muslims from a list of notable Indians. The move was criticized by Congress politicians as a blatant attempt to turn the education department of the Rajasthan government "into a 'laboratory of Hindutva.'"[169] Other examples of experiments from such laboratories include stricter state laws on cow-slaughtering and more funding for cow shelters, both of which fueled cow vigilantism among the BJP's core supporters.[170]

Indian states' experimentation with Hindutva policies is a prime example of the potential divergence between a power holder's and a third party's perspectives on the measures of policy success, as mentioned in the first chapter. From the view of the power holders—in this case, most states' predominantly Hindu electorates—the Hindutva policies advanced by the BJP fulfilled their political demand for a Hindu-centric national identity. Consequently, they rewarded many experimenters handsomely, paving the way to one-party dominance by the BJP. In this sense, the Hindutva experiments were mostly successful. On the other hand, many third-party observers, including scholars and journalists from both inside and outside India, find these experiments antithetical to India's constitutional and democratic values.[171] From this perspective, it is important to reflect upon potential institutional deficiencies that enable such manipulation of India's constitutional mechanism.

Indeed, Modi and the BJP's on-again, off-again relationship with radical anti-Muslim electoral tactics holds some important lessons about India's model of experimentation. As the Gujarat example illustrates, subnational experiments in a democratic system can be used to

168. Chowdhury, "BJP Government in Rajasthan."

169. Iqbal, "Rajasthan to Purge 'Distortions.'"

170. Siddiqui et al., "In Modi's India"; Safi, "Cow Slaughter."

171. For example, Jaffrelot, "India's Democracy at 70"; Siddiqui et al., "In Modi's India"; Wilkinson, *Votes and Violence*; Mishra, "The Gujarat Massacre."

test populist policies that target or disadvantage minorities. This raises the question of how much power subnational units should have when it comes to issues like policing and minority rights. As James Madison famously argues in Federalist No. 10,

> The smaller the society, the fewer probably will be the distinct parties and interests composing it; the fewer the distinct parties and interests, the more frequently will a majority be found of the same party; and the smaller the number of individuals composing a majority . . . the more easily will they concert and execute their plans of oppression. Extend the sphere, and you take in a greater variety of parties and interests; you make it less probable that a majority of the whole will have a common motive to invade the rights of other citizens; or if such a common motive exists, it will be more difficult for all who feel it to discover their own strength, and to act in unison with each other.[172]

Madison's argument, like Wilkinson's, lends support for a more centralized system. Under such a system, the diverse interests on the national stage will check the communal passions at the lower levels, thereby reducing anti-minority "innovations" and their wider diffusions. Modi's shelving of communal politics during his pre-2014 pursuit of national leadership also supports this proposition, as the fragmented partisan landscape and the resulting coalition politics constrained his ability to repeat his 2002 "success" in the laboratory of Hindutva.

However, when a nation becomes less politically diverse overall, this benefit of a centralized system decreases. For example, as coalition politics became less necessary for the BJP to maintain its rule, it reverted to its Hindutva roots, scaling up the policies that led to the Gujarat riots. This is where federalism's function of preventing central tyranny becomes more pronounced. For example, resistance to the Citizenship Amendment Act from opposition-ruled state governments became a major headache for Modi, especially because the states are responsible for administering it.[173] Moreover, as long as the states remain

---

172. Madison, "The Federalist Papers: No. 10."

173. Mansoor, "What Kerala's Challenge to Indian Citizenship Law Signals"; Kuchay, "Many Indian States."

powerful in their own right, the BJP—even with a comfortable majority in the Lok Sabha—must be careful with its policies to avoid losing in future state assembly elections, many of which are still up for grabs. In this sense, Indian federalism is serving as a useful check against the BJP's increasingly bold Hindu nationalist policies.

In sum, federalism plays a nuanced and shifting role in preventing "bad" innovations against minorities, such as the Hindutva policies that led to the 2002 Gujarat riots. If states become too autonomous— as the U.S. south before the Civil War (or even before the civil rights movement)—they risk becoming pockets of ignorance and populism that blatantly infringe minority rights without regard to national sentiment. On the other hand, if they become too dependent on the center, the risk of central tyranny may become too great, especially in the case of national dominance by an anti-minority populist party. Which risk is greater depends on the specific partisan dynamic, which is highly volatile and difficult to predict. Therefore, the combination of cooperative federalism (in which states hold considerable power, especially in implementing central laws and policies) and national political parties (which must compete for power at both levels) provides a middle-of-the-road solution by ensuring that all decisions by central and state governments are interconnected, which forces decision-makers at both levels to consider the broader political consequences of their actions. To be sure, this solution is highly imperfect, as both the Gujarat riots and recent national events illustrate. However, one can easily imagine worse scenarios if India were a loose confederacy or a completely unitary state.

Conclusion

The Indian case studies illustrate the pros and cons of the various elements of the country's model of experimentation. Although initially established as a highly centralized structure, India's federal system experienced a decentralization process in the late twentieth century due to rapid marketization and political fragmentation. This created an interesting combination of the union's powerful constitutional prerogatives and the states' increasing economic and political leverage that proved powerful for experimentalism—though not without some major caveats. For example, the panchayati raj case demonstrates both the potential and the shortfalls of the newly decentralized system. While some states (e.g., Madhya Pradesh and Kerala) utilized their vast discretion to devise innovative ways to create and operate grassroots democratic institutions, many others refused to empower their panchayats as the Seventy-Third Amendment mandated.

This lack of forceful central coordination—largely due to decades-long political fragmentation—was partially mitigated by the increasing power and prestige of the Supreme Court. In the right to food case, the Court successfully compelled the states to quickly adopt Tamil Nadu's famous scheme, though they had ignored similar demands from the union's executive branch for years. The decentralized system also evidences both advantages and disadvantages with regard to "bad" policy experiments in the example of the Gujarat riots. While a decentralized system might encourage certain states to infringe upon minority rights through "innovative" populist policies, an overcentralized one could be even more dangerous when the national electorate is dominated by anti-minority sentiment.

The Indian model also provides other takeaways that are particularly interesting when compared to its U.S. or Chinese counterparts. For example, MGR's decision to launch the expensive midday meal program despite Tamil Nadu's poor economy and finances provides a stark contrast to the priorities of the Chinese provincial governments. It is clear that MGR's all-in effort was at least partially driven by an expectation that the welfare program would boost his popularity among the rural poor—a key electorate for the chief minister in future state assembly elections. In contrast, innovations in China during the same period were almost exclusively focused on production and gross domestic product (GDP) growth, the most important performance metrics used by the center to evaluate a subnational or local leader for promotion. This comparison illustrates how the accountability structures of different models of experimentalism affect the priorities of subnational innovators. These comparative themes are explored in more detail in the final chapter.

CHAPTER THREE

The China Model

This chapter provides a theoretical framework for the mechanisms behind China's unique government innovation process.[1] This framework aims to address the shortcomings of both the decentralization theory and the factional competition theory by combining an analysis of China's constitutional arrangements with that of its intra-elite competition. In other words, it aims to answer the following questions: Is China's center-local structure decentralized, centralized, or both? How does this structure shape the behaviors of different factions when it comes to policy innovations? And conversely, how does the changing factional dynamic affect the system's ability to generate policy changes? In the case study section, this framework is applied to reexamine earlier examples of experimentation, including decollectivization and the Special Economic Zones (SEZ). It also includes an analysis of China's political innovations during the twenty-first century, such as those concerning competitive elections and civil society, thereby extending the scope of the experimentation theory across different times and subjects.

---

1. A version of this chapter previously appeared in the *Stanford Journal of International Law* 57 (2021): 137–90. When possible and appropriate, please cite that version. For information, visit https://law.stanford.edu/stanford-journal-of-international-law-sjil/.

Laboratories of Authoritarianism:
The Theoretical Framework

Like in the federal laboratories, China's cycle of experimentation results from the interplay between constitutional and political factors, particularly China's center-local structure and the political competition among party factions. The relationship of these two factors is analogous to that of the Colosseum and the gladiators: The former sets the stage and the rules, and the latter fight one another for prizes and spectator favor. Gladiatorial games—or in this case, the experimental cycle—cannot exist without both elements. It is therefore critical that any study of laboratories of authoritarianism understand both the functioning and interconnection of the constitutional framework and factional dynamics as well as their respective effects on the experimentation process.

Constitutional Structure

Just as Brandeis's idea of laboratories of democracy is based on the various institutions of federalism, China's laboratories of authoritarianism are premised upon a set of constitutional principles and institutional arrangements. Among them is the principle of "Two Initiatives" (两个积极性), which sets the overarching framework for the interaction between central and subnational governments. Under this principle, China's provincial governments—like some subnational governments in federal democracies—have broad discretion across many important policy fields; however, unlike in federal democracies, the central government has the power to appoint and remove top provincial leaders. In other words, while preserving the division of policy powers under formal federalism, the Chinese system completely reverses political accountability, which has significant implications for its ability to generate and spread policy innovations. This unique combination provides an arena for intraparty competition among political factions and forms the basis for the cycle of policy experimentation.

However, before diving into specific constitutional norms, one must clarify what defines "constitutional" in the Chinese context. Some assert that the text of the People's Republic of China (PRC) Constitution is the only legitimate source of constitutional law.[2] This proposition is supported by the Constitution itself, which declares itself the only "fundamental law of the state" and as having "supreme legal authority" over all other laws.[3] It also stipulates that the Constitution can only be amended by a supermajority vote of the National People's Congress (NPC), not the majority vote required by other legislation.[4]

One obvious issue with this textualist view is the clear divergence between constitutional texts and practices. For example, while the Constitution stipulates that the NPC is "the highest organ of state power,"[5] in practice, it mostly acts as a rubber stamp and is infinitely less powerful than the executive branch (i.e., the State Council)—not to mention the Communist Party. Therefore, such a proposition marginalizes the study of Chinese constitutional law, as it limits the subject to little more than window dressing—or, at best, "blueprints" or "billboards."[6] A less stringent view is that China's constitutional norms also include a series of laws with constitutional significance,[7] such as the Legislation Law, the Basic Law of Hong Kong, and laws regarding the organizational structure and election of the NPC.[8] Although immensely more inclusive than strict adherence to constitutional texts, this view does not completely solve the fundamental problem of the textualist approach, as many important and entrenched institutions and practices, such as the party's complex relationship with the government, are not captured by formal legislation. These omissions inevitably create significant gaps in understanding China's constitutional structure.

Some take a different approach by arguing that certain political decisions and norms—written or unwritten—should also be considered parts of China's Constitution. According to these scholars, China's

2. See generally Yao, "Guanyu Zhongguo Xianfa Yuanyuan."
3. Xianfa Preamble (1982).
4. Xianfa art. 64 (1982).
5. Xianfa art. 57 (1982).
6. See Ginsburg and Moustafa, "Introduction," 5–9.
7. See, e.g., Lin, "Constitutional Evolution through Legislation."
8. See, e.g., Ministry of Education of People's Republic of China, "Jiaoyubu Guanyu Zai Guojia."

Constitution often takes the form of political customs and precedents rather than formal legislation, a practice similar to those in countries with uncodified constitutions (e.g., the United Kingdom). For example, in his article "The Party's Leadership as a Living Constitution in China," He Xin claims that answers to the most important questions about the Chinese Constitution do not lie in its texts or the law but in "CCP documents, party practices, speeches of party leaders, and empirical evidence."[9] Along similar lines, Wen-Chen Chang and David Law argue that China practices "politics-centered constitutionalism," under which actions by political actors—such as the party and the State Council—serve as the primary form of constitutional implementation.[10] Jiang Shigong also argues that China is a country with "unwritten constitutional laws," including several "constitutional principles," such as the leadership of the party; the "trinity" principle that the head of the state, commander-in-chief, and head of the party should be vested in one person; and the principle of Two Initiatives.[11]

This chapter takes the position that the Chinese Constitution includes all the elements mentioned above—the Constitution, the statutes, and the other rules and practices of the party-state—as long as they meet certain thresholds. The inclusion of nonlegislative norms is especially important when studying China's constitutional practices across different periods, as the extensive use of formal legislation in areas of constitutional significance is a relatively recent phenomenon. However, for a norm to become constitutional, several requirements must be met to distinguish it from ordinary laws and policies. First, it must concern the role, powers, or structures of different entities within a state, the relationship between different levels of government, or the fundamental rights of the people. Second, it must be entrenched enough, either legally or politically, that it cannot be changed as easily as ordinary laws or policies (like a U.K. "constitutional" statute cannot be changed as easily as regular legislation despite being subject to the same parliamentary rules). Third, even under authoritarianism, a constitutional norm must function—as Tushnet suggests in his article on

9. He, "The Party's Leadership."
10. See Chang and Law, "Constitutional Dissonance in China," 28–33.
11. Jiang, "Written and Unwritten Constitutions."

authoritarian constitutionalism—as a constraint on the arbitrary use of government power (central or local).[12] Based on these criteria, the remainder of this section explores the constitutional principle of Two Initiatives and the ensuing institutional arrangements that characterize China's center-local relations.

"TWO INITIATIVES": THE CONSTITUTIONAL PRINCIPLE GOVERNING CENTER-LOCAL RELATIONS

Unlike the U.S. Constitution, which assigns enumerated powers to the federal government and (theoretically) reserves the remaining powers for the states, the PRC Constitution provides a vague statement regarding center-local relationship in its General Principles Chapter:

> The divisions of functions and powers between the central and local state organs is guided by the principle of giving full scope to the initiative and enthusiasm of the local authorities under the unified leadership of the central authorities.[13]

This so-called Two Initiatives concept (i.e., initiatives from both localities and the center) is deemed by many as the guiding principle—in theory and practice—for the constitutional relationship between China's central and subnational governments.[14] However, despite its prominence in the Chinese Constitution and official rhetoric, this principle has received limited attention in the English literature.[15] This is likely due to a general lack of interest in most of the articles of the PRC's Constitution among English legal scholars, who traditionally focus on judicially enforceable constitutional clauses. This disregard may also be due to the minimal political and legal controversy surrounding the

12. Tushnet, "Authoritarian Constitutionalism," 420.

13. Xianfa art. 3 (1982), http://www.npc.gov.cn/zgrdw/englishnpc/Constitution/2007-11/15/content_1372963.htm.

14. See, e.g., Zhu, "The Division of Power," 46–47; Jiang, "Written and Unwritten Constitutions," 33.

15. One notable exception is an English translation of Zhu Suli's influential 2004 article. Zhu, "Federalism in Contemporary China."

Two Initiatives principle. Unlike contentious constitutional issues, such as the market economy, protection of private property, and presidential term limits, this principle is rarely opposed or used to make politicized arguments. Nevertheless, Two Initiatives has been a critical component of China's constitutional order, though understanding the full range of its practical implications requires some digging.

From the text of the Constitution, it is easy to understand the meaning of "unified leadership of the central authorities," given China's formal status as a unitary state. Indeed, the Constitution clearly stipulates that (1) the NPC has the power to make laws in all domains and to annul local legislation that contravenes national laws,[16] and (2) the State Council (the executive branch of the central government) has the power "to exercise unified leadership over" the work of local governments.[17] In contrast, the rest of the Constitution provides little support for "giving full scope to the initiative and enthusiasm of the local authorities." One must therefore find other means to understand the meaning of the concept and track how the clause was implemented in historical practices.

In his famous article on the Two Initiatives principle, Zhu Suli summarized the principle's basic features based on his reading of relevant historical texts, in particular Mao Zedong's *On the Ten Major Relationships* (论十大关系). According to Zhu, "the initiative and enthusiasm of the local authorities" mainly include the following requirements:

a. Although the powers of the center are supreme, the center should consult the localities whose interests will likely be affected.
b. Local governments should be given considerable discretion in forming and implementing policies.[18]

Some scholars view these ideas as overly opaque and thus contributing to the under-institutionalization of China's center-local relations. For example, Zhu himself argues that the Two Initiatives

16. Xianfa art. 62, sec. 3, art. 67, sec. 2, 8 (1982).
17. Xianfa art. 89, sec. 4 (1982).
18. Zhu, "The Division of Power," 47.

principle—especially the directive to always consult local authorities—represents a conscious rejection of institutionalization in favor of a more flexible arrangement (though Zhu also notes that such a rejection was probably a reasonable choice during early PRC periods).[19] Similarly, Hu and Wang view Two Initiatives as being too "vague" and "policy-like," signifying that "the 1982 Constitution still rejects the institutionalization of center-local relations."[20] According to these scholars, the principle is increasingly impeding China's development, as it causes both unpredictability in its center-local relations and the severe problem of "where there is a policy from above, there is a countermeasure from below."[21]

On the other hand, some claim that Two Initiatives is an alternative—and better—way of institutionalizing China's center-local relations. Using the NPC's oversight power as an example, Lin Yan argues that China's center-local constitutional dynamic is not characterized by clear-cut power divisions and zero-sum games but by mutually beneficial collaboration among different levels of government.[22] Ding Yi similarly claims that Two Initiatives forms the important constitutional basis for flexibly adjusting center-local relations through repeated negotiation between the center and localities, thereby mitigating the problems associated with running a formally unitary system in a large and diverse country.[23]

Indeed, some of the core features of Two Initiatives are similar to certain constitutional principles associated with established federal systems. For example, the idea that the central government should always consult relevant local authorities before instituting policies that concern them brings to mind Canada's "executive federalism." Under this system, disputed issues concerning the provinces are often resolved through negotiations between the federal and provincial governments

---

19. Zhu, "The Division of Power," 47.
20. Hu and Wang, "Infrastructure Power," 56.
21. See Zhu, "The Division of Power," 49–50; Hu and Wang, "Infrastructure Power," 56.
22. See Lin, "Cooperative Federalism," 847.
23. See generally Ding, "Contract-Based Governance."

rather than by single authoritative decision-makers.[24] In other words, Canadian federalism is based on "practical stances like bargaining and compromise, to work out the bounds of central and state/provincial power."[25]

Similarly, the idea that local governments assume responsibility for implementing broad central directives is reminiscent of Germany's "administrative federalism." Article 83 of the German Basic Law provides that states "shall execute federal laws in their own right insofar as this Basic Law does not otherwise provide or permit."[26] Exclusive federal administrative structures exist only in limited areas, such as foreign affairs and armed services.[27] This means that states "predominate in the field of public administration because they establish and operate nearly all the country's administrative agencies."[28] This arrangement thus "encourages flexibility in adjusting national policy to local conditions."[29] Moreover, since the federal government relies heavily on state governments to implement its laws, the system also gives states substantial power to influence federal legislation.[30]

As a constitutional principle, therefore, Two Initiatives is not inherently anti-institutionalization despite its apparent vagueness. After all, there are some indeterminacies in the allocation of competences even in established federations such as Canada and Germany.[31] Therefore, on a purely theoretical level, Two Initiatives could serve as the constitutional principle for an institutionalized government structure. However, China does lack the kind of institutional guarantees typical

24. Field, "The Differing Federalisms," 118–19; see also Cameron and Simeon, "Intergovernmental Relations in Canada."

25. See Field, "The Differing Federalisms," 119.

26. Art. 83 GG.

27. See Kommers and Miller, *Constitutional Jurisprudence*, 144; Halberstam and Hills, "State Autonomy," 176.

28. Kommers and Miller, *Constitutional Jurisprudence*, 143.

29. Kommers and Miller, *Constitutional Jurisprudence*, 120.

30. Jackson and Tushnet, *Comparative Constitutional Law*, 1010.

31. See, e.g., Field, "The Differing Federalisms," 108–9. However, it should be noted that both Canada and Germany have extensive systems of checks and balances that prevent federal overreach—something absent in the Chinese system. This theme will be explored in more detail in the comparative chapter of this book.

of established federal democracies (most notably judicial review) that can theoretically help enforce such constitutional principles. It is therefore crucial to examine how Two Initiatives has been practiced by the party-state in real life.

Since the start of the Reform and Opening in the late 1970s, Two Initiatives did become China's official principle governing center-local relations, in both constitutional text and official rhetoric. Under the reign of Deng Xiaoping, it was incorporated into the General Principles Chapter of the 1982 Constitution and has remained in place ever since.[32] The concept also emerged repeatedly during speeches by top government leaders, often as the guiding principle for dealing with major reforms involving local governments. For example, during his last major speech as the general secretary of the CCP, Jiang Zemin discussed how the government should be guided by the Two Initiatives principle when restructuring China's vast state-owned enterprise sector:

> We should give full play to the initiative of both the central and local authorities on the precondition of upholding state ownership . . . The Central Government should represent the state in performing the functions as investor in large state-owned enterprises, infrastructure and important natural resources . . . while local governments should represent the state in performing the functions as investors with regard to other state property.[33]

Similarly, President Hu Jintao cited Two Initiatives as the overarching principle for reforming China's fiscal and taxation system, which aimed to strengthen the fiscal capacities of local governments.[34]

More importantly, unlike many other parts of the Chinese Constitution that serve primarily as window dressing, Two Initiatives remained an active component of China's political order throughout the studied period. Despite disagreements about the principle's merits, many scholars agree that it has profoundly shaped the institutional arrangements

32. Xianfa art. 3 (1982); see Jiang, "Written and Unwritten Constitutions," 36.
33. Jiang, "Full Text of Jiang Zemin's Report."
34. "Zhengzhiju Jiu Caishui Tizhi."

surrounding China's center-local relations.[35] The following subsections examine the divisions of policy-making and appointment/removal powers between the center and subnational governments under Two Initiatives, which have led to the formation of China's unique center-local structure. It also discusses the potential impacts of this structure on policy experimentation.

DECENTRALIZED POLICY-MAKING POWERS: DE FACTO FEDERALISM?

Similar to Montinola, Qian, and Weingast's formula of "federalism, Chinese style,"[36] Zheng Yongnian claims that China's central-local relationship can be defined as "de facto federalism" because it satisfies the following conditions:

a. A hierarchical political system in which the activities of government are divided between the provinces and the center in such a way that each kind of government has some activities on which it makes final decisions.

b. Intergovernmental decentralization is institutionalized to such a degree that it is increasingly becoming difficult, if not impossible, for the national government to unilaterally impose its discretion on the provinces and alter the distribution of authority between governments.

c. The provinces have primary responsibility over the economy and, to some extent, politics within their jurisdictions.[37]

According to Zheng, the division of policy-making power between China's center and subnational governments is similar to that in federal democracies. Certain powers, such as foreign policy and national defense, are exclusive to the national government, while responsibility for other issues, including local public security and most economic

---

35. See, e.g., Ding, "Contract-Based Governance"; Zhu, "The Division of Power," 48–49; Hu and Wang, "Infrastructure Power"; Jiang, "Written and Unwritten Constitutions," 37.

36. Montinola, Qian, and Weingast, "Federalism, Chinese Style," 55.

37. Zheng, "Explaining the Sources," 107.

matters, is reserved for the subnational governments.[38] Consequently, Zheng argues that "there is no essential difference between China's de facto federalism and other forms of federalism in the world in terms of policy formation and implementation, except that China is not democratic."[39]

Indeed, China's economic structure during the Reform and Opening era seems to provide a solid basis for such de facto federalism. Qian and Xu find that China's economic structure is much more decentralized than that of other communist states. They claim that Eastern Europe and the Soviet Union adopted a "U-form hierarchy," under which the role of local governments was limited to collecting information for and implementing directives from the central government.[40] Although China initially copied the centralized Soviet hierarchy, Mao announced China's turn toward Two Initiatives in a famous 1956 speech during which he dismissed the Soviet model and urged China to learn from "some capitalist countries."[41] China thus began a process of "administrative decentralization," which saw the central government's bureaucracy trimmed and the authority to supervise many state-owned enterprises delegated to local governments.[42] These changes, along with further economic decentralization during the Deng Xiaoping era, ultimately resulted in an "M-form hierarchy," which meant China's economy became organized into "a multi-layer-multi-regional form mainly according to territorial principle, in which each region at each layer can be regarded as an operating unit . . . [that is] relatively self-contained."[43] This decentralized structure was further strengthened as economic development became the central task of the party-state, in which the provinces played a central role.

The federalism arguments also find support from the theory of fragmented authoritarianism. Introduced by Lieberthal and Oksenberg in 1988, the concept depicts China as being characterized by disjointed

---

38. Zheng, "Explaining the Sources," 108.
39. Zheng, "Explaining the Sources," 108.
40. Qian and Xu, "Why China's Economic Reforms Differ," 143.
41. Mao, "On the Ten Major Relationships."
42. Qian and Xu, "Why China's Economic Reforms Differ," 145.
43. Qian and Xu, "Why China's Economic Reforms Differ," 144.

decision-making between the central and local governments.[44] According to this theory, although the different levels of government generally share the same overarching mandate from the central authority, policy outcomes in China are often shaped by the specific interests and preferences of the local governments.[45] This is particularly true because most local bureaucracies are not under the direct leadership of their functional superiors (described in Chinese as "leadership along a line" or 条上领导) but instead receive orders from local governments at the same administrative level ("leadership across a piece" or 块上领导).[46] Though China tried to strengthen the leadership of functional superiors in the late 1990s, the reforms only centralized "line" leadership from the township/county to the provincial level, which made subnational governments even more powerful.[47]

China's fiscal arrangements also reflected a decentralized policy-making structure. Throughout the Reform and Opening period, subnational governments occupied an increasingly large share of government spending. In 1978, the subnational governments were responsible for 52.6 percent of total expenditures; this number rose to 66.1 percent in 1988, 71.1 percent in 1998, 78.7 percent in 2008, and 85.1 percent in 2012.[48] In comparison, U.S. states and lower governments only accounted for 34 percent of U.S. government spending in 2022.[49] These numbers show that Chinese subnational governments were given extensive responsibilities in spending and that the center relied heavily on them to implement its national programs.

China's revenue collection system was also fairly decentralized, especially during the early part of the studied period. From the early 1980s through 1994, China maintained a "fiscal contract regime" (财政包干制), under which the center did not directly collect taxes but instead contracted with subnational governments—who were responsible for revenue collection—on the total amount or share of fiscal revenue

44. Lieberthal and Oksenberg, *Policy Making in China*.
45. Mertha, "'Fragmented Authoritarianism 2.0.'"
46. Mertha, "China's 'Soft' Centralization," 797.
47. Mertha, "China's 'Soft' Centralization."
48. National Bureau of Statistics of China, "Central and Local."
49. Bureau of Economic Analysis, "National Income."

to be remitted to the center during the subsequent several years.[50] This system greatly boosted subnational governments' fiscal power vis-à-vis the center. In 1993, localities accounted for 78 percent of revenue collection, while the center accounted for only 22 percent—not even enough to cover its own expenditures.[51] Such a system naturally "induce[d] a strong positive relationship between local revenue and local economic prosperity"[52] and further strengthened the self-contained nature of the subnational units.

The 1994 tax-sharing reform abolished the fiscal contract regime and gave the center much more control over revenue collection, but China's fiscal system remained relatively decentralized even compared to many federal systems. To remedy the exceedingly weak financial position of the center, the tax-sharing reform established the national tax collection system, thus giving the central government direct control over some important revenue sources, including value-added and customs taxes.[53] The localities retained exclusive access to several types of tax, however, including business and personal income taxes, as well as income from selling rights to state-owned lands.[54] Although these changes tilted the balance in favor of the center, the localities still held considerable revenue power, as they continued to collect around half of each state's income even after 1994.[55] By contrast, U.S. state and lower governments only collected about 34 percent of total U.S. revenue (excluding federal grants-in-aid) in 2022.[56]

However, although some "federalism" arguments rightfully point out the decentralized nature of China's center-local structure during the studied period, they fail to fully capture the complex interactions between the center and the localities. China's division of policy-making powers has never been as clear-cut as that in the U.S. Constitution, which is known for its "separation of functions or clear definition of

50. Montinola, Qian, and Weingast, "Federalism, Chinese Style," 63.

51. National Bureau of Statistics of China, "Central and Local."

52. Montinola, Qian, and Weingast, "Federalism, Chinese Style," 64.

53. Wong, "Central-Local Relations Revisited," 55.

54. Wong, "Central-Local Relations Revisited," 55–56.

55. Local governments accounted for 44.3–51.5 percent of total revenue collection between 1994 and 2001. National Bureau of Statistics of China, "Central and Local."

56. Bureau of Economic Analysis, "National Income."

boundaries" even among Western federal systems.[57] Instead, the power divisions between different levels of the Chinese government have been heavily shaped by the subnational governments' implementation (or lack thereof) of central directives and their continual negotiations with the center, as the Two Initiatives principle demands.

One prominent example is the spread of privatized agricultural production across provinces. As will be discussed in more detail later in this chapter, between 1979 and 1981, provinces chose different strategies for implementing the center's decollectivization plan. Some became "pioneers" by allowing grassroots innovation in privatization;[58] some acted as "bandwagoners" that closely followed the center's written directives;[59] and some were "resisters," lagging far behind others in the decollectivization process.[60] According to Chung, this great policy variation was due to Beijing's "painful realization that implementation was the key to successful reforms and enlisting local support was indispensable."[61]

In other words, the policy powers of the subnational governments are twofold. First, on matters where no clear national directives are present, localities can typically determine their own courses. Second, when faced with a central directive, localities often have substantial discretion regarding how—and to what extent—it will be carried out. Although this power-sharing arrangement is not as dualist as Montinola, Qian, and Weingast's or Zheng Yongnian's theories suggest, it gives the subnational governments extremely broad discretion in running their own jurisdictions. This is especially true because localities' power to implement central policies often allows them to effectively resist or substantially alter the center's instructions. Such discretion is what leads to frequent accusations of local protectionism[62] and—allegedly—the failure of various centrally mandated reforms in areas

57. Field, "The Differing Federalisms," 118.
58. Chung, *Central Control*, 101.
59. Chung, *Central Control*, 129.
60. Chung, *Central Control*, 137.
61. Chung, *Central Control*, 174.
62. See Zhu, "The Division of Power," 49–50; Hu and Wang, "Infrastructure Power," 56.

such as the judiciary and environment.[63] However, as will be discussed in detail later, the subnational governments' extensive authority to form their own distinct ways of governing can be a major boon for policy innovation, especially when such innovation risks violating political or legal norms.

CENTRALIZED APPOINTMENT/REMOVAL POWERS: CCP'S NOMENKLATURA AND DISCIPLINARY SYSTEMS

Decentralization, however, is only part of the story, as the Two Initiatives principle demands simultaneous local discretion and central supremacy. Although China's policy-making powers remained relatively decentralized during the studied period, the center maintained its institutional supremacy over localities mainly through the personnel management and disciplinary systems. To be sure, the Constitution provides other seemingly powerful mechanisms of central control, such as Article 67, which stipulates that the Standing Committee of the NPC can review and veto local legislation and government decisions that contravene national legislation.[64] In reality, however, this power is rarely used and thus has no substantial effect on the center's control over localities.[65] A second mechanism of central supremacy is provided by Article 89, which states that the State Council has the power "to exercise unified leadership over" all local governments and "to formulate the detailed division of functions and powers between the Central Government and [subnational governments]."[66] Although this provision offers more bite than Article 67, the State Council's control over local governments is not nearly as unified as Article 89 suggests. As discussed in the previous section, local governments enjoy considerable policy discretion, including the ability to deviate from central directives. Consequently, one is hard-pressed to find within the texts of the Constitution a mechanism of central control sufficiently strong to hold the vast country together.

63. See, e.g., Ng and He, *Embedded Courts*, 195.
64. Xianfa art. 67, sec. 8 (1982).
65. Jiang, "Written and Unwritten Constitutions," 32.
66. Xianfa art. 89, sec. 4 (1982).

That said, one need look no further than the most powerful political entity in the party-state to find such a mechanism. Though mentioned only in the preamble of the PRC Constitution until 2018,[67] the CCP has always been the elephant in the room, one that casts a long shadow over every aspect of China's constitutional order. The most important mechanism for the party's leadership over the state is the party committee system. A party committee exists for each government at every level of the state, from the center to the townships. Under the leadership of the party secretary (and in the center, the general secretary), each committee, mostly through a standing committee that consists of the main party and government leaders at the same level, makes the most important decisions for the jurisdiction.[68] Therefore, the party is not merely an integral part of China's constitutional structure but the very core. As discussed below, it serves not only as the center of political life for governments at each level but also as the primary vertical link connecting the levels. In other words, the party is the web that holds the entire state together.

More specifically, the Constitution's failure to provide a central control mechanism is primarily remedied by the party's relatively centralized appointment and removal system. Jiang Shigong notes that the key to the center's power over localities does not lie within the PRC's Constitution but rather in the CCP Constitution.[69] Article 10 of the CCP Constitution (which sets its organizational principle of "democratic centralism") stipulates that "lower-level Party organizations defer to higher-level Party organizations, and all organizations and members of the party defer to the National Congress and the Central Committee of the Party."[70] Such deference is primarily achieved through the nomenklatura system, under which the CCP controls the appointment of officials at all government levels. Since the early 1980s, the CCP has maintained a "one-level-down system" of

67. The 2018 Constitutional Amendment added to Article 1 of the Constitution the declaration that "leadership by the Communist Party of China is the defining feature of socialism with Chinese characteristics." Xianfa Preamble (1982); Amendment to the Constitution of the People's Republic of China of 2018.

68. He, "The Party's Leadership," 246–47.

69. Jiang, "Written and Unwritten Constitutions," 32.

70. "Constitution of the Communist Party of China."

cadre management that stipulates that key government and party officials at each local level are appointed by the party officials posted at the
level immediately above.[71] This means that the careers of subnational
leaders, including provincial party secretaries and governors, are
tightly controlled by the central party leadership.[72] The same is true for
top officials at lower administrative levels (e.g., county), who are appointed by the subnational party leadership. The nomenklatura system
thus serves as the center's trump card over localities and the basis of
its political and institutional supremacy, as subnational officials care
deeply about their own career advancement. In the rare event that a
subnational official openly defies a *politically unified* central government on a key priority, the center can use this system to remove the
obstructing official.[73]

Aside from being relatively centralized, another notable feature of
China's nomenklatura system is its meritocracy. Nathan claims that an
important source of the Chinese regime's resilience is the increasingly
meritocratic nature of China's cadre evaluation system, under which
top leaders "rose to the top predominantly because of administrative
skill, technical knowledge, educational background, and Party, rather
than personal loyalty."[74] This view is supported by empirical evidence
that suggests a strong positive correlation between economic performance (as measured by indicators such as GDP growth or revenue
collection) and promotion, including the promotion of subnational
officials to central government positions.[75] Besides economic performance, indicators such as stability maintenance[76] and environmental
protection[77] play increasingly important roles in the cadre evaluation

---

71. Landry, Lü, and Duan, "Does Performance Matter?," 1100.

72. It should be noted, however, that most other officials (such as those working
for various government agencies) are appointed by the party leadership at the same
administrative level.

73. See, e.g., Chung, *Central Control*, 161.

74. Nathan, "Authoritarian Resilience," 10.

75. See, e.g., Li and Zhou, "Political Turnover"; Shih, Adolph, and Liu, "Getting
Ahead"; Jia, Kudamatsu, and Seim, "Political Selection in China," 631.

76. See He, "Maintaining Stability by Law," 849.

77. Kostka, "Command without Control."

process.[78] Consequently, the nomenklatura system creates a kind of political tournament among local leaders at the same administrative level who compete on performance indicators for limited promotion opportunities.[79] The origin of this meritocratic feature is likely both cultural-historical and instrumental. The ancient Chinese idea of "Mandate of Heaven" dictates that rulers must be able and just or otherwise lose their legitimacy to rule. It is also widely perceived that, as the revolutionary ideologies have given way to economic development, the party has increasingly relied on performance legitimacy, thus making meritocracy an essential component of its political resilience.[80]

Another important mechanism of central control is the party's disciplinary system, which determines the removal and subsequent prosecution of most officials. According to the party's Constitution, subnational leaders can be disciplined and removed from their party posts by the Central Committee or the Politburo based on reports from the Central Commission for Discipline Inspection.[81] Since this commission "function[s] under the leadership of" the Central Committee and the Politburo, the disciplinary power over subnational officials is—like the power over their appointment—institutionally centralized.[82] Although much less frequently utilized than the appointment mechanism, the disciplinary system functions as a sword of Damocles for subnational actors. Indeed, the party's top leadership has used this power to remove and prosecute several high-profile provincial party secretaries for challenging the center's authority.[83]

Adding the party's nomenklatura and disciplinary systems into the mix fulfills the requirements of the Two Initiatives: The subnational governments enjoy substantial policy discretion within their own

78. Some studies, however, find that performance plays a larger role in the promotion of lower-level officials, and political factors—particularly factional affiliations—become more dominant as officials rise in rank. See, e.g., Landry, Lü, and Duan, "Does Performance Matter?," 1074; Choi, "Patronage and Performance," 965.

79. See generally Li and Zhou, "Political Turnover."

80. Nathan, "Authoritarian Resilience," 10.

81. "Constitution of the Communist Party of China."

82. "Constitution of the Communist Party of China."

83. For example, South China Morning Post, "Disgraced Officials Zhou Yongkang."

jurisdictions, while the center retains its supremacy through power over appointment and removal. On the one hand, the division of policy powers between the central and subnational governments is similar to— or even more decentralized than—many formal federal systems. On the other hand, because the key subnational leaders are appointed and removed by the central government rather than elected by their own constituents, the flow of political accountability is turned upside down. This reversal carries a series of important consequences, many of which are beyond the scope of this study. The following section will explore the structure's implications for policy experimentation and how it forms the institutional basis for the laboratories of authoritarianism.

AN EXPERIMENT-FRIENDLY SYSTEM?

The cycle of experimentation described by Heilmann includes two distinct but interrelated processes—local policy entrepreneurship and national adoption.[84] However, there is apparent tension in this formula: Local policy innovation requires local discretion in a given policy sphere, but national adoption of such innovation requires eliminating this discretion. To achieve the cycle of experimentation, a constitutional structure must allow the power over a specific issue to flow from a subnational government to the center when a local innovation is deemed successful, thus allowing the innovation to become a national policy.

China's unique center-local structure offers a possible answer. When an issue arises, and no apparent national solution exists, the subnational governments' broad policy discretion enables them to devise different policy tools to tackle the problem. More specifically, China's decentralized policy structure has several advantages when it comes to subnational policy entrepreneurship:

a.   Their self-contained economic structures and broad fiscal powers give subnational governments more resources to make and implement innovative programs without seeking approval or assistance from the center.

84. Heilmann, "Policy Experimentation in China's Economic Rise," 9–12.

b. Extensive policy discretion lets subnational officials explore a wide range of policy alternatives to achieve broadly defined national goals (e.g., economic growth or social stability), even when such policies might counter central directives or violate national laws.

c. Broad economic policy-making discretion creates opportunities for corruption by officials, which ironically increases policy experimentation. Since their material interests are closely tied to local economic development, subnational and lower-level officials have strong incentives to innovate as a way to attract investment and boost growth.[85] This effect is especially pronounced when media and institutional scrutiny against rent-seeking are weak, as was the case during the studied period in China.

d. Decentralization facilitates interjurisdictional competition, which further incentivizes local officials to experiment with new policies and to imitate the successful innovations of their peers.

e. Experiments—especially failed ones—are less disruptive to other jurisdictions and the entire system, as local governments operate independently of both the center and other localities.

In an ideal world, the center's power over subnational personnel would perfectly complement policy entrepreneurship. Assuming a *unified* central party leadership favors policy experimentation, the nomenklatura system provides an extremely useful tool for incentivizing local leaders to be creative. Since performance indicators play an important role in the promotion of local cadres, officials have a strong incentive to innovate—and to learn from others' innovations—in order to excel in the political tournament. Moreover, when the center decides that a successful local innovation should become a national policy, it can leverage its personnel power to encourage or even force subnational leaders to adopt the innovation. In this scenario, both the decentralized policy powers and centralized personnel powers work jointly, thus creating ideal conditions for completing the cycle of experimentation.

However, the centralized appointment/removal system also has the potential to stall the experimental process. If the party center is generally averse to policy experimentation—for reasons such as political

---

85. See, e.g., Heilmann, "Policy Experimentation in China's Economic Rise," 22.

conservatism or preference for centralized governance—and punishes local leaders who launch new policies, then the nomenklatura and/or disciplinary system may easily hold up the entire experimental cycle. Indeed, if one pushes the centralized personnel system to its extreme, a *unified* central government could simply replace all subnational leaders with sycophants who do nothing but steadfastly implement its explicit orders.

This two-sidedness is the curse (or blessing) of the Chinese system. The reversal of political accountability means that the system's operation is often determined not by the diverse preferences of voters living in different subnational units but by the political inclinations of the central government. Therefore, the functioning of the experimental process is highly susceptible to the vicissitudes of central politics, compelling those interested in China's approach to experimentalism to not only study its constitutional structure but also pay close attention to its elite politics. As discussed in the following section, the actions of the center largely reflect the political dynamics among various factions within the party. Consequently, the functioning of the laboratories of authoritarianism can fluctuate wildly with China's fast-changing factional landscape.

Intraparty Competition

China is similar to federal democracies in the sense that political competition plays a critical role in its center-local relationships and, by extension, in its experimentation process. However, instead of rival political parties, China has competing factions within the highest echelons of the CCP. After the death of Mao Zedong, who dominated Chinese politics for decades, intraparty competition became an important trend following the development of collective—instead of dictatorial—leadership over the CCP.[86] Prominent examples include the rivalry between Deng Xiaoping's reformist faction and Chen Yun's relatively conservative faction in the 1980s, as well as the conflict between the faction of President Hu Jintao (the Tuanpai) and the faction of former

86. Li, *Chinese Politics*, 250.

President Jiang Zemin (the "Shanghai Gang") in the 2000s.[87] These factions are often linked to various interest groups, representing different regions, bureaucracies, and populations.[88] For example, Li Cheng claims that the Tuanpai represented the interests of poor inland provinces and consequently emphasized economic equality and social justice. The Shanghai Gang, on the other hand, represented the elitist interests of the affluent coastal regions and was thus economically libertarian and politically conservative.[89] Li argues that such dynamics resulted in "a Chinese-style bipartisanship" that was "similar to systems found in other countries."[90]

China's intraparty competition, however, differs from partisan competitions in the West in one important aspect: Chinese factions are generally more personalist and thus less institutionalized than political parties in established democracies. In his groundbreaking 1973 paper on Chinese factionalism, Nathan claims that a faction "is based upon personal exchange ties rather than authority relations" and therefore "does not become corporatized after recruitment but remains structured along the lines of the original ties which formed the bases of recruitment."[91] To be sure, China's factions became more institutionalized in the late 1990s and 2000s, as the main factions increasingly relied on geographic or bureaucratic ties rather than purely personal ones to hold themselves together.[92] However, despite this gradual shift, factions in China still depend heavily on the personal connections, abilities, and ideologies of their top leaders, such as Deng Xiaoping, Chen Yun, Hu Jintao, and Jiang Zemin. Therefore, changes to these leaders' political stances, official positions, or health often have tremendous effects on factional dynamics. Consequently, factional politics in China has remains highly volatile, resulting in the observation of different phases within the laboratories of authoritarianism during the studied period.

---

87. See generally Fewsmith, *Elite Politics*.
88. See Shih, *Factions and Finance in China*.
89. Li, *Chinese Politics*, 251–52.
90. Li, *Chinese Politics*, 250.
91. Nathan, "A Factionalism Model," 42.
92. See generally Cheng, "Leadership Transition."

China's experimentation process enters a coordinated phase when the faction with a superior—but not completely dominating—position in the center is a strongly penetrating faction (i.e., a faction whose power base includes a substantial number of subnational leaders). In such a situation, faction patrons in the center have a strong incentive to safeguard the powers and discretion of the subnational units, as subnational leaders constitute a substantial part of their political alliance. They will also likely provide strong support for subnational experimentation since successful policy innovations can enhance faction members' performance in the localities and thus increase the faction's political capital. Furthermore, such a faction can use its superior position and the center's constitutional supremacy over localities to scale up successful experiments, forcing its political rivals to comply with its preferred policies and further consolidating its power. Under this coordinated phase, the cycle of experimentation thrives, as central and subnational leaders within the faction work closely to produce decentralized policy experiments and, when the experiments prove successful, their centrally coordinated expansion. This was the dominant mode from 1978 to 1989, during which Deng Xiaoping's subnational supporters conducted many important innovations that later became national policies, including privatization of agricultural production and marketization of many coastal cities. Such vibrant experimentation was largely due to Deng's superior—though by no means unchallenged—position in the center vis-à-vis the more conservative factions during this period.[93]

The laboratories of authoritarianism are in a muted phase when the more powerful faction in the center is weakly penetrating or non-penetrating, often one whose power is based on central ministries or party apparatus (e.g., the CCP Central Commission for Discipline Inspection) rather than subnational leadership. In this scenario, the factional leaders have little incentive to empower subnational units or to support their policy innovations, as such a faction stands to gain very little from the success of subnational units. Indeed, a weakly penetrating or non-penetrating faction is likely to be politically impaired if

93. Vogel, Deng Xiaoping; Cai and Treisman, "Did Government Decentralization Cause China's Economic Miracle?"

successful innovations come from members of rival factions with greater subnational penetration. Consequently, the center will likely use its constitutional supremacy to forestall subnational innovation, thereby thwarting the cycle of experimentation. The only example of this phase during the studied period is between the Tiananmen Incident in 1989 and re-liberalization in 1992, during which the more conservative and nonpenetrating faction had a clear upper hand against its more liberal and penetrating rival, which was accused of bringing about the political upheaval. The conservatives were able to substantially slow the process of China's Reform and Opening by discouraging the coastal provinces from policy innovation, fearing that further "capitalist" changes might revive momentum for their rivals.[94]

A third phase—the fragmented mode—occurs when the contest for supreme power remains close, with no single faction having clear political superiority. Under such circumstances, central patrons of penetrating factions still provide some political support, such as shielding experiments from rivals' political attacks, for their faction members' subnational experiments. However, unlike during a coordinated phase, the factions are far less capable of scaling up these experiments, especially when they address issues that are contentious among the political elites. Due to China's decentralized policy-making structure, it is difficult for the center to coerce subnational units to adopt policy innovations without utilizing its supreme power over subnational personnel. Therefore, when the center's power is fractured, no single faction can effectively use the appointment/removal powers against noncompliant subnational leaders. Consequently, the experimentation landscape becomes highly fragmented. Subnational units will compete by devising novel policies and learning from peers' successful innovations, but since the center can't turn these innovations into national policies, the experiments increasingly diversify China's policy landscape across regions. A prime example of this phase is the period between 2002 and 2012, during which the factions of Hu Jintao (the Tuanpai) and Jiang Zemin (the Shanghai Gang) battled bitterly for political supremacy.[95] The result was the emergence of several politically salient innovations, including

94. Fewsmith, *China since Tiananmen*, 21–47.
95. Li, *Chinese Politics*.

competitive local elections in Sichuan and Jiangsu and different models of civil society management in Beijing, Yunnan, Guangdong, and other provinces. However, despite yielding improved public goods provision and stability, such initiatives rarely became national policy, largely due to factional gridlock in the center.

The phases described above elucidate how laboratories of authoritarianism function under different factional dynamics. Although not an exhaustive list of possible scenarios, these three phases cover most of the periods between 1978 and 2012, during which no single faction gained complete political dominance in the center. Each phase thus serves as a subhypothesis for the case study section, which aims to answer one question: Do the studied experiments, which range from decollectivization to managing civil society, confirm the theories about how China's experimental mechanism performs under different political scenarios?

Case Studies

To test the theory about China's laboratories of authoritarianism, this section analyzes the major subnational policy innovations that occurred during the Reform and Opening era. To achieve their analytical purpose, the cases must meet two requirements. First, the innovation must meet the definition of experimentation, which means that: (1) its success can be objectively measured[96] in an institutionalized fashion,

96. Here, objectivity has two different meanings: First and foremost, it means that those who have the ultimate political power over the experimenters (e.g., the CCP center) must be able to evaluate the merit of the experiments based on certain concrete indicators in an institutionalized fashion, so that they can make decisions over the experimentation (e.g., whether to scale up the innovation and/or promote the experimenter). In the Chinese case, the measurement process often takes the form of cadre evaluation, and the indicators used in this process include GDP growth, revenue collection, number and magnitude of protests by local residents, number and severity of petitions against the local governments, and pollution indicators. For example, local officials sometimes tried to recruit NGOs to help them provide social services in the hope that it would help satisfy the local population and thus lower the number of protests and petitions. For the purposes of this study, objectivity also means that a third-party observer without any personal stake in the experiments can also obtain

such as through the cadre evaluation system;[97] (2) it must be repeatable by other political actors, which precludes policies too difficult (politically or financially) to be imitated;[98] and (3) it must be useful to other localities or the nation as a whole (i.e., the innovation must address an issue shared with other localities).

In addition, this study focuses on experiments that heavily involve China's provincial governments (including province-level municipalities such as Beijing and Shanghai) rather than innovations that concern only town and municipal governments. One consideration is comparability, as most literature on federal laboratories examines state-level policy innovations because states are the primary constituent units under federal systems. Experiments from states and provinces are also easier to scale up since central governments generally have much closer political connections with subnational governments than with lower-level governments. The larger sizes and populations of states/provinces also make their experiences with new policies more valuable to the center than those of municipalities or towns. This does

---

sufficient information to measure the merit of the innovations. Under some circumstances, the criteria for such measurements would be the same as or similar to the indicators for power-holders—for example, in the case of Special Economic Zones, the main criteria for both would likely include sustainable GDP growth. But where the self-interest of the power holders is drastically different from the public interest, such as in the case of civil society management, a third-party perspective can help comprehensively evaluate and understand the experimentation process.

97. One prominent example of an innovation being too politicized to be objectively measured is the Chongqing Model. Part of what made the Chongqing Model more politicized than other policy experiments was its wholesale and radical nature, as it negated many basic assumptions (economic and political) of the Reform and Opening era. As a result, it was hard to measure the merits of the model purely based on established indicators within the cadre evaluation system, such as GDP growth and stability maintenance. Whether to support the model, therefore, depended overwhelmingly upon the factional affiliation of the top leaders rather than on the merit of the experiment itself. Other experiments usually had narrower policy focuses, making them easier to evaluate with more objective and often quantifiable metrics.

98. For example, many popular components of the Chongqing Model, such as infrastructure, relied heavily on money borrowed from state-owned banks with which Bo Xilai had strong personal connections. This made it hard for these components to diffuse to other localities.

not mean, however, that lower local administrative units play no part in the experimental process. In fact, some of the most important experiments have been either initiated by municipal or lower governments (e.g., decollectivization) or executed by them (e.g., election experiments). In these cases, however, provincial governments provide crucial political protection and sponsorship of the experiments. More importantly, provincial leaders serve as the critical link between local policy entrepreneurs and the center, the latter of which has the final say on the fate of experiments.

The case studies include four sets of experiments: (1) the decollectivization reform (1978–1983), which supplanted the egalitarian People's Commune system with a household responsibility system; (2) the SEZ reform (1979–early 1990s), which introduced market mechanisms and opened coastal regions to foreign trade and investment; (3) the election experiments (1998–early 2010s) that introduced local elections in many regions across China; and (4) the civil society management systems (early 2000s–early 2010s) adopted by provinces to simultaneously utilize and control the booming social sector. These cases cover the two main productive phases of laboratories of authoritarianism during this period: The first two exemplify how the system works during the coordinated phase, while the latter two illustrate its functioning under the fragmented phase.

Decollectivization of the Rural Economy

One of the earliest and most successful examples of China's institutional experiments was the decollectivization of its vast rural economy. After the Great Leap Forward in 1958, most rural populations in China were organized into collective units called People's Communes (人民公社).[99] Under this system, almost all land and production belonged not to individuals but to the collectives and, ultimately, to the state.[100] Famers' compensation was based on their labor contribution and had little to do with agricultural output.[101] Unsurprisingly, this translated

99. See Lin, "Collectivization and China," 1234.
100. See Lin, "Collectivization and China," 1231–35.
101. See Lin, "Collectivization and China," 1234–35.

into extremely low incentive for farmers to produce and long-term nationwide food deficiencies (even famines) throughout this period.[102]

Despite their obvious deficiencies, the People's Communes, which were closely associated with communist orthodoxy and Mao Zedong, retained strong support from political elites in 1978, two years after Mao's death.[103] In the central government, their main defender was the relatively conservative faction led by party President Hua Guofeng, who advocated for the infamous "Two Whatevers" policy: "We will resolutely uphold whatever policy decisions Chairman Mao made, and unswervingly follow whatever instructions Chairman Mao gave."[104] On the other side of the political spectrum was the more reform-minded faction headed by Vice President Deng Xiaoping, a highly respected revolutionary war veteran. Due to his extensive connections in the party and the military, Deng's faction included many high-level officials in both the center and the provinces.[105] Although many reformists were dissatisfied with the inefficient collective mechanism, Deng was wary of directly opposing it in the central government, which would risk a serious accusation of "pursuing the capitalist road" and weaken his position.[106] The reformists therefore needed an alternative way to break the impasse.

The breakthrough came in the form of provincial experiments under the leadership of Deng's subnational protégés. In the late 1970s, the province of Anhui, then led by Deng's protégé Wan Li, became the first to attempt decollectivization. The experiment for household-based farming started in the now-famous Xiaogang village. In November 1978, driven by extreme poverty, eighteen local farmers secretly signed a "blood contract" that unlawfully divided the collective lands and assigned them to each household for family-based farming. According to the contract, each household would turn over some of its harvests to the government to satisfy the normal production quota but would

102. See, e.g., Lin, "Collectivization and China," 1229; Chang and Wen, "Communal Dining," 28–29.
103. Xu and Du, "Baochandaohu Tichu Guocheng"; Vogel, *Deng Xiaoping*, 436.
104. Xu and Du, "Baochandaohu Tichu Guocheng."
105. Shih, *Factions and Finance in China*, 89.
106. Vogel, *Deng Xiaoping*, 436.

keep the rest for its own consumption. Similar practices quickly spread to other localities in Anhui, with explicit endorsements from Wan and the rest of the provincial leadership.[107]

Anhui's experiments soon began to draw political backlash from the conservatives at the center, but Wan was able to withstand the pressure and carry on with his initiative. On March 15, 1979, the party's official newspaper, the *People's Daily*, published an article criticizing the experiment for undermining the collective system.[108] It was reported that Vice President Wang Dongxing, another key figure in the conservative faction, had even made direct calls to Anhui county officials to condemn their "serious deviations" from central policies.[109] However, lacking direct control over provincial policies, the conservatives could only hope that Wan would cave to the pressure and abandon his plans. Feeling the political heat, Wan asked Deng for his endorsement during a meeting in June 1979.[110] Although Deng was not ready to publicly back decollectivization at that point, he privately told Wan to "go ahead" and "seek the truth from the facts."[111] With Deng's acquiescence secured, Wan mostly disregarded conservative opposition and continued to encourage local officials in Anhui to expand the household responsibility system.[112] Before long, his perseverance paid off: Anhui enjoyed an exceptionally successful autumn harvest in 1979 in areas that adopted the new system, with Xiaogang village registering crop production that equaled the combined output during the first five years of the Cultural Revolution.[113]

Encouraged by the results in Anhui and similar successes in other provinces,[114] Deng and his allies in the center began to push for the expansion of decollectivization. In fall 1979, the party center issued an

107. Chung, *Central Control*, 93.
108. Chung, *Central Control*, 95.
109. Chung, *Central Control*, 96.
110. Vogel, *Deng Xiaoping*, 439.
111. Vogel, *Deng Xiaoping*, 439.
112. Chung, *Central Control*, 96–97.
113. Vogel, *Deng Xiaoping*, 440; Zhang, "Nongcun Gaige Qi Damu."
114. A similar but less bold experiment was conducted by Sichuan Party Secretary Zhao Ziyang, another of Deng's protégés, in 1978. Vogel, *Deng Xiaoping*, 438.

official document that relaxed adherence to collective principles by allowing the household responsibility system in "distant and mountainous areas."[115] More successes of the new system followed, and in May 1980, Deng finally voiced his unequivocal support for the household-based system, citing Anhui's achievements and criticizing the "unwarranted" fears of conservatives.[116] Around the same time, Wan was promoted to the position of vice premier and director of the State Agricultural Commission, giving him the authority to expand his innovation to other parts of the nation.[117] Riding on the momentum, the reformists further liberalized household farming, and most provinces—which had been closely monitoring the shifting political winds—soon voluntarily jumped on the bandwagon.[118] The nationwide percentage of production units under the household responsibility system rose from 1 percent in January 1980 to 78.2 percent in December 1982—a stunning increase considering decollectivization had been illegal just a few years earlier.[119]

Further emboldened, the reformists went on a full offensive to turn decollectivization into a mandatory national policy. In 1982, Wan and other reformist leaders stopped allowing provinces a choice, forcefully pushing for unified adoption of the household responsibility system across the country.[120] In a speech, Wan warned against "some people who resist [decollectivization]" and vowed to "help them to correctly understand the situation."[121] In 1983, Yang Yichen, the Party Secretary of Heilongjiang province and the most stubborn opponent of decollectivization was removed from his post and replaced by a reform supporter.[122] By the end of 1983, all sluggish provinces had submitted to the center's pressure, and 98.3 percent of the nation's production teams were under the household farming system.[123]

115. "1982 Nian Zhongyang."
116. *People's Daily Online*, "Lishi Xuanze."
117. Vogel, *Deng Xiaoping*, 441.
118. Chung, *Central Control*, 57.
119. Chung, *Central Control*, 111.
120. Chung, *Central Control*, 59–60.
121. Chung, *Central Control*, 60.
122. Chung, *Central Control*, 161.
123. Chung, *Central Control*, 60.

Overall, the household responsibility system reform proved a huge success. Studies show that the change significantly accelerated agricultural production and almost instantly improved the rural population's standard of living.[124] By 1984, some farmers began to produce more grain than they could sell, stocking state grain storehouses—a stark contrast to the decades-long food shortages during the Mao years.[125] Zhao Ziyang, then the premier and a key reformist figure, conceded in his memoir that the effect of decollectivization was so "magical" that even the reformers themselves could not have imagined it.[126]

These experiments were not only a significant policy achievement for the reformists but also an extraordinary political victory against their factional rivals. Along with other liberalizing reforms, the expansion and success of decollectivization dealt a serious blow to the old guards of Mao's legacies. In 1980, Hua Guofeng and several other conservative leaders who opposed decollectivization were relieved of their positions for their "leftist" mistakes, in particular their advocacy of "Two Whatevers."[127] With the promotion of Wan and several other liberal officials, the reformists headed by Deng Xiaoping substantially consolidated their hold on power, gaining them clear political superiority over their conservative rivals during most of the 1980s.

In many ways, the decollectivization reform was the prototypical case of China's laboratories of authoritarianism within a coordinated phase. The reform process included all three stages of the experimentation-based policy cycle, including discretionary experimentation, centrally coordinated diffusion, and unified national adoption.[128] More importantly, it perfectly illustrates how China's constitutional structure and factional politics interact to produce this cycle. For example, Wan utilized subnational policy discretion to push the unorthodox reform despite conservative objections, and the reformists used the center's personnel power to remove the obstructing provincial party secretary after gaining the political upper hand. It is therefore

124. See generally Prosterman, Hanstad, and Ping, "Can China Feed Itself?"; Yifu Lin, "Institutional Reforms," 202.

125. Zhao, *Prisoner of the State*, 97–98.

126. Zhao, *Prisoner of the State*, 97.

127. Vogel, *Deng Xiaoping*, 441.

128. Heilmann, "Policy Experimentation in China's Economic Rise," 9–12.

befitting that decollectivization is repeatedly hailed by the party leadership and the official media as the very spearhead of China's Reform and Opening.[129]

Special Economic Zones

Though rural decollectivization played an important role in creating momentum for the reformist agenda, it was the marketization experiments in the urban regions that directly caused the economic miracle that lifted China from an impoverished country to the second-largest economy. Among these experiments, the arguably most significant are the SEZs in Guangdong, which served as a marketization model for the rest of China. Similar to the collective economy in the rural regions, China's urban economy was highly nationalized and planned by the late 1970s, with the state owning almost all entities in the manufacturing and service sectors. There were also few transactions between China and Western industrialized countries, making it impossible for China to capitalize on its vast inexpensive and relatively well-educated labor force. The country's Soviet-like model caused extreme imbalances in economic development. While China saw a dramatic increase in its fixed asset investment between 1952 and 1980, its abysmal performance in per capita consumption during the same period meant that its living standards barely improved.[130]

Like with the decollectivization process, a political struggle ensued over marketization and opening the Chinese economy. On one side were the reformists led by Deng Xiaoping, whose position gradually gained the upper hand—and ultimately triumphed around 1980—over Hua Guofeng and his old guards. The reformist cause was championed by two of Deng's lieutenants in the center: Hu Yaobang, who served as the formal leader of the Communist Party from 1981 to 1987, and Zhao Ziyang, who was the premier and then secretary-general[131] between

129. For example, *Xinhua News*, "Xi Jinping Kaocha Xiaogangcun."
130. Zhao, *Prisoner of the State*, 124; Lin, "History and Future," 12.
131. After 1982, Secretary-General replaced Chairman as the title of the top leader of the Chinese Communist Party. Zhao replaced Hu Yaobang as the Secretary-General in 1987.

1980 and 1989. On the other side was Chen Yun, the head of the Central Commission for Discipline Inspection and the reformists' main opponent on the issue of marketization. Chen was not a conservative in the same way Hua Guofeng was—Chen opposed "Two Whatevers" and even Mao Zedong himself on multiple occasions, and he had been a strong ally of Deng and Wan in the decollectivization campaign.[132] However, Chen was more suspicious of rapid marketization than his reformist colleagues, preferring a more planned economy.[133] He was also more cautious about utilizing Western capital and allegedly wary of the imperialist intentions of Western investments.[134] Like Deng, Chen was a veteran of the revolutionary wars and commanded tremendous respect within the party, making him the focal point of those who opposed the marketization reforms.[135] According to a study, the core members of Chen's relatively conservative faction were mostly high-level officials who spent most of their careers in the central bureaucracies that managed China's vast planned economy, which made them natural opponents of marketization.[136] Again, Deng and his allies needed compelling evidence to demonstrate that their economic plan was superior to that of their opponents.

This time, Guangdong took the lead to become the undisputed vanguard of the Reform and Opening. Located on the southern coast of China, Guangdong was a natural starting point for marketization due to its long history of international trade and close proximity to Hong Kong, the trading and financial center of the region. In late 1978, Xi Zhongxun was appointed as the party secretary of Guangdong. Upon arriving in the province, Xi was shocked by the magnitude of poverty-driven illegal immigration to Hong Kong, prompting him to look for creative ways to improve the province's economy.[137] In April 1979, Xi asked Deng and other central leaders for more liberty to open Guangdong's economy to foreign investments.[138] In particular, Xi proposed

132. Vogel, *Deng Xiaoping*, 439.
133. Zhao, *Prisoner of the State*, 133.
134. Zhao, *Prisoner of the State*, 119–20.
135. Shih, *Factions and Finance in China*, 90–91.
136. Shih, *Factions and Finance in China*, 91.
137. Wu, "Xi Zhongxun"; Vogel, *Deng Xiaoping*, 395.
138. Wu, "Xi Zhongxun"; Vogel, *Deng Xiaoping*, 398.

setting up three "trade collaboration zones" with relaxed economic planning and regulations in the coastal areas of Guangdong.[139] Deng famously replied: "Let's call them Special Zones... We will give you a policy that allows you to charge ahead and cut through your own difficult road."[140]

Following Deng's approval, four Special Zones[141] (three in Guangdong and one in the adjacent Fujian province) were established in August 1979. A few months later, Deng, under pressure from Chen, changed the name to "Special Economic Zones" to assure conservatives that the experiments were not political.[142] The SEZs enjoyed many unprecedented privileges compared to the rest of China, including protection of private property rights, freedom to establish foreign-owned enterprises and joint ventures, and generous tax incentives.[143] Although companies could only export their products overseas (selling them domestically required special permission), they could obtain everything they needed from China, including land rights, raw materials, and workers.[144] Due to these attractive terms and the almost unlimited supply of cheap and educated labor, Guangdong's SEZs soon began to draw large numbers of foreign investors, especially overseas Chinese from Hong Kong and Southeast Asia.[145]

However, like the decollectivization experiments, the SEZs generated considerable political backlash from Deng's more conservative colleagues. Chen and his allies in the central planning bureaucracies were concerned that the spread of the SEZ model would cause the disintegration of the planned economy and ultimately turn China into a capitalist country.[146] After the SEZs were established, Chen repeatedly voiced his reservations: "Four SEZs are sufficient. We should not

139. Wu, "Xi Zhongxun"; Vogel, *Deng Xiaoping*, 398.
140. Wu, "Xi Zhongxun"; Vogel, *Deng Xiaoping*, 398.
141. Vogel, *Deng Xiaoping*, 402.
142. Vogel, *Deng Xiaoping*, 402.
143. *Beida Fabao*, "Regulation on Special Economic Zones."
144. *Beida Fabao*, "Regulation on Special Economic Zones."
145. Wu, "Xi Zhongxun."
146. Vogel, *Deng Xiaoping*, 400; Zhao, *Prisoner of the State*, 101–2.

establish any more," otherwise "foreign capitalists as well as domestic speculators at home will come out boldly and engage in speculation and profiteering."[147] The conservatives soon found the perfect opportunity to attack the SEZs. As head of the Central Commission for Discipline Inspection, Chen received a report detailing rampant smuggling and corruption among Guangdong's officials in January 1982.[148] Chen seized the opportunity to immediately launch a full-fledged assault against the SEZ marketization policies, calling the economic crimes in Guangdong "reflections on class struggle under new circumstances."[149] The conservatives even threatened to reinstall economic planning in the SEZs and cancel many of their privileges.[150]

Again, China's decentralized policy powers and the political fracture in the center saved the reformists' most prized innovation. As in the case of decollectivization, the conservatives in the center—despite having political momentum—lacked the power to bypass the subnational governments and directly control the experimental policies. Instead, Chen and his allies summoned Guangdong Party Secretary Ren Zhongyi—who recently succeeded Xi—to a Discipline Inspection conference in February 1982 to answer for his failure to stop economic crimes, hoping to pressure him into submission.[151] However, Ren had been lobbying the reformist factional patrons in the center, who privately ensured him that they supported his continuation of the SEZ experiments.[152] Their endorsements soon proved crucial to the SEZs and Ren's position. In March 1982, Chen requested removing Ren from his post in Guangdong because Ren was too "clever" and not principled enough on issues of economic crime.[153] It was reported that Hu and Zhao "repeatedly appealed" to Chen until Chen gave up the plan.[154] Finally, in December, Deng forwarded to the Politburo a field report that

147. Vogel, Deng Xiaoping, 412.
148. Liu and Fang, "Chen Yun."
149. Zhao, Prisoner of the State, 120–21.
150. Zhao, Prisoner of the State, 121–23.
151. Vogel, Deng Xiaoping, 362.
152. Vogel, Deng Xiaoping, 415–16.
153. Zhao, Prisoner of the State, 104.
154. Zhao, Prisoner of the State, 105.

praised Ren's efforts to deal with smuggling and corruption.[155] Based on the report, the Politburo promptly issued a document endorsing Guangdong's work to battle economic crime and confirming its support for the SEZs.[156] The SEZs were saved.

With the threat of the anti-smuggling campaign behind them, the reformists began to take advantage of the SEZs' tremendous economic success to push the spread of the model. Shortly after SEZ's establishment, the combination of foreign investment and local economy marketization brought almost miraculous changes. For example, the Shenzhen SEZ registered an average annual GDP growth of more than 60 percent between 1979 and 1984 (and 22.4 percent from 1979 to 2017), transforming it from an impoverished county into one of China's wealthiest municipalities in a matter of years.[157] These achievements generated strong momentum within the party leadership to further expand the SEZ model.[158]

In January 1984, Deng made a highly symbolic trip to the Shenzhen SEZ.[159] Deng, along with the millions of Chinese who watched him on TV, was excited by the city's mushrooming skyscrapers and factories.[160] He immediately announced that the "development and experience of the Shenzhen SEZ prove that our policy of establishing such zones is correct."[161] After his return to Beijing, Deng assembled his team and ordered them to prepare to set up more SEZs.[162] In May, the central government officially declared that fourteen more coastal cities, including Tianjin, Shanghai, and Guangzhou, would become open to foreign investment and marketization based on SEZ outcomes.[163] Unlike Shenzhen, which had been a small and poor county prior to becoming an SEZ, the fourteen cities included China's largest

---

155. Vogel, *Deng Xiaoping*, 417.
156. Vogel, *Deng Xiaoping*, 417.
157. Shenzhen Bureau of Statistics, "1979 Nian Yilai Shenzhen."
158. Vogel, *Deng Xiaoping*, 417.
159. Vogel, *Deng Xiaoping*, 418.
160. Vogel, *Deng Xiaoping*, 418–19.
161. Vogel, *Deng Xiaoping*, 418.
162. Vogel, *Deng Xiaoping*, 419.
163. *Xinhua News*, "1984 Nian Guowuyuan."

municipalities, responsible for a huge part of the Chinese economy.[164] Expanding the SEZ model to these regions thus represented a complete vindication of the experiments and of the Reform and Opening itself. Following the economic success of the newly opened cities, expansion of the SEZ model continued. According to a study, the proportion of municipalities with SEZ-like policies was 9 percent in 1985, 24 percent in 1990, 69 percent in 1995, and 92 percent in 2008.[165] It is not an over-statement to claim that China's status as the "factory of the world" and later as an economic superpower is due largely to the bold policy experiments in Guangdong. Like decollectivization, the SEZ experiments showcase the functioning of the laboratories of authoritarianism within a coordinated phase.

Local Elections

The experiments on local elections refer to the trials of direct or semi-direct elections of township-level government and/or party leaders between the late 1990s and early 2010s. These experiments were a direct response to the growing social unrest since the late 1990s, which was closely associated with the growing corruption, inequality, and other socioeconomic issues that accompanied China's rapid marketization.[166] Local governments were increasingly pressured by the center to deal with such sentiments and achieving "social stability" gradually became one of the most important criteria for promotions.[167] Social unrest became especially acute in rural regions, where township officials were tasked with collecting taxes and fees, implementing birth control, and enforcing bans on the traditional burial of the dead.[168] Consequently, some local officials began to contemplate elections as a way to improve the responsiveness of local governments and appease residents.[169]

In the late 1990s, the inland province of Sichuan became the nation's pioneer in this sensitive policy area. In March 1998, the party's

164. *China Information News*, "14 Ge Yanhai Chengshi."
165. Wang, "The Economic Impact," 136.
166. Ma and Wang, "Governance Innovations and Citizens," 374.
167. Li, "The Politics of Introducing Direct Township Elections," 707.
168. Li, "The Politics of Introducing Direct Township Elections," 706.
169. Ma and Pang, "The Rise and Fall," 610.

Sichuan Provincial Committee announced its unprecedented plan to adopt competitive elections at the township level.[170] In September, it issued the Interim Measures for Selection and Appointment of Sichuan Township Party and Government Officials, which stipulated that township leaders could be chosen by "popular nomination" and "self-nomination."[171] These actions by the provincial leadership became a rallying call for local leaders, who began to experiment with various competitive mechanisms. In December 1998, Buyun, a rural township located in Sichuan's Suining Municipality, held the first competitive township election since the founding of the People's Republic in 1949.[172] It included an open nomination process that required only thirty voters' signatures to participate in the primary, a primary election in which village representatives voted to generate finalists, and a popular election in which 6,236 of 11,347 eligible voters chose their leader from three candidates.[173] News of the election was first reported by the liberal newspaper *Southern Weekend* in early 1999 and was soon picked up by many other outlets, including both commercial and government-owned news websites.[174] However, the election was also criticized as unconstitutional by an official newspaper, which argued that the Chinese Constitution explicitly stipulates that government heads must be elected by their same-level People's Congress rather than by direct popular vote.[175]

Despite the criticism, other localities began to experiment with novel ways to inject competitive elements into the selection of state and party officials. However, to avoid similar controversies about the constitutionality of direct elections, many subsequent experiments took the form of *gongtui* (public nomination), in which the popular

170. Organizational Department of Chinese Communist Party Sichuan Provincial Committee, "Guanyu Gongxuan/Zhixuan."

171. Organizational Department of Chinese Communist Party Sichuan Provincial Committee, "Guanyu Gongxuan/Zhixuan."

172. Florini, Lai, and Tan, *China Experiments*; Organizational Department of Chinese Communist Party Sichuan Provincial Committee, "Guanyu Gongxuan/Zhixuan."

173. Florini, Lai, and Tan, *China Experiments*.

174. Florini, Lai, and Tan, *China Experiments*.

175. Li, "The Politics of Introducing Direct Township Elections," 121.

vote generates candidates rather than winners.[176] The local People's Congress—or, in the case of electing the party secretary, the local Party Congress—then formally elects officials as required by the Constitution and other laws.[177] Despite their obvious downgrade from Buyun's direct-election model, these experiments represent a major departure from the traditional practice of exclusive party nomination and appointment of officials and a significant step toward political participation. According to some scholars, these competitive or semicompetitive elections serve as venues of deliberative democracy that improve local governments' responsiveness and capacity.[178]

Although towns across many provinces adopted versions of election experiments, two provinces—Sichuan and Jiangsu—stand out as forerunners of this initiative during the 2000s. According to a 2010 study, of the 108 towns that conducted election experiments for party secretaries, Sichuan and Jiangsu were responsible for 29 and 21, respectively, while town elections in other provinces did not exceed single digits.[179] Even more noteworthy, Jiangsu expanded competitive elements from townships to counties and municipalities, a politically bold move considering the increased sensitivity to "democratizing" the selection of higher-level officials.[180]

Sichuan's and Jiangsu's audacity with election experiments can be largely attributed to the factional affiliations of their provincial leaders. During the height of the experiments, the provinces were led by Sichuan Party Secretary Zhang Xuezhong (2002–2006) and Jiangsu Party Secretary Li Yuanchao (2002–2007), both of whom belonged to the Tuanpai faction.[181] The Tuanpai, then led by President Hu Jintao and Premier Wen Jiabao, was based on its members' shared experience in the Communist

176. It should also be noted that these experiments varied significantly in terms of the openness of the nomination process and levels of public participation. Wang and Ma, "Participation and Competition," 304.

177. Wang and Ma, "Participation and Competition," 304.

178. See He and Warren, "Authoritarian Deliberation," 280–82; Nathan, "Authoritarian Resilience," 14; but see generally Ma and Wang, "Governance Innovations and Citizens."

179. Tsai, "Explaining Political Reform" 111.

180. "Li Yuanchao Dui Jiangsusheng."

181. Tsai and Dean, "Experimentation under Hierarchy."

Party's youth wing, the Youth League.[182] Many of its top leaders had extensive experience working in inland and underdeveloped provinces, which facilitated close ties between them and the many vulnerable groups in these regions.[183] Consequently, the Tuanpai was considered a "populist" faction in terms of its political and policy orientations.[184] This is demonstrated by its "putting people first" rhetoric and emphasis on equality and social justice, as opposed to previous administrations' focus on economic development.[185] Relatedly, the faction also showed more interest in introducing electoral mechanisms, which it considered potentially powerful tools for improving government responsiveness and promoting the faction's populist agenda.[186] Indeed, it was reported that Hu showed strong interest in Jiangsu's election experiments during his 2004 trip to the province.[187] During the trip, Hu met with Qiu He, a protégé of Li Yuanchao and the most prominent pioneer of electoral reforms in Jiangsu, requesting details about the new election system.[188] Hu's actions were viewed as a tacit endorsement of the experiments.[189] One of Hu's subordinates even explicitly confirmed that Hu acquiesced due to reports showing the positive social effects of the elections, including Qiu's popularity and the development of jurisdictions with competitive elections.[190]

A few years after the visit, Hu and his faction ramped up their support for the election experiments, particularly the intraparty variation. Most notably, in his keynote speech during the Seventeenth Communist Party Congress in 2007, Hu announced that the party would:

expand intra-Party democracy to develop people's democracy and increase intra-Party harmony to promote social harmony . . . We will

182. Li, *Chinese Politics*, 252.

183. Li, *Chinese Politics*, 279.

184. Li, *Chinese Politics*, 252.

185. Li, *Chinese Politics*, 252; Tsai, "Explaining Political Reform," 133.

186. Florini, Lai, and Tan, *China Experiments*, 75; Tsai, "Explaining Political Reform," 131–34.

187. Tsai, "Explaining Political Reform," 131; *Sina News*, "Qiu He."

188. Tsai, "Explaining Political Reform," 131; *Sina News*, "Qiu He."

189. Tsai, "Explaining Political Reform," 131.

190. Tsai, "Explaining Political Reform," 131.

reform the intra-Party electoral system and improve the system for nominating candidates and electoral methods. We will spread the practice
in which candidates for leading positions in primary Party organizations
are recommended both by Party members and the public in an open
manner and by the Party organization at the next higher level, gradually
extend direct election of leading members in primary Party organizations
to more places, and explore various ways to expand intra-Party democracy at the primary level.[191]

Due to the political prominence of the venue, Hu's speech was widely
perceived as strong support for the election experiments.[192] Perhaps
more importantly, Li Yuanchao, the party secretary of Jiangsu known
for his sponsorship of election experiments, was promoted to head of
the powerful CCP Organizational Department, which oversees the
appointment of high-level government and party officials.[193] After his
ascension, Li immediately announced his plan to push for the expansion of competitive local elections, specifically calling for the nation
to follow the examples of Jiangsu and Sichuan.[194] Using the power of
the Organizational Department, Li encouraged Jiangsu's provincial
leaders to extend the competitive process to the appointments of
higher-level officials and promoted several key reformers to higher
positions.

However, despite Hu's and Li's strong endorsements, the election
experiments did not become national policy like decollectivization and
SEZs did. To be sure, the experiment did diffuse to other areas, albeit
only for a limited time: Competitive nominations and elections for
township leaders and higher positions continued to thrive and expand
in pioneer provinces such as Sichuan and Jiangsu and spread to localities
in other provinces such as Hubei and Yunnan during the studied period
(they were mostly canceled by the center after the rise of Xi Jinping
in 2012).[195] However, the magnitude of diffusion was quite limited.

191. Hu, "Full Text of Hu Jintao's Report."
192. Qiang, "'Dangnei Minzhu.'"
193. *People's Daily Online*, "Li Yuanchao Tongzhi Jianli."
194. Li, "Li Yuanchao."
195. Wang and Ma, "Participation and Competition," 310; Ma and Pang, "The Rise
and Fall," 616.

According to one study, only about 1,000 competitive elections or selections had taken place by the end of 2013, which is a small percentage of the approximately 40,000 townships in China.[196] Why did the election experiments fail where the decollectivization and SEZs succeeded?

The difference lies largely in factional dynamics: While the decollectivization and SEZ experiments took place when China was within a coordinated phase, the election experiments emerged during a fragmented phase. During the late 1970s and 1980s, Deng and his reform-minded allies generally maintained political superiority in the central government, which enabled them to effectively utilize the center's supreme constitutional power to expand their preferred innovations despite opposition from conservative factions. In contrast, Hu and his Tuanpai faction were in a much weaker position, even though Hu was the official leader of both the party (as the secretary-general) and the state (as the president). Throughout his reign (2002–2012), Hu and the Tuanpai were entangled in a bitter political conflict with former President Jiang Zemin and his faction, the Shanghai Gang.[197] Unlike the populist Tuanpai, the Shanghai Gang had its political base in the rich and coastal provinces (especially Shanghai) and thus had a more elitist policy orientation.[198] It was economically libertarian but politically conservative and wary of free media and competitive elections.[199] Indeed, Jiang himself explicitly voiced his objection to township elections during a 2001 NPC session, saying that competitive elections at the village level "must not be extended to higher levels (including the township level)."[200] Although Jiang formally retired from politics in 2004, members of his faction continued to occupy many important positions both in the center (including in the highest decision-making body, the Standing Committee of the Politburo) and in the provinces.[201] Given the CCP's principle of "collective leadership," Hu and his allies were

196. Ma and Pang, "The Rise and Fall," 402.

197. Li, *Chinese Politics*, 250. For more detailed studies of pre-2012 factional politics in China, see, e.g., Bo, *China's Elite Politics*; Li, *China's Leaders*.

198. Li, *Chinese Politics*, 251.

199. Li, *Chinese Politics*, 251.

200. Li, "The Politics of Introducing Direct Township Elections," 704.

201. Li, *Chinese Politics*, 250.

unable to push the nationwide expansion of the election experiments past direct opposition from a similarly powerful faction.[202]

This result showcases how China's laboratories of authoritarianism function within a fragmented phase. As mentioned previously, when no single political faction claims clear political superiority and the experiments involve issues that are contentious among political elites, the experimental landscape will likely remain open and unsettled. Although political support from factional patrons such as Hu and Li might be sufficient to maintain the momentum of local reforms, it is not enough to overcome political opposition from other factions in the center. This renders the faction sponsoring the experiment unable to use the central government's supreme constitutional position to force localities to adopt the innovation. Consequently, no definitive national policy will come of the process, and the experiments will remain local and diverse across regions.

Civil Society

A similar story unfolded as the regime applied different models to manage China's growing civil society. As the marketization of the Chinese economy progressed during the 1990s, the old welfare system—which was based on the planned economy—declined rapidly, leading to the emergence of many new vulnerable groups. Charged with providing social services to their constituencies, many local governments lacked the resources to manage these mushrooming social issues and thus turned to NGOs—which were often well-funded by international sources—by either tolerating their operations or actively collaborating with them. During the earlier stage (the 1990s to mid-2000s), most NGOs operated within a depoliticized sphere, as they avoided openly confronting authorities.[203] However, in the 2000s, some NGOs began to pursue more fundamental changes, as demonstrated

---

202. See, e.g., *Deutsche Welle*, "Chuchuang Xiu Haishi Dongzhenge"; for general discussion on collective leadership, see generally Li, *Chinese Politics*; Hu, *Zhongguo Jiti Lingdao Tizhi*.

203. Schwartz, "Environmental NGOs in China."

by increases in PIL,[204] environmental campaigns,[205] and similar activities that created tension or hostility between civil society groups and authorities.

This created a dilemma for subnational leaders. While "the linkage of public goods provision to promotion . . . motivates local officials to cooperate with civil society to deliver public service,"[206] after the color revolutions and Arab Spring, officials were also under increasing pressure from the central government to "maintain stability"—often through asserting stricter control over internationally funded NGOs working in sensitive policy areas.[207] As Stern and O'Brien observe, with the exception of a few "no-go zones," China's central government has not enforced a consistently drawn boundary for civil society operations.[208] Rather, "the norm is granting local officials discretion to judge if a boundary has been crossed."[209] Since both public goods provision and stability maintenance are important criteria for promotion, subnational officials in different provinces began to experiment with various approaches to managing civil society with the aim of maximizing gains while containing political risks. For example, in 1998, the central government enacted the Regulation on Registration and Administration of Social Organizations, which required NGOs to register with the local Bureau of Civil Affairs and find a government or government-approved entity to be its supervising organization (业务主管部门).[210] However, the enforcement of the regulation was almost completely left to the local party-state, and some local governments even actively collaborated with unregistered NGOs.[211]

204. Wang and Gao, "Environmental Courts"; Jia, "China's Constitutional Entrepreneurs."

205. Johnson, "Regulatory Dynamism"; Van Rooij, "The People vs. Pollution."

206. Teets, "Let Many Civil Societies Bloom," 23.

207. Teets, "Let Many Civil Societies Bloom," 30–31.

208. Stern and O'Brien, "Politics at the Boundary," 15; see also Fu, "Fragmented Control"; Fu and Distelhorst, "Grassroots Participation and Repression."

209. Stern and O'Brien, "Politics at the Boundary," 15; see also Fu, "Fragmented Control"; Fu and Distelhorst, "Grassroots Participation and Repression."

210. "Regulation on Registration and Administration of Social Organizations."

211. Teets, "Let Many Civil Societies Bloom," 33.

Under these circumstances, a new dominant model of civil society management emerged during the 2000s. This new approach to the state-civil society relationship, which Teets terms "the consultative authoritarianism model," combines "a pluralistic society participating in policy formation and implementation and the use of multiple nuanced tools of state control."[212] Beijing, under the leadership of Shanghai Gang member Liu Qi (2002–2012), became a prominent pioneer of this approach by adopting a model of "broad registration, tight supervision" (宽审批，严监管). The capital city was one of the first province-level units to formally loosen the restrictive NGO registration requirements.[213] Starting in the late 2000s, the municipal government gradually eased regulations by allowing groups working in charity, welfare, and social services to register with the local Bureau of Civil Affairs without having a supervising organization.[214] In addition, the city provided resources for select NGOs in the form of incubators, funding, and training in project management, auditing, and accounting.[215] In exchange for registration and funding, however, the NGOs were required to make their finances more transparent, which some believe allowed "overt state control over previously gray areas allowing for more operational autonomy."[216] Moreover, the government used various methods to assert control over groups it deemed threatening to social stability or national security, including inviting NGO leaders to "have tea" to discuss the groups' activities,[217] banning colleges from supplying these groups with student volunteers,[218] and even temporarily shutting them down.[219] In these ways, the Beijing model tried to create a supervised civil society with indigenous financial sources, thus reducing the political risks associated with NGOs while maintaining

212. Teets, *Civil Society under Authoritarianism*, 97.

213. See Yin, "China's Attitude toward Foreign NGOs," 523; Wang, "NGO Zhucenan De Xianzhuang."

214. Simon, *Civil Society in China*, 330; Teets, *Civil Society under Authoritarianism*, 99.

215. Teets, "The Evolution of Civil Society," 171.

216. Teets, "The Evolution of Civil Society," 172.

217. Teets, *Civil Society under Authoritarianism*, 95.

218. Teets, *Civil Society under Authoritarianism*, 74.

219. Teets, *Civil Society under Authoritarianism*, 95.

their service-providing functions. In the late 2000s and early 2010s, this model gradually spread to other provinces, including Sichuan and Jiangsu, thus becoming the dominant form of civil society management in the authoritarian country.[220]

Again, the province of Guangdong served as the boundary pusher for the liberal-leaning reformers. In late 2011, Guangdong announced that "unless specific regulation provide[d] otherwise," it would eliminate the requirement that NGOs have a supervising organization starting in 2012.[221] This represented a significant step beyond Beijing's already relaxed registration rules, which still demanded that NGOs operating outside the fields of charity, welfare, and social services have a supervising organization.[222] Moreover, Guangdong seemed to advocate for a more fundamental change in the state-society relationship. In a famous 2012 speech, Guangdong Party Secretary Wang Yang—a prominent Tuanpai member—declared that Guangdong was aiming for "big society" and "small government"—phrases in obvious discord with the orthodox party-state approach.[223] Specifically, he announced that the government would separate itself from social organizations as a way to "vitalize the self-ruling function of the society" and encourage the public to participate in their work.[224] He even promised to transfer or outsource to these groups any government functions "that social organizations can handle and handle well."[225] Reports show that both reforms yielded considerable tangible effects. Registration became significantly easier for most civil society groups in 2012, resulting in many organizations being officially registered within a few months.[226] Some municipalities, including Guangzhou and Shenzhen, set up hundreds of "service centers" as platforms for systematically outsourcing social services to NGOs, leading to "explosive expansion" in certain civil society sectors.[227]

220. See Teets, *Civil Society under Authoritarianism*, 113–44; Stern and O'Brien, "Politics at the Boundary," 5.
221. Zhang, "Fazhi Ribao: Shehui Zuzhi."
222. Zhang, "Fazhi Ribao: Shehui Zuzhi."
223. *Sina News*, "Wang Yang: Jianshe Da Shehui."
224. *Sina News*, "Wang Yang: Jianshe Da Shehui."
225. *Guangzhou Daily*, "Wang Yang: Fan Shehui Zuzhi."
226. Niu, "'Songbang' Hou De Guangdong."
227. Simon, *Civil Society in China*, 277–80.

While Guangdong's actions secured some degree of political endorsement from Tuanpai central patrons, Wang Yang perfectly under-
stood the source of the challenges to his reforms. He said during a
meeting of the National Congress: "The biggest problem of decentralizing powers [to the social organizations] is . . . the barrier caused by
central laws and regulations."[228] To tackle this problem, Guangdong
officials visited Beijing in 2011 to seek the support of Li Liguo, who was
then the minister of civil affairs and consequently responsible for issues
related to civil society.[229] Li, who was considered a Tuanpai member due
to his earlier career in the Youth League, expressed strong approval for
Guangdong's reforms and a willingness to use its experience as a model
for national regulations.[230] The most significant endorsement, however,
came from higher up the political hierarchy: Wen Jiabao, then the Chinese premier and another prominent Tuanpai member, voiced his support for "society self-rule" in the high-profile 2012 National Civil Affairs
Conference.[231] During his speech, Wen urged the government to support the development of social organizations and to transfer more of its
administrative work and social service functions to these groups.[232]
Wen's words, broadly in line with the Tuanpai's populist policy orientation, signified the faction's backing of Guangdong's experiments and,
more generally, its approval of a bigger role for China's civil society.

Guangdong's liberal approach to civil society, however, also faced
strong opposition from the other side. In a widely reported article published in the party-owned journal *Qiushi*, Zhou Benshun, then the
secretary-general of the Central Political and Legal Affairs Commission[233] and a member of the Shanghai Gang, launched a direct attack
against the Guangdong experiments.[234] In the article, he warned about
"the trap of 'civil society' designed by some Western countries against

228. *Southern Metropolis Daily*, "Zhengfu Fangquan Gaige."
229. Simon, *Civil Society in China*, 330–31.
230. Simon, *Civil Society in China*, 330–31.
231. *Sina News*, "Wen Jiabao: Gongong Fuwu."
232. *Sina News*, "Wen Jiabao: Gongong Fuwu."
233. The Central Political and Legal Affairs Commission is a party entity overseeing all judicial, prosecutorial, and law-enforcement institutions and activities in
China. It reports directly to the party's Central Committee.
234. Zhou, "Zou Zhongguo Tese," 37; Qian, "'Gongmin Shehui.'"

us" and—without mentioning Guangdong by name—pointedly criticized the two main "mistakes" of the liberals: the idea of "small government, big society" and the separation of government from social organizations.[235] Stressing the importance of party leadership, he advocated a dominant role for government in social service provision and tight regulations over civil society to "prevent some social groups with ill intentions from multiplication."[236] Zhou Benshun's positions were supported by his direct superior, Zhou Yongkang, who was the head of the Central Political and Legal Affairs Commission and a member of the all-powerful Standing Committee of the Politburo. Around the time it published Zhou Benshun's article, *Qiushi* published Zhou Yongkang's speech on the same subject, in which he emphasized the "fundamental differences" between China's social organizations and Western civil society, declaring that China's management of these groups must "adhere to the Party's leadership"[237] As Zhou Yongkang was a key patron of the Shanghai Gang and one of the most powerful men in the country at the time, his speech—along with the article by his protégé—signified the elitist faction's strong opposition to the Guangdong experiments and its tacit endorsement of Beijing's more managed approach. This illustrates the significant interfactional rift within the central government regarding how to deal with China's burgeoning social sector.

As a result of the center's political gridlock, the regime's approach to civil society remained fragmented across regions. As with the election experiments, no single faction could scale its preferred version of civil society management to the national level. Under such circumstances, provincial party secretaries utilized their broad policy discretion to choose how to deal with civil society in their own jurisdictions. Teets observes that by the end of Hu Jintao's term, Beijing and Guangdong had become the standard-bearers of "two dominant competing models of civil society management" that were "represent[ing] a spectrum of possible relationships with the government."[238] As the models

235. Zhou, "Zou Zhongguo Tese," 37.
236. Zhou, "Zou Zhongguo Tese," 37.
237. Zhou, "Jiaqiang He Chuangxin Shehui Guanli," 7.
238. Teets, "The Evolution of Civil Society," 159.

of civil society management "diffused from pioneers such as [Guangdong] and Beijing to other provinces,"[239] each was free to position itself anywhere on the spectrum by combining different elements. Consequently, while some provinces chose to adopt either Guangdong's more autonomous approach or Beijing's more restrictive model, others took a middle path.[240] For example, while Yunnan emulated the Beijing model by placing heavier supervision on NGOs, it also preserved the historically significant presence of international NGOs and government-NGO collaborations to maintain its level of public goods provision.[241] This outcome illustrates that the fragmented phase can be advantageous for the regime. Since each province has its own distinct social issues and experiences with civil society, a unified national approach would likely be less efficient than localized solutions in providing social services and maintaining political stability.

Like the Indian experiments on Hindutva, Chinese provinces' new approaches to civil society management created another potential divergence between different measurements of success. From the perspectives of the power holders, that is, the central patrons of different factions, some of the experiments likely represented promising means to balance the risk and benefit of China's emerging civil society. Such favorable perceptions were illustrated by the political endorsements from the central political figures for both the Beijing and Guangdong models. On the other hand, from the perspectives of some domestic and international observers, such attempts to manage the civil society constituted a violation of citizen's constitutional right to freedom of association[242] and were inherently problematic.[243] However, unlike the Gujarat government's violent policies toward Muslims during the 2002

239. Teets, *Civil Society under Authoritarianism*, 174.

240. Teets, "The Evolution of Civil Society," 172. It is worth noting that, after Xi Jinping's successful consolidation of power, the Chinese central government has adopted a more restrictive model of civil society management, in many ways similar to that of Beijing toward the end of the Hu Jintao administration. By contrast, Guangdong's more liberal approach has largely been sidelined at the national level. See generally Diana and Greg Distelhorst, "Grassroots Participation and Repression."

241. Teets, "The Evolution of Civil Society," 169.

242. Constitution of People's Republic of China, Article 35.

243. For example, Human Rights Watch, "World Report 2012: China."

riots, which significantly made the minority group's lives worse than in previous decades, it was not clear that all models of civil society management would ultimately make the NGOs fare worse under China's authoritarian context. For instance, it was plausible that the Guangdong government was genuinely trying to establish a less repressive model, which, if imitated by others, might actually give certain NGOs more space to operate than before. Even some of the more prohibitive models, such as the one adopted by Yunnan, might be considered an effort to "harmonize" the civil society with the state so as to avoid more sweeping restrictions preferred by staunch conservatives like Zhou Benshun (and seemingly by more and more autocrats around the world). The case thus highlights the importance of evaluating subnational experiments in a more context-specific fashion—even for third-party observers who hold little stake in the process.

Conclusion

China's combination of a unique center-local constitutional structure and vibrant factionalism has produced one of the largest and most important laboratories of government policy in history. By selectively adopting and adapting Western policies and institutions, the experimental system has played a critical role in lifting hundreds of millions of people from poverty, turning one of the world's poorest countries into the second-largest economy in a span of a few decades. Even during the 2000s, when the system's ability to scale up innovations was significantly hampered by factional struggles, it nevertheless continued to incentivize subnational leaders to venture novel—and often norm-shattering—policies. The laboratories of authoritarianism were thus the key mechanism behind China's rapid transformation from a state plagued by extreme poverty and a personality cult to the wealthiest and likely most sophisticated authoritarian regime in history. However, it also suffered from poor functional stability, with factional dynamics in the center substantially affecting the operation of the laboratories of authoritarianism.

The four case studies illustrate these themes. On a broad level, they show that China's policy innovations have been generated by the dynamic interactions between China's center-local structure and its intra-elite factional politics. More specifically, the cases illustrate how the laboratories of authoritarianism function under different political circumstances. The decollectivization and SEZ reforms both occurred during a time when a penetrating faction—Deng Xiaoping and his reformist allies—held a superior position over their competitors. With such political superiority, the reformist patrons in the center could provide political cover for subnational experimenters, who used their broad discretion to initiate norm-defying policies. Moreover, by combining their superior position with the center's constitutional supremacy, the reformists forcefully expanded these innovations despite objections from opponents by seizing the political momentum created by the subnational experiments.

In contrast, most of the election and civil society experiments occurred when the central government politics was characterized by neck-and-neck rivalry between two penetrating factions, the Tuanpai and the Shanghai Gang. The standstill led to a decade-long policy gridlock, as neither side could make major national decisions when the other strongly objected. Consequently, controversial policies initiated by subnational members of the two dueling factions were unlikely to be either vetoed or scaled up by the center. This created a situation in which subnational leaders had great freedom to venture novel policies for managing problems in their own jurisdictions as well as opportunity to learn from innovations initiated by peers in other regions. The result was a highly diverse policy landscape, with subnational units often adopting different—sometimes almost diametrically opposed—schemes based on varied local conditions and leaders' policy orientations.[244]

---

244. See generally Mulvad, "Competing Hegemonic Projects."

CHAPTER FOUR

Experimentalist Constitutions

Comparison and Implications

This chapter compares the approaches of the United States, India, and China to subnational policy experiments. It pays special attention to the similarities and differences between the U.S. and India's democratic experimentalism and China's authoritarian approach, attempting to identify each model's comparative advantages and disadvantages. It is divided into five parts. The first discusses the three countries' constitutional systems—including their regime types and center-local structures—and how these arrangements affect their ability to experiment. The second part explores how political parties (in the United States and India) and factions (in China) compete under these constitutional frameworks as well as how this competition influences the functioning of the subnational laboratories. The third part examines the secondary but substantial roles of courts and nongovernment actors in the federal laboratories and what the lack of such influences means for the Chinese model. The fourth part summarizes the key takeaways from the comparison. The chapter concludes by discussing the study's implications for understanding policy experimentation under the Xi Jinping administration.

Constitutional Systems: Democratic/Authoritarian and Center-Local Structure

The constitutional infrastructure of a country's approach to experimentalism has two main components: the regime type (e.g., democratic or authoritarian) and the center-local structure. As the term "laboratories of democracy" indicates, being democratic is a key characteristic of the U.S.—as well as India's—approach to subnational experimentalism and center-local relations more generally. A core feature of the modern federal bargain is that the de facto leader of a subnational government should be democratically elected (directly or indirectly) by the constituents of the subnational unit.[1] This ensures that leaders are accountable to the people they govern, not to national leadership. Such accountability means that policy experiments conducted by the subnational government must be justified in local terms (i.e., that a venture's benefits should outweigh its costs and risks to the voters of a subnational unit).

The direction of accountability is largely reversed under China's laboratories of authoritarianism. Under the one-level-down appointment system, key provincial party and government leaders—including the party secretary and the governor—are nominated by the party center. In addition, these officials are within the jurisdiction of the party's Central Commission for Discipline Inspection, which has the power to remove them for corruption or other charges. These mechanisms ensure that a provincial government is primarily accountable to the center rather than to those living in the provincial constituencies—though subnational officials do attend to the needs of their jurisdiction to the extent that they are evaluated by the center on the outcomes of their policies.

Unlike the relatively black-and-white democratic/authoritarian distinction, a federal/unitary dichotomy is less helpful when comparing these countries. Facing the dual challenge of vast regional diversity and growing interregional connectedness, mega-nations like the United States, India, and China increasingly adopt a mixed approach

---

1. In India, the governor of a state is appointed by the president, while the chief minister is elected by voters of the state (under the Westminster system). Like the president, the governor's powers are nominal under most circumstances.

when it comes to center-local relations. As discussed in the previous chapters, the U.S. federal system has centralized considerably since the Civil War (especially during the New Deal). India was initially considered "quasi-federal" due to its heavily pro-union Constitution and only partially (and possibly only temporarily) "federalized" after significant changes in the political and economic landscape. On the other hand, the supposedly unitary Chinese system has devolved a great deal of fiscal and policy-making power to the subnational governments, in some ways more than its formally federal counterparts. In other words, the three countries' center-local relations are less distinctive than they might first appear to be.

These structural designs set the institutional framework under which subnational policy laboratories function. As a result, the three countries' vastly different constitutional systems offer a good opportunity to study the advantages and disadvantages of different arrangements in terms of their impacts on policy experiments. The following sections approach this issue from four different angles: incentive, priority, capacity, and diffusion.

Incentive to Experiment

One important implication of the difference between the democratic and authoritarian models is subnational officials' incentive to experiment. Freeriding is considered a potentially serious impediment to policy experimentation under the democratic model. The reasoning is simple: Subnational experiments provide valuable information to other actors (subnational or national) about the efficacy and potential risks of new policies, creating a positive information externality[2] that leads to free-rider problems and under-experimentation. Since subnational leaders in a democratic federal system are evaluated by constituents based on their local policy performance through gubernatorial elections, rational leaders wait to learn from their peers' experiments rather

2. See Rose-Ackerman, "Risk Taking and Reelection," 594; Galle and Leahy, "Laboratories of Democracy?"

than bear the costs and risks of experimenting themselves.[3] As Rose-Ackerman famously argues, because the American federal system—at least in its current form—cannot sufficiently address the externality problem, "few useful experiments will be carried out in [the federal laboratories]."[4] One possible mitigating factor, however, is heterogeneity among the states. More socially or economically advanced states may serve as hubs of policy innovation for neighboring states or the country as a whole, allowing a decentralized system to address the externality problem without outside interference.[5] For instance, states such as Wisconsin and California are often more innovative in areas like welfare and environmental policy. They thus naturally serve as hubs of policy experiments—as illustrated by the unemployment insurance and CAA case studies—thereby mitigating the incentive problem. Another issue to consider is governors' ambitions to run for higher offices. For example, governors aspiring to the U.S. presidency may be more willing to conduct experiments that provide a model for the national government, as this could benefit a governor's eventual run for the presidency.

China's authoritarian and more top-down model represents a more fundamental solution to the positive externality problem. In China, the appointment and removal of subnational leaders are determined by the central government rather than by subnational constituents. Therefore, the system can overcome positive externality by rewarding behaviors associated with policy experimentation. For example, the center can promote a subnational leader who initiated a successful experiment not only for the innovation's positive local outcome but also for the information generated. Along similar lines, the center can apply lighter or no penalties to those who fail at their creative initiatives, as even failed experiments generate useful information for both the center and other local governments. In other words, the Chinese system can—at least in theory—internalize the positive externalities associated with

3. See Rose-Ackerman, "Risk Taking and Reelection," 594; Strumpf, "Does Government Decentralization Increase Policy Innovation?," 208.

4. See Rose-Ackerman, "Risk Taking and Reelection," 594.

5. Walker, "The Diffusion of Innovations," 893; Strumpf, "Does Government Decentralization Increase Policy Innovation?," 228.

subnational experiments via its top-down accountability structure, thereby adjusting experimentation closer to the optimal level.

Evidence suggests that China's central government has indeed used this mechanism to encourage subnational experiments during the studied period. For example, some of the main innovators in the de-collectivization and SEZ reforms, including Wan Li (Anhui party secretary), Zhao Ziyang (Sichuan party secretary), and Xi Zhongxun (Guangdong party secretary), were promoted to prominent positions in the central government immediately after their initiatives started to produce favorable outcomes.[6] Similarly, Li Yuanchao was appointed to head the powerful CCP Organizational Department after his provincial career in Jiangsu, during which he pioneered various election reforms.[7] After his promotion, Li used the new position to promote other subnational leaders who experimented with competitive elections. Similarly, other studies show that the Chinese regime places considerable value on innovative behaviors when evaluating local cadres, even establishing the prestigious national Government Innovation Award to honor the best local experimenters.[8] This suggests that the Chinese approach might have an advantage in eliciting innovative behaviors *when the center prefers them*—a criterion that, as discussed later in this chapter, is not always present.

Priorities of Experiment

Another significant issue related to the democratic/authoritarian distinction is the political priorities of experimentation. Since subnational governments are accountable to different actors in democratic and authoritarian systems (local constituencies versus the central government), it is only natural that they will prioritize differently in the experimental process. Of particular relevance to this issue is the comparison between India and China. As the two countries had roughly similar levels of socioeconomic development at the start of the studied period (around 1980), they likely needed reforms in similar sets of

6. For example, Vogel, *Deng Xiaoping,* 441.
7. *People's Daily Online,* "Li Yuanchao Tongzhi Jianli."
8. See Zhu, "Mandate versus Championship," 124; Chen, "A U-Turn," 664–65.

policy areas. Therefore, their divergent choices of subnational experiments may reflect their different accountability structures.

India's democratic system contributes to the diversity of its experimental policies. Many Indian politicians—most notably Indira Gandhi—have mobilized people of lower socioeconomic status, often in an effort to expand their own voter base. This process has increasingly opened India's political process to more diverse—and sometimes more populist—demands from different social groups, and this diversity is reflected in the wide range of experiments subnational leaders have conducted. Manor notes that Indian politicians "believe that while growth may inspire popular support, much more will be gained from new initiatives on several of the other fronts," such as democratization, poverty reduction, and land reforms.[9] Tamil Nadu's midday meal reform is a good example. Chief Minister MGR launched the expensive program despite knowing that it would take already scarce fiscal resources from critical growth-oriented projects, as he believed—rightly— that the reform would make him immensely popular with his most important political base, the rural poor. Similarly, Kerala's People's Campaign for Decentralized Planning and Gujarat's "laboratory of Hindutva" were both attempts to draw popular support through experiments catering to the demands of the incumbents' target voters.

In contrast, China's authoritarian system results in an experimental approach focused on a limited set of objectives. Under the one-level-down appointment system, local officials are evaluated based on criteria such as economic growth, revenue collection, and social stability. Unlike subnational officials in India, who must respond to bottom-up demand from diverse social forces, Chinese provincial officials need only focus on the relatively stable criteria set by the center. The experiments from the late 1970s to the late 1990s are particularly illustrative. Given the central leadership's (especially Deng Xiaoping's) strong emphasis on boosting production and economic growth, almost all major local experiments during this period (including the decollectivization and SEZ reforms) focused on these objectives. It would be unimaginable for a provincial leader to use limited financial resources to launch a large-scale welfare program like India's midday meal scheme,

9. Manor, "Politics and Experimentation in India," 11–12.

as such behavior would be unlikely to increase GDP—or their chances of promotion.

In the late 1990s and the 2000s, as China's economy continued to grow, promoting social stability or a "harmonious society" became another important criterion for cadre evaluation. This prompted experiments geared toward enhancing government responsiveness and finding new ways to interact with emerging social forces, such as the election experiments and the civil society management reforms. Despite being more diverse than those in the 1980s, the experiments in the 2000s were nevertheless a direct and focused response to the center's political priorities at the time.

This top-down focus has its advantages and disadvantages compared to the diversity produced by the democratic model. A more focused model can often achieve its objectives sooner and more effectively, as illustrated by the early experiments' immense contribution to China's economic "miracle." The inherently elitist nature of the Chinese approach might also help avoid certain kinds of populist experiments, such as the Gujarat government's incitement of communal violence in 2002. However, this focused approach may also deprive the country of many possible policy options. For example, the election experiments—which represented a potential path toward democratization—were completely abandoned when the new administration decided against them in the early 2010s. This lack of diversity is inherently in tension with the spirit of experimentalism, the purpose of which is to offer new and varied policy choices.

Capacity to Experiment

With motivation and political priorities set, the next question is whether a subnational unit has the capacity to carry out its intended experiments. Generally speaking, a subnational unit's ability to launch policy experiments is positively associated with system decentralization; the more financial resources and policy discretion a subnational unit commands, the more capable it is of conducting experiments.[10]

10. As discussed below, this general rule is sometimes complicated by the development of cooperative federalism in certain countries (under which the center often

However, it is difficult to compare levels of decentralization among the United States, India, and China. Not only has the line between federal and unitary systems (especially in large and diverse countries) blurred considerably during the past century, but each of the studied countries has also shifted substantially between decentralization and centralization during the same period. It is nevertheless possible to make some helpful observations by juxtaposing the three systems.

Over the past century, the U.S. states' ability to generate policy experiments has increasingly relied upon conditional federal assistance due to the country's general centralizing trend. The U.S. Constitution assigns extremely expansive legislative power to the states, as the federal government can exercise only enumerated powers with the residual powers reserved for the states. Historically, this system provided considerable leeway for individual states to try out new policies based on their unique local demands and circumstances. This resulted in great innovative potential in some states, as illustrated by the pioneering roles of the western states during the women's suffrage movement and of Wisconsin in the development of unemployment benefit legislation. However, since the late nineteenth century, states' legislative capacities in many important areas have been limited as a direct result of Congress's rapidly expanding portfolio. Consequently, the states' ability to independently generate innovative economic policy has probably diminished to at least some degree, especially in areas where federal legislation has preemptive force. However, any such loss of experimental capacity has been offset by the federal government's extensive use of grants-in-aid, which provide funding and other forms of assistance (such as data and research) to the states in exchange for their compliance with federal requirements. Such funding can help states develop institutions and programs that they often lack the resources to properly create and operate themselves. These federally sponsored institutions and programs, in turn, boost the states' ability to innovate in relevant areas. A prominent example is the CAA, under which states became important sources of innovative environmental policies thanks

funds the subnational units' policy initiatives while requiring them to conform to certain guidelines), as such conditional funding simultaneously limits the subnational units' policy discretion and boosts their experimental capacities.

partly to the support provided by the federal law. On the other hand, the conditions that come with such grants also limit states' policy autonomy, as illustrated by the ACA's original requirement for Medicaid expansion. In other words, while centralization has not necessarily made the states less capable of experimentation, it has constrained which policies they can experiment with.

By contrast, the experimental capacities of the Indian states have received a significant boost from recent decentralization. Following India's Independence, the Congress Party's political dominance and a centrally planned economy severely limited the range of policies states were allowed to or capable of exploring on their own. Since the late 1980s, however, economic liberalization and the Congress Party's political fragmentation have significantly increased the states' policy and fiscal autonomy, enabling them to launch experiments that reflect the country's vast interregional diversity. Notable examples include the Gram Swaraj reform in Madhya Pradesh and the People's Campaign for Decentralized Planning in Kerala, both of which represent ambitious and innovative ways to devolve substantial authority and financial resources to grassroots democratic institutions. Similarly, Gujarat's status as the "Hindutva laboratory" (exemplified by its massive government-sponsored communal violence in 2002) at a time when the BJP-ruled union government was moderate on communal issues illustrates the states' considerable autonomy in pursuing policies distinctive from the center. This capacity to experiment has been further enhanced by the country's accelerating economic development since the 2000s, though it remains unclear whether (and to what extent) the BJP's recent exponential rise in national politics will constrain states' political options for experimentation.

Throughout the studied period, China's decentralized fiscal and policy-making powers provided a strong basis for local experimentation. Despite being within a nominally unitary system, the Chinese provinces wield respectable fiscal power that is comparable to (in some ways even superior to) that of their counterparts under federal systems like the United States and India. For example, in 1998, the Chinese subnational and local governments accounted for 71.1 percent of total government expenditures, while this percentage was 49.9 percent and

55.7 percent for the United States and India, respectively.[11] In the same year (which was after China's 1994 fiscal recentralization), the percentage of subnational and local revenue to total government revenue was 50.5 percent in China, 40.8 percent in the United States and 38.9 percent in India.[12] Although this does not necessarily mean that China was more fiscally decentralized than its federal counterparts,[13] it does show that the Chinese provinces had extensive responsibility for spending and revenue collection and that the center relied heavily on them to implement its national programs. The provinces also had considerable policy-making autonomy. On matters where no clear national directives were present, localities could typically set their own courses, and when faced with a central directive or law, they usually had substantial discretion regarding how—and to what extent—it would be carried out.

These decentralized fiscal and policy-making powers were critical enabling factors for most important subnational experiments during the studied period, including all four of the Chinese case studies. For example, during the early phase of the decollectivization reform, Provincial Party Secretary Wan Li defied both national law and the conservatives at the center to continue his controversial reform plan until it was proven effective. Other than Deng Xiaoping's private acquiescence on the matter, the key to Wan's perseverance and ultimate success was the inability of the conservative central leadership to directly interfere with the province's economic policies. Similarly, in the late 1990s and 2000s, the provinces' autonomy allowed them to try various social and political innovations that were in tension with China's established authoritarian norms, such as Jiangsu's election experiments for high-level government positions and Guangdong's relatively tolerant stance toward the booming civil society. In some sense, Chinese provincial leaders probably had more power to deviate from central policies than their counterparts in the United States and India. While

11. OECD, "OECD Fiscal Decentralisation Database"; Rao, "Incentivizing Fiscal Transfers," 46; National Bureau of Statistics of China, "Central and Local."
12. OECD, "OECD Fiscal Decentralisation Database"; Rao, "Incentivizing Fiscal Transfers," 46; National Bureau of Statistics of China, "Central and Local."
13. For a comparison of fiscal decentralization in China and the United States, see Zhao, "Fiscal Decentralization."

governors and chief ministers in the federal systems were generally bound by the supremacy of the national laws, a provincial secretary could often launch policies that conflicted with laws or even the Constitution. However, as discussed earlier, such law-defying ability has diminished considerably over the past few decades as China's administrative and legal systems have become more institutionalized.

Diffusion of Experiments

There are two basic ways an innovation can spread to other jurisdictions. The first is the peer-to-peer model, under which subnational units independently decide whether to adopt innovations that originated in another jurisdiction. The second is the scaling-up model, under which the central government turns a subnational innovation into a national policy, thereby compelling all subnational jurisdictions to adopt it.[14] Each model has pros and cons. Peer-to-peer diffusion allows each subnational unit to choose innovations based on local circumstances and if an innovation is adopted, to tailor it to local needs. Under a democracy, the peer-to-peer model also brings the policy-making process closer to the people, making it easier to hold decision-makers accountable. However, the scaling-up model can be useful in addressing the issues of race-to-the-bottom and positive externality. When a subnational innovation increases the taxes or other costs of doing business in the jurisdiction, other subnational units are likely to avoid adopting it, as it could disadvantage them in interstate competition—even if the policy itself is otherwise cost-effective. Similarly, when an innovation has positive spillover effects (such as reducing air pollution in neighboring regions), states' voluntary adoption will likely be less than optimal because the decision-makers cannot sufficiently reap the policy's benefits. Under these circumstances, the center's intervention—

14. The two models of diffusion are not mutually exclusive and are often mixed and matched in practice: The center may decide to let a policy spread through peer-to-peer learning for a period of time before deciding whether to make it a national policy; the center could also opt to encourage the peer-to-peer diffusion of an innovation through financial incentives without compelling all jurisdictions to adopt it.

often through scaling the innovation to national policy—becomes necessary to overcome the system's ineffectiveness. As issues involving race-to-the-bottom and positive externalities (such as healthcare and climate change) have become increasingly important since the early twentieth century, it is inevitable that countries will increasingly use the scaling-up model for policy diffusion. The following section discusses how the three studied countries differ in their ability to utilize these two models.

The evolution of the U.S. federal system has generally boosted the national government's ability to scale up state innovations. Under the early dual federalism structure, the center lacked the power to interfere with the states' exclusive policy spheres; it could do little to force them to adopt a specific innovation. As a result, the federal laboratories largely operated without federal intervention during this period, mostly relying on peer-to-peer learning as the means of diffusion. The women's suffrage movement is a good illustration of this dynamic. During most of the movement, the center remained relatively idle on the matter, forcing activists to focus attention on spreading universal suffrage on a state-by-state basis—not least because voting eligibility was considered firmly within the states' prerogatives at the time. The unemployment benefit reforms encountered similar problems before the New Deal. With the federal government doing little to advance the cause, the states were largely left on their own to legislate on the matter.

As the U.S. federal system became more cooperative in the twentieth century, so did the experimental process. Through the Commerce Clause and the Taxing and Spending Clause, Congress started to legislate on matters that had been regulated only by the states. These practices became more aggressive during and after the New Deal, as the Supreme Court began to largely defer to Congress's exercise of such powers. The development gave the center almost plenary power to scale up its preferred policies, with little regard for whether such authority originally belonged to the states. An early example is the Social Security Act, which turned Wisconsin's unemployment benefit policy into national legislation. Despite constitutional doubts expressed in a closely divided 1918 decision about whether the federal government could directly regulate unemployment insurance in the states, the act effectively compelled all states to enact unemployment benefit schemes.[15] This expansive federal power has taken a hit in recent decades due to the combined effect of the Supreme Court's new federalism jurisprudence and a polarizing partisan landscape. Despite this, the Medicaid expansion example illustrates that the center remains able to strongly influence states' decisions (though not to legally compel them) to adopt its preferred policies—largely thanks to its massively superior fiscal resources that can be used to induce state action.

Since the late 1980s, India has been characterized by an interesting combination of pro-union constitutional structure and rapid decentralization. The Indian Constitution contains many arrangements that allow the union government to rein in the states, including President's Rule—the power to unilaterally dismiss a state government—and the ability to amend the Constitution with relative ease. In addition, the structure of India's Union, State, and Concurrent Lists has resulted in "the effective dominance of the Union government over state governments in terms of legislative powers."[16] These Union-centric features, however, have been undermined since the late 1980s due to increasing political fragmentation and economic liberalization, which led to the so-called federalization of center-local relations. During this process, states gained substantial political autonomy and economic resources, giving them unprecedented ability to pursue their own policy preferences and initiatives.

Such a system has both advantages and disadvantages when it comes to policy diffusion. India's pro-union Constitution provides an institutional edge in spreading innovations through central intervention. For example, thanks to the relatively low bar for making constitutional amendments, the union government was able to force the states to create their own panchayati systems through the Seventy-Third Amendment. Similarly, the expansive powers of the Supreme Court enabled it to compel the states to adopt the midday meal scheme by

15. The decision in *Hammer v. Dagenhart* was closely divided (5–4), with Justice Holmes dissenting. The decision was overturned by *United States v. Darby*, in which a unanimous court embraced the reasoning of the dissent. Hammer v. Dagenhart, 247 U.S. 251 (1918); United States v. Darby, 312 U.S. 100 (1941).

16. Tillin, *Indian Federalism*; Singh, "The Federal Scheme," 454–55.

creatively recognizing a justiciable right to food. Neither of these achievements would be plausible within the U.S. system. A constitutional amendment that forced the states to create a specific type of local government would not likely be ratified by three-fourths of the states, and the U.S. Supreme Court does not typically recognize socioeconomic rights, such as the right to food. In other words, the Indian union government has a wider range of institutional tools than its U.S. counterpart for scaling up its preferred innovations. India's decentralization, however, has somewhat undermined this advantage. Despite the Seventy-Third Amendment's mandate, for example, many states refused to devolve sufficient powers and resources to the panchayati institutions. Similarly, before the Supreme Court's intervention, most states did little to enforce compliance with the union government's midday meal program, which required them to provide cooked food (rather than dry rations) to students. These examples illustrate the union's lack of control over the implementation of scaled-up policies, which can be largely attributed to India's political and economic decentralization.

Of the three countries, China has the constitutional structure that gives the center the greatest power to incentivize the spread of innovative policies at the subnational level. Despite their vast policy discretion, the provincial governments are ultimately beholden to the central government, which possesses the power to appoint and remove key subnational officials. Such institutional supremacy enables the center to reward prompt adoption of successful innovations and punish lack of compliance.

In practice, however, such power takes different forms depending on factional dynamics, particularly when an innovation is politically contentious. When one faction holds a clearly superior position in the central government, it can usually leverage the center's full constitutional power to pressure subnational units to adopt its preferred innovations— as illustrated by the reformists' successful national expansion of both the household responsibility system and the SEZs.[17] However, factions are less capable of forcing controversial innovations on subnational units when the central government is politically gridlocked. For example,

17. Chung, *Central Control*, 111; Wang, "The Economic Impact of Special Economic Zones," 136.

despite his own promotion and the backing of other Tuanpai patrons, Li Yuanchao was unable to scale the election experiments to the national level over objections from the rival Shanghai Gang.[18]

That said, even in the second scenario, where the center lacks coercive power over the provincial governments, it can still encourage subnational leaders to adopt successful innovations by setting broad policy objectives and rewarding those who achieve them. For example, in the late 2000s, many subnational governments chose to follow Beijing's municipal government in adopting the consultative authoritarianism model, which combines broader public participation with more sophisticated state control.[19] This was not achieved through central coercion, as the central government itself was badly divided over which model of civil society management was superior.[20] Rather, provincial leaders tried to mimic what they viewed as a successful new approach for improving public goods provision and social stability—two performance metrics that the central government uses to determine future promotions.

Political Parties and Factions

When discussing the issue of federalism, judges and legal scholars mostly focus on constitutional structure, especially the division and sharing of various powers between the center and subnational governments. In his seminal book, Riker challenges this emphasis by arguing that "the federal relationship is centralized according to the degree to which the parties organized to operate the central government control the parties organized to operate the constituent governments."[21] According to Riker, this degree of control can be further divided into two measurements: "(1) the degree to which one party controls both levels of government; and (2) the degree to which each potential governing

18. Ma and Pang, "The Rise and Fall," 402.

19. See Teets, *Civil Society under Authoritarianism*, 113–44; Stern and O'Brien, "Politics at the Boundary," 5.

20. Zhou, "Zou Zhongguo Tese," 37; Qian, "'Gongmin Shehui.'"

21. Riker, *Federalism: Origin, Operation, Significance*, 129; see also Riker and Schaps, "Disharmony in Federal Government."

party at the national level controls its partisan associates at the level of constituent governments."[22] In addition, Riker mostly dismisses the importance of constitutional arrangements, suggesting that "the division and sharing of administrative responsibilities, which is often said to be at the heart of federal arrangements, has little or nothing to do with maintaining the [federal] bargain."[23] Essentially, Riker argues that the partisan dynamic is what really matters in center-local relations and that the institution of federalism has little real-world impact on political outcomes.

Partisan/Factional Competition under Constitutional Frameworks

This study provides some support for Riker's emphasis on parties in the sense that it suggests that partisan politics has significant impact on the experimental process. In each of the three studied countries, changes in partisan dynamics have resulted in substantial changes in the functioning of subnational "laboratories." However, the study argues that constitutional arrangements—including "the division and sharing of administrative responsibilities" that Riker dismisses—are also greatly important. Indeed, these three countries' experiences indicate that such arrangements serve as the foundations upon which political parties or factions compete and assert their influence on the state. Consequently, constitutions strongly affect *how* partisan/factional competition impacts subnational experimentation.

As the U.S. Medicaid expansion example shows, a relatively decentralized constitutional arrangement can be a powerful instrument for an opposition party in the center to resist an incumbent from below. The Medicaid ruling in *NFIB v. Sebelius* was a significant development in federalism doctrine, as it was the first constitutional limit on Congress's use of its spending power in many decades. However, like the other new federalism rulings before it, *NFIB* should have had limited capacity to effect major political or economic change due to the federal government's expansive portfolio and vastly superior fiscal capacities.

22. Riker, *Federalism: Origin, Operation, Significance*, 131.
23. Riker, *Federalism: Origin, Operation, Significance*, 135.

Yet it had significant effect, used mostly by Republican-ruled states to resist the Medicaid expansion, which was a key Democratic agenda. This resistance caused delays or refusals of the expansion in more than half the states, resulting in the uninsured population increasing by millions, despite the generous fiscal incentives offered by the federal government to states willing to participate. This example shows that the United States's relatively federalized constitutional structure—even what's left of it today—can serve as a battleground for partisan conflict, as scholars like Jessica Bulman-Pozen have argued.[24] This is especially true when the parties are polarized and/or the policy issue is politically contentious. In this sense, political parties are indeed what keeps the "federal bargain" alive in the United States today, although in a very different fashion than Riker described in the mid-twentieth century.[25]

By contrast, a politically pro-center structure affords a subnational government controlled by the opposition relatively few options for resisting the center's key decisions. This, in turn, means that the partisan/factional dynamic in the center is more likely to be of paramount importance to the functioning of the system, including the experimental process. China generally falls into this category due to its politically centralized structure. Since the center holds the power to appoint and remove key provincial leaders, a politically unified center can theoretically overrule subnational governments on most important matters. However, such political unification was not the norm during the studied period, as political factions at the center were often competing for influence. As a result, the functioning of the experimental system in the examples studied here largely depended on the factional dynamic in the center, entering (1) a coordinated mode when the superior faction in the center was strongly penetrating, (2) a muted mode when the more powerful faction in the center was weak or nonpenetrating, or (3) a fragmented mode when the contest for supreme power remained close, giving no single faction clear political superiority over the others.

24. Bulman-Pozen, "Partisan Federalism."
25. Riker believed political parties in the United States are decentralized and therefore place decentralizing pressures on the entire federal system. Riker, *Federalism: Origin, Operation, Significance*, 91. See also Bulman-Pozen, "Partisan Federalism."

Compared to the steadiness of the post–New Deal U.S. federal system, China's fluctuation among these three modes within a relatively short period (1978 to 2012) highlights not only the vicissitudes of its factional politics but also the center-heavy nature of its political structure. With provincial leadership politically dependent upon its central patrons, any major changes in the center's factional dynamics likely meant corresponding changes at the subnational level. Xi Jinping's rise in recent years and the ensuing rapid demise of many important local experiments (such as the election experiments) serve as another example of how China's pro-center structure has made its experimental system relatively unstable.

India sits somewhere between the United States and China in the political centralization of its constitutional structure. As discussed above, the Indian Constitution is highly pro-center compared to its U.S. counterpart. However, because the state assemblies—and thus the state chief ministers—are elected by their constituents, India is more politically decentralized than China. This means that while partisan politics at the center plays a defining role in the operation of India's federal (and thus experimental) system, the states remain meaningful venues of political competition, even when a single party dominates the center. The decades-long decline of the Congress Party's dominance and the rise of regional parties are among the core reasons for India's decentralization, which in turn has made India a fertile ground for subnational experimentation. Given the union's constitutional supremacy over the states, the expansion of regional parties in the Lok Sabha—rather than just in the state assemblies—was central to this transformation. The need to coalesce with regional parties to form a national government made it politically difficult for the center to coerce the states—such as through the President's Rule—as it had when the Congress Party dominated. As the case studies on the midday meal and panchayati raj programs demonstrate, such decentralization has led to vibrant policy entrepreneurship at the state level and has constricted the union government's ability to enforce its policy objectives.

India's federal system is experiencing another wave of change due to the BJP's growing electoral dominance in the center. Due to the political realignment around the Hindu identity, the BJP has consolidated its power, independently winning more than 50 percent of the

Lok Sabha seats in both the 2014 and the 2019 general elections. This makes it much less necessary for the BJP to coalesce with regional parties at the union level. As a result, the central government can use its constitutional powers against the states more assertively, as illustrated by the Modi government's abolition of Jammu and Kashmir's special status and its imposition of the Citizenship Amendment Act soon after the 2019 election. However, the active resistance from some non-BJP-ruled states against these policies shows that Indian federalism can sometimes serve as useful checks against the center's power abuses. This is especially true because the states are often responsible for administering union laws and policies (such as in the case of the Citizenship Amendment Act).

Political Polarization and "Laboratories of Partisanship"

One notable issue in both the U.S. and India case studies is the effect of political polarization on experimentalism. As mentioned above, political polarization—often in the form of deep ideological divisions among a country's major parties—can incentivize the parties lacking power at the national level to leverage their ruling positions in subnational units to resist central policies. In some ways, this federalizing effect may help preserve the decentralized features of a given polity, potentially creating more space for subnational experimentation. However, under a polarized political environment, such experiments are likely driven less by commonly shared public objectives and more by partisan interests and ideologies.

This political polarization effect is apparent in the Medicaid expansion case. After *NFIB v. Sebelius*, seven states with at least one legislative chamber controlled by the Republican Party opted to use the Section 1115 waiver to innovate their own Medicaid programs. The goal was to sufficiently distinguish their programs from the standard Democratic Medicaid expansion to pacify the Republican opposition, which insisted that only a small, truly deserving population should be eligible for Medicaid. The waiver was used to install new policy components in the states' Medicaid programs, such as premium charges and voluntary work incentives, thereby making the newly eligible population members of the working poor to satisfy the conservative demand for deservingness.

Political polarization may have a similar effect on Indian sub-national government policies toward religious minorities (especially Muslims). As illustrated by Modi's relatively moderate minority policies after the 2002 Gujarat riots, the BJP could ill afford to alienate its regional partners by adopting extreme Hindu nationalist policies when coalition politics remained the norm. However, as the BJP became independently capable of securing a majority in the Lok Sabha (and an increasing number of state assemblies), it grew bolder in pursuing its anti-minority ideology. This not only allowed other BJP-ruled states to follow Gujarat's early example in using communal policies for electoral gains but also enabled them to likewise become innovators of Hindutva policies. Rajasthan, for example, became a pioneer in comprehensively overhauling primary school textbooks according to communal principles in an effort to promote Hindu nationalism through public education. In effect, the BJP's intensifying right-wing stance has turned more states into "laboratories of Hindutva" when it comes to identity-related policies.

Such partisan turns pose a serious challenge to the technocratic foundation underlying the idea of federal laboratories (and experimentalism more generally). As mentioned at the beginning of this study, embedded in the terms "laboratory" and "experiment" is the implication that this policy-making mechanism bears resemblance to the scientific process. In other words, federal laboratories should be more than states freely developing their preferred policies; they should embody the ideal of striving to determine the objectively best policies through extensive trial and error.[26] Within a polarized political environment, however, subnational experiments instead often aim to enhance particular partisan or ideological positions. This is especially true in highly divisive policy fields, such as climate change and identity politics. As such issues increasingly take center stage in many countries due to intensifying political divisions, it is often more accurate to characterize these subnational units as laboratories of partisanship rather than as laboratories of democracy.

26. Tarr, "Laboratories of Democracy."

The Institutionalization of Political Parties/
Factions and System Stability

In addition to the centralized/decentralized features of its constitutional structures, the institutionalization of a country's political parties/factions affects the stability of its experimental system. Scott Mainwaring, Fernando Bizzarro, and Ana Petrova define an institutionalized party system as one in which "a stable set of parties interacts regularly in stable ways."[27] Generally speaking, more institutionalized parties mean more stable patterns of political competition,[28] which translate into less turbulence in the federal system. In this sense, the U.S. federal laboratories have long benefited from a relatively stable two-party system. Despite occasional political turbulence and even realignment, the Democratic and Republican parties have largely maintained structural and ideological consistency since the New Deal, at least until the recent partisan polarization. This has helped ensure a consistent pattern of two-party competition, which reduces political disruptions to the experimental structure.

India's political parties are generally less institutionalized than their U.S. counterparts, which has contributed to the turbulence in its experimental system in recent decades.[29] Many major changes in the partisan landscape can be attributed to Indian parties' heavy reliance on charismatic leaders. For example, Indira Gandhi's dictatorial control over the Congress Party ensured that its electoral success or failure was largely tied to her personal decisions, including the party's first-ever defeat after the Emergency, which foreshadowed its slow decline and India's political regionalization during the 1990s. Although India's parties have become less personalist in recent decades, the emerging dominance of the BJP in the 2010s can be partially attributed to the personal appeal of Modi as well as to general public distaste for Rahul Gandhi

27. Mainwaring, Bizzarro, and Petrova, "Party System Institutionalization," 19; see also Mainwaring and Scully, *Building Democratic Institutions.*

28. Mainwaring, Bizzarro, and Petrova, "Party System Institutionalization," 19.

29. One such sign is that the partisan composition of the Lok Sabha often swings dramatically from one election to the next. For example, the Congress Party's seat count dropped from 414 in the 1984 election to 197 in 1989; it similarly fell from 206 in 2009 to 44 in 2014. Election Commission of India, "Election Results."

(the great-grandson of Jawaharlal Nehru and thus the Congress's heir apparent). Reliance on specific individuals—especially under the Congress's dynastic system—makes India's partisan competition more unstable, adding to the vicissitudes of its experimental mechanism.

That being said, China's factions are more centered around specific political patrons—and thus less institutionalized—than the main political parties in both the United States and India. Most factions in China center around a single central patron, which means that the individual's declining health or death likely results in severe weakening (if not dissolution) of the entire faction. For example, Chen Yun's once-powerful conservative faction rapidly disintegrated in the early 1990s after he stepped down due to advanced age and withering health. The same happened to Deng Xiaoping a few years later, marking the end of the revolutionary generation's influence in Chinese politics. The next generation of factions—including the Shanghai Gang and Tuan-pai—became a little more institutionalized, as they tried to groom younger officials (often provincial leaders) who could take over when the old patrons left the political scene. However, the factions remain highly personalist, as the power and influence of the senior-most patron remains paramount. Generally speaking, factions can rise and fall relatively easily, depending on their leaders' personal attributes, including health, political skill, and charisma. This means that China is unlikely to maintain a stable factional dynamic, which translates into constant turbulence in its center-local relationship. It is therefore unsurprising that China's laboratories of authoritarianism often fluctuate among the different modes discussed above.

Other Players: Courts and Nongovernmental Actors

Although this study argues that the interaction between constitutions and political parties/factions is a primary factor in the functioning of subnational laboratories, the case studies show that several other factors also assert considerable influence on the experimental process. Chief among them are the judiciary and civil society. While these are both present in all three countries, the authoritarian nature of the

Chinese regime severely limits their significance in government policy-making. This distinction thus provides an interesting opportunity to identify their impacts on experimentalism.

The Role of the Courts

The courts' role in shaping center-local relations is somewhat limited even in a democratic context. Legal scholars sometimes credit land-mark cases such as *NLRB v. Jones & Laughlin Steel* and *NFIB v. Sebelius* with monumental shifts in the U.S. federal system.[30] However, as dis-cussed earlier, the real driving force behind these shifts were not the Court rulings themselves but the major political, economic, or social changes of the time. For example, it would be misleading to attribute the U.S. turn toward a more cooperative federal structure to pro–New Deal Supreme Court decisions, such as *West Coast Hotel Co.* Rather, these rulings were themselves responses to the Great Depression and the decade-long shift toward greater national power. Another example is new federalism jurisprudence. *NFIB v. Sebelius* would have been unlikely to make much difference in the Medicaid expansion context without the recent partisan polarization, which drove Republican-leaning states to use the case against the Obama administration's healthcare agenda, even though resistance made little fiscal (or human-itarian) sense. In other words, the judiciary plays a junior role, as it mostly serves as a vehicle through which greater forces project their influence on the federal system.

That being said, such a vehicle can matter a lot in countries where the judiciary enjoys high levels of legitimacy and prestige. The courts' impact can also be particularly significant in times of political gridlock. Although court rulings are unlikely to make systematic differences on their own, they can have significant consequences when one of the two major political parties supports their decisions. This effect is augmented when parties are in neck-and-neck competition, which can make a pop-ular judiciary a critical force in tipping the political balance. *NFIB v. Sebelius* again serves as a good example. Without the Court's restriction

30. NLRB v. Jones & Laughlin Steel Corp., 301 U.S. 1 (1937); NFIB v. Sebelius, 567 U.S. 519 (2012).

on Congress's spending power, Republican-leaning states would have had no choice but to comply with the Medicaid expansion plan laid out by the Democratic Party in the ACA. In this way, the recent political polarization has made the Supreme Court more relevant than before— at least concerning the functioning of the federal system.

The expansion of the midday meal scheme in India offers an even more powerful illustration of a court's influence under the "right" political circumstances. The fragmentation and regionalization of electoral politics since the 1980s had severely weakened the national parties and the union executive branch as a whole. As illustrated by the states' poor enforcement of the NP-NSPE before the judicial intervention, this made it difficult for the center to coerce states into adopting its preferred policies despite India's pro-union Constitution. On the other hand, the Supreme Court had become highly popular thanks to its civil rights jurisprudence and increased accessibility through the PIL system. Such prestige enabled the Court to break the political impasse between central and state powers. In *PUCL v. India*, the Court boldly established a constitutional and justiciable right to food, including schoolchildren's right to a cooked midday meal. Pursuant to this right, the Court ordered all state governments to provide cooked meals instead of grain rations under the midday meal schemes. In contrast to their response to the NP-NSPE, the state governments soon fell in line, implementing the order in just a few years, as it would be politically costly for them to be seen by voters as being at odds with the popular Court.

How does the judiciary's role (or lack thereof) affect the experimental process? Obviously, the Chinese court system cannot match its U.S. or Indian counterparts in perceived legitimacy, nor does it have the power to adjudicate constitutional matters related to center-local relations. But how does an insufficient judiciary disadvantage (or advantage) China's ability to generate and diffuse policy innovations? One intuitive answer is that a more powerful judiciary could stabilize China's center-local relations, making the laboratories of authoritarianism function more consistently. But is that really true?

Whether under democracy or authoritarianism, courts are unlikely to become a reliable force of stability against major political, economic, or social change. Hamilton's claim that the judiciary is the "least dangerous" branch generally holds true across political systems.

With rare exceptions (e.g., when the Turkish Constitutional Court had military backing against the elected parliament),[31] courts generally lack sufficient political backing to hold themselves against changing tides. As discussed earlier, the courts in the United States and India mostly work on the margins in defining the relationship between center and local governments. Even when the judiciary plays a balance-tipping role when other political actors are locked in a stalemate, there is no guarantee that it will be a stabilizing rather than disturbing force. For example, the new federalism jurisprudence of the U.S. Supreme Court was a clear attempt to change the legal status quo established after the New Deal, and *PUCL* was both a bold centralizing move and a power grab for the judiciary. The reason behind such judicially induced "disturbances" is simple: Like other branches of government, the courts are not immune to changes. New federalism was the direct result of several judicial appointments made by President Reagan, and *PUCL* stemmed from the Indian High Court's post-Emergency legal activism and rapidly growing power vis-à-vis other state institutions.

Consequently, one should not expect that courts (or the power of judicial review) would have a major stabilizing effect on China's experimental process or general center-local relations. Even if the current Chinese regime developed a reasonably independent court system that could review center-local relations based on constitutional law, it is unlikely that such courts would substantially reduce the vicissitudes of China's center-local relations. As mentioned previously, the disturbances are largely caused by the centralized political structure and under-institutionalization of factional politics. As long as these two factors remain unchanged, China's center-local relations will continue to be determined by which personalist faction has the upper hand within the center. There is little chance that the Chinese judiciary— however powerful it becomes—will substantially counter the political wave caused by major changes in factional dynamics, just as courts in democratic countries usually cannot hold themselves for long against significant shifts in public opinion or the economic landscape. The best one can hope for from an empowered Chinese judiciary is the regularization of the day-to-day relationship between the central and local

31. Shambayati, "Courts in Semi-Democratic/Authoritarian Regimes."

bureaucracies *within* a particular factional equilibrium—but not across different factional dynamics.

The Role of Nongovernmental Actors

Another distinguishing feature between the democratic and authoritarian experimental models is the role of NGOs. As a vibrant civil society is a key feature of a consolidated democracy, it is unsurprising that NGOs sometimes play an important secondary role in the experimental process. Although experimentalism mainly concerns the inner functioning of the state, NGOs can assert great influence on how various governmental actors set their experimental agendas and priorities. For example, the various women's associations were key drivers behind the successful state suffrage movements in the United States around the turn of the twentieth century. These NGOs' tireless and often well-organized activities—such as lobbying, parades, and picketing—proved highly effective in putting women's suffrage onto state legislature agendas. Similarly, the successful national expansion of India's midday meal scheme was initiated by NGOs such as the People's Union for Civil Liberties, which launched the famous public interest lawsuit (*PUCL v. India*) in the Supreme Court and argued for a constitutional right to food. In both these cases, rather than directly acting on the relevant issues, the NGOs moved strategically by persuading or pressuring key institutions (i.e., state legislatures and the judiciary) to act on the matters. They spread their preferred policies more effectively by leveraging the country's existing experimental mechanism.

This interaction between nongovernmental actors and state organs is almost completely lacking in the Chinese cases due to the country's top-down authoritarian accountability structure and less tolerant policies toward civil society. Under the Chinese system, subnational leaders are evaluated by their superiors in the center, so the center is the primary agenda-setter in prioritizing subnational experiments. This contrasts with the federal laboratories, in which each subnational unit mostly (though not always) sets its own agendas based on the demands of its constituency. China's top-down accountability structure makes it more difficult for civil society to participate in the experimental process. Since most NGOs are grassroots or local in nature, they are generally better at exerting influence on local governments than on the center. Furthermore, as discussed in the civil society management case, the regime also severely limits—and sometimes outright forbids—the operation of many types of NGOs. Common tactics, such as organized demonstrations, that are employed by NGOs elsewhere to influence government policy are prohibited in China, making it hard for these entities to assert influence on local governments, much less the central government.

This limited participation in civil society further constrains the diversity in the agenda of the laboratories of authoritarianism. As discussed earlier, China's top-down accountability system focuses its experimental process on specific policy objectives, while India's bottom-up structure is driven by diverse electorates. This difference is augmented by the stark contrast in the role of NGOs under the two systems. In democratic systems, NGOs often give voice to those not adequately represented in the electoral process and highlight issues neglected by the government, making the government's experimental agenda more inclusive and diverse. However, one must be cautious about the potential flip side of such NGO-induced diversity. Although civil society is positively associated with liberal values, the rise of various forms of populism in recent decades has considerably altered the landscape of nongovernmental actors in many countries. Consequently, it is conceivable that NGO participation in such places may increasingly bring illiberal or even authoritarian elements into the experimental process, as illustrated by the active role of the VHP and other Hindu nationalist organizations in the 2002 Gujarat riots and various states' recent surge of Hindu nationalist "innovations."

Conclusion

The picture that emerges from this comparison is complex. On the one hand, the Chinese Constitution seem to have many potential advantages over its democratic counterparts in developing and disseminating useful subnational innovations. Largely thanks to its top-down accountability structure, the Chinese model can more easily overcome the incentive problem caused by the positive information externality of subnational experiments. It also boasts the ability to focus the system's experimental energy on a set of strategically chosen objectives, especially economic development. China's centralized political powers also allow the center to effectively diffuse the subnational innovations it deems successful, through either rewarding voluntary adoption or making them compulsory national policies. At the same time, its relatively decentralized fiscal and policy-making structure gives the provinces substantial ability to formulate innovative policies based on their own unique preferences and circumstances. Together, these factors explain why China's approach to experimentalism has generated and spread many successful policy innovations, transforming the country from one of the poorest in the world to a global superpower.

On the other hand, the federal laboratories have certain advantages over the Chinese model. The most significant is consistency. For example, as the prototype of the democratic model, U.S. experimentalism has remained relatively productive for more than a century, despite profound transformations of the country's political, economic, and social landscapes. A key reason for this functional stability is that state governments have maintained some political independence from the federal government because they are locally elected rather than centrally appointed. This gives them a strong incentive to respond to local demands for innovative policies, whether or not the federal government favors experimentation. In addition, a democratic system has the benefit of established systems of political competition, often in the form of institutionalized political parties openly competing for power. This institutionalization of partisan politics guarantees some level of predictability and consistency across administrations. By contrast, in China's top-down political structure, the functioning of the experimental mechanism is determined by political dynamics in the center, which in turn are decided by the struggle among the various highly personalist factions. Consequently, the Chinese model has experienced much more functional turbulence during the past forty years than its democratic counterparts. This is also why some of its most important achievements during the studied period—such as the election experiments—failed to survive into the subsequent political era.

The policy diversity produced by broad political participation is another advantage of the federal laboratories. This effect is achieved through both gubernatorial elections and civil society. In diverse mega-countries like the United States and India, state elections inevitably put significant political pressure on subnational officials to develop new policies that reflect the diverse demands of their local electorates. In addition, the active civil society in many democratic countries increases the heterogeneity of experimental policies by representing the interests and voices of those underrepresented in the electoral process. Both these mechanisms serve to make the experimental process more diverse—a quality aligned with the broad objective of experimentalism. However, diversity comes with the risk of producing populist and divisive experiments that threaten liberal democracy itself, especially given the dangerous political trends in many countries.

A more general takeaway from the comparison is that the functioning of subnational laboratories—democratic or authoritarian—is determined largely by the interaction between constitutional arrangements and partisan/factional politics. Focusing on constitutions alone—as jurists and institutionalists sometimes do—fails to capture how the laboratories operate in reality. The role of the courts is a good example. Despite its formal role as the final arbiter of constitutional matters in some countries, the judiciary normally plays a marginal part in shaping center-local relations. It is thus unrealistic to expect that an empowered judiciary—no matter how professionalized or well-respected—can substantially mitigate the instability of China's experimental mechanism, which is caused by drastic changes in the center's factional dynamics. Tackling the consistency issue requires changing more fundamental aspects of China's authoritarian system, such as altering the top-down nature of the nomenklatura system or institutionalizing the various political factions within the party—both of which present much greater challenges than reforming the courts.

Although this study does not directly engage with other key features of federalism—such as enhancing democratic participation and empowering subnational governments to check the center—its findings nevertheless bear on how such features may play out differently under varying political circumstances. For instance, many experimental policies showcase the benefit of local participation. As mentioned earlier, the state-level democratic process was the driving force behind both the early success of the women's suffrage movement in the West and MGR's

single-minded push for a midday meal program in Tamil Nadu. However, federalism's virtue in giving voice to subnational voters becomes
less clear in other instances, such as the rejection of the Medicaid expansion by Republican-ruled states and the anti-Muslim experimental
policies in BJP-run subnational governments. Federalism's promise to
empower subnational governments can also be a double-edged sword,
especially when it comes to personal liberties. While the non-BJP states'
resistance to Modi's Citizenship Amendment Act is a classic example
of the right-enhancing property of federalism, the 2002 Gujarat riots
also demonstrate its potential to enable populist sentiment. The study
thus illustrates how political circumstances can profoundly shape the
output of federalism and calls for more thorough discussion on the constitutional implications of recent changes in the partisan landscape in
many countries—just as Bulman-Pozen calls for more discussion about
this issue in the United States in *Partisan Federalism*.

This study represents an early attempt at studying subnational experimentation through the lens of comparative constitutional law, leaving many important variables central to the functioning of democratic
and authoritarian laboratories underexplored or unexplored. One such
variable is intracountry diversity. As California's pioneering policies in
reducing air pollution show, such diversity can facilitate experimentation. However, a very high level of intracountry diversity can also hinder the spread of ideas. For example, Kerala's long history of Communist
Party rule has made it so politically and socially unique that many of
its innovative policies (e.g., its bold move to greatly empower the panchayats) are too difficult for other states to imitate. Other types of disparities—such as the tremendous linguistic and cultural barriers
among Indian states—may also constrain the flow of new ideas across
subnational governments. This dual effect of diversity raises the interesting question of whether there is an ideal level (or type) of intracountry diversity for facilitating the initiation and diffusion of policy
experiments—and to what extent this variable explains the performance of different experimental systems.

Historical legacies, especially recent revolutionary experiences, are
another set of variables that may critically influence this study's comparisons. As pointed out by Sebastian Heilmann, the pre-1949 communist movements in China created a pattern of point-to-surface

policy-making that later became a foundation for the reform-era experimental process. Similarly, the various legacies of India's anticolonial struggle—such as Gandhi's idea of Gram Swaraj and Nehru's modernist visions—constituted the basis for many of its experimental policies. Moreover, the political parties born of these revolutions (e.g., the CCP and the Indian Congress Party) may serve as powerful vehicles for transformative changes long after the revolutions have ended. These examples suggest that countries with a recent revolutionary history might have a unique advantage in promoting policy experimentation over those with more established polities.

Several other factors are also worth exploring. For example, the appointment system of the CCP seems to be largely based on performance, making it a powerful tool for incentivizing experimentation. A less meritocratic system, such as one heavily reliant on nepotism or corruption, would be much less effective in this regard. This raises a question about the extent to which this meritocracy—and the resulting productivity of the laboratories of authoritarianism—is specific to China's cultural heritage. A plausible argument can be made that the emphasis on performance can be at least partially attributed to Confucian ideologies, such as the "mandate of heaven," which dictates that a ruler's legitimacy rests primarily on just and able performance. It follows that laboratories of authoritarianism might fail to produce a similar level of benign experiments in countries without comparable moral and ideological constraints on their officials. These questions call for more countries—such as Russia, a large authoritarian country with a formally federal structure—to be included in future comparisons.

Implications for Contemporary China

Are any of the above conclusions meaningful for understanding China under the Xi Jinping administration? Despite some recentralization efforts, such as the 1994 tax-sharing reform, China was in a relatively decentralized phase during the period covered by this study (i.e., from the late 1970s to early 2010s)—which, as discussed above, was crucial to the effectiveness of the Chinese experimental model. However, the current administration seems to have brought an end to this period, as its policies and political campaigns have steadily chipped away the vast discretion once enjoyed by the local governments. Drawing most attention has been the anti-corruption campaign, widely considered the most prolonged and sustained of its kind in the post-Mao era. This sweeping campaign has "removed powers and discretion from local governments . . . and signaled a zero-tolerance approach to noncompliance with central directives."[32]

Scholars point out that these recent changes have seriously weakened local officials' incentives to innovate, thereby undermining China's pattern of experimentation. For instance, Heilmann argues that "under conditions of a concentration of power at the top levels and in combination with sustained and intense campaigns to enforce intraparty discipline, there are no longer any credible or powerful incentives to permit local policy makers to embrace the political risks inherent in bottom-up policy experimentation."[33] More specifically, Chen finds that under the current administration, "instead of being primarily assessed based on relatively objective indicators like . . . performance in securing local GDP growth . . . the promotions of local cadres are heavily affected by their upper-level leaders' subjective views."[34] Consequently, "the incentives for local officials to engage in policy innovations or experimentations are indeed significantly curbed, if not completely eliminated."[35] Teets and Hasmath similarly conclude that local experimentation has decreased significantly during the Xi administration due to lack of formal and informal incentives, with only "pockets of policy experimentation" remaining due to "ineffective institutional incentives, influence of peer groups, and variations in the personalities of policymakers."[36]

This lack of incentive for local experimentation can be at least partially traced to changes in the factional landscape. As discussed in the China chapter, during earlier eras of fierce factional competition,

32. Kostka and Nahm, "Central-Local Relations," 568.
33. Heilmann, Red Swan, 210.
34. Chen, "A U-Turn," 663.
35. Chen, "A U-Turn," 664.
36. Teets and Hasmath, "Evolution of Policy Experimentation," 49.

experimentation was often used to further a particular faction's policy agenda and, by extension, its political status. In particular, factions used local experiments to advance policies they could not successfully push through at the national level due to intense opposition from rival factions (e.g., the decollectivization policy). However, as Xi assumes a dominating position in the party center, he has less incentive to use local innovation to boost his political prospects. Similarly, the administration no longer needs to utilize experimentation to circumvent objections to its reforms thanks to the absence of meaningful factional challengers.

At the same time, however, the current factional dynamic does not preclude China's experimentalist tradition from continuing in a systematic, albeit much more restricted, fashion. Despite its diminishing political returns, experimentalism continues to provide a relatively low-risk venue for trying out new reforms prior to national adoption—a potent policy tool frequently utilized by the CCP to deal with uncertainties since the pre-1949 revolutionary period.[37] It is particularly useful to the current leadership, which vows to tackle some of China's deeply entrenched and emerging problems with sweeping new policies. These technocratic needs will likely help keep the experimentalist tradition alive—albeit in a "quarantined" fashion that limits its application to policy fields related to the administration's key agendas. Indeed, the current administration—including Xi himself—has repeatedly stressed the importance of local experiments in successfully implementing its priorities.[38] Recent examples of such quarantined experimentalism include the social credit system and the procuratorial PIL system. In both cases, the central government authorized the provinces to establish the new systems without giving detailed instructions, resulting in diverse innovations and significant peer-to-peer learning across the provinces.

Perhaps more importantly, there is reason to believe that the current decline in experimentation is temporary. As previously discussed, the functioning of the three examined experimentalist models—whether democratic or authoritarian—depends on the interaction

37. Heilmann and Perry, "Embracing Uncertainty."
38. Lu, "Xi Jinping Chairs."

between their respective constitutional structures and partisan/ factional dynamics. Specifically, this study argues that the turbulent nature of the Chinese model results largely from the vicissitudes of the factional struggles within the central government—rather than from any fundamental changes in China's center-local constitutional structure. If this argument holds true today, one could conclude that the current decline in China's experimentation is similar to its low productivity between 1989 and 1992, a period when the conservative faction got the upper hand. In other words, it may likewise be a temporary—albeit much longer—setback caused by drastic shifts in the factional landscape and may reverse relatively easily when the political dynamic changes (as it did after Deng's 1992 southern tour). On the other hand, if the recent changes in center-local relations are constitutional in nature (e.g., the establishment of powerful centralizing agencies capable of reining in localities), the damage to experimentalism will likely be much more difficult for new leadership to undo.

It is therefore critical to identify the nature of the centralization under the Xi Jinping administration. Is it due primarily to the consolidation of factional power or to fundamental changes to China's Two Initiatives constitutional structure? This is not an easy question to answer, as in China, the line between politics and law is often blurred. However, some key causes of this centralization clearly fall on the factional/political end of the spectrum. Chief among these is the sweeping anti-corruption campaign—a classic example of an ad hoc campaign-style centralization drive—which some scholars identify as the primary reason that local cadres dare not resist central orders and have become less proactive in their work.[39] Other examples of non-institutionalized centralization measures include the appointment of Xi's protégés to key subnational positions and the general trend of promoting cadres based on upper-level leaders' subjective views. Although these measures have been highly effective in ensuring compliance from local officials (and reducing their incentive to experiment with bold policies), their potency will likely fade when the political wind changes. Indeed,

39. Wang and Yan, "Bureaucratic Slack in China"; Kostka and Nahm, "Central-Local Relations."

there are signs that the current administration has been reducing the intensity of some of the more disruptive centralization pushes.[40]

Even some of the more institutionalized forms of centralization still rely on certain factional conditions to be effective. Some studies identify the various newly empowered leading groups (notably the Central Comprehensively Deepening Reforms Commission) as representing a critical institutional turn toward political centralization.[41] However, these groups do not provide highly institutionalized checks on local power, as they are mostly coordination devices and possess no enforcement authority. They can influence only via other sources of power, such as a leader's personal prestige or influence (through their primary official position) over group members' careers.[42] Therefore, the effectiveness of the leading groups will likely depend heavily on the factional dynamics, especially the political authority of the groups' leaders.

Some reforms, however, are clearly designed to alter center-local relations in an institutionalized and thus permanent fashion. The most "constitutional" among these is probably the establishment of the Supervisory Commission by the 2018 Constitutional Amendment, which made the discipline inspection institution one of the top state organs at all government levels. China also saw a recent series of reforms over its judicial system that aimed to make the courts and procuratorates more professional and independent, including those that established cross-jurisdiction tribunals and centralized powers over local judicial personnel and budgets. This revamping of disciplinary and judicial bodies was designed to strengthen enforcement of centrally made rules, which theoretically would permanently decrease the institutional autonomy of local bureaucracies. Another example is the merging of local tax agencies (地税) into national tax agencies (国税), which completely centralized all tax-collection power and reduced local governments' revenue autonomy. If successfully implemented, these and similar reforms could create powerful pro-centralization institutions and vested interests that will be difficult for future administrations to undo.

40. Wang and Hou, "Breaking the Cycle?"
41. Lee, "An Institutional Analysis," 334; Tsai and Zhou, "Integrated Fragmentation."
42. Tsai and Zhou, "Integrated Fragmentation," 6–11.

However, it is still too early to definitively assess whether these institutional changes will be effective or long-lasting, given their implementation setbacks and high maintenance costs. For instance, attempts to centralize the judiciary have faced major obstacles, as higher governments lack sufficient incentives, information, and financial resources to properly manage lower courts, forcing them to seek help from the local party-state. Moreover, even if the center assumed full fiscal and personnel control over specific local institutions—such as the disciplinary, judicial, and tax entities—these institutions would likely still rely on the local party-state for many informal types of assistance, ranging from security provision to land allocation for new buildings.[43] More fundamentally, the cost of managing a country as large and diverse as China in an overly top-down fashion may become prohibitively high, which could cause the center to modify or even reverse its power grabs. Jaros and Tan argue that the central party-state's insufficient organizational and informational capacities to govern the vast and diverse political economy often force the center (including the current administration) to resort to "soft centralization" (i.e., centralization to the subnational rather than the central level).[44] Indeed, as the newly centralized governing structure continues to incapacitate the daily functioning of the local party-state, backlashes become increasingly likely. For example, the fifth plenary session of the Nineteenth CCP Central Committee announced a plan to increase local revenue by establishing new local taxes and increasing the local share of some national taxes (e.g., the consumption tax). The move reflects the severe fiscal imbalance created by the recent centralization of revenue powers and the resulting demand for re-decentralization among localities. As the current administration pushes its centralizing agenda, similar backlashes are likely to occur, which may further pressure the center to halt or even reverse some of its advances.

In sum, there is currently insufficient evidence to suggest that the drastic centralization under Xi—and the resulting decline of China's experimental model—is institutionally (not to mention constitutionally) entrenched. So far, the most potent centralizing measures—such

43. Wang, "'Detaching' Courts from Local Politics?"
44. Jaros and Tan, "Provincial Power,'" 83–84.

as the anti-corruption campaign, the subjective promotion criteria, and the various leading groups—largely rely on the continuous factional dominance of Xi Jinping and his allies. Although the administration has recently attempted reforms that have the potential to institutionalize central dominance, the efficacy and sustainability of these changes are still very much in question. Consequently, it is premature to suggest that Xi has fundamentally altered the Two Initiatives center-local constitutional framework on which China's experimental model is based. Rather, the administration is largely functioning within the existing framework, though the consolidation of the factional landscape makes the Constitution's top-down features (especially the centralized appointment and removal powers) much more salient, causing diminished local experimentation. One therefore cannot rule out a return of China's experimentalism in the not-so-distant future. If history is any guide, just as its subnational innovation rapidly declined in the 2010s, China's experimentalist model may rejuvenate as soon as the political wind begins to change.

Bibliography

Scholarly Sources

"1982 Nian Zhongyang Diyige Yihao Wenjian" [No. 1 Document of the Party Center in 1982]. January 1, 1982. http://www.crnews.net/zt/zyyhwj /lnzyyhwjhg/440269_20210209111856.html.

Abeyratne, Rehan. "Enforcing Socioeconomic Rights in Neoliberal India." *Minnesota Journal of International Law* 29 (2020): 1–63.

Ablavsky, Gregory. "Empire States: The Coming of Dual Federalism." *Yale Law Journal* 128, no. 7 (2019): 1792–2121.

Abramowitz, Alan. *The Disappearing Center: Engaged Citizens, Polarization, and American Democracy.* New Haven, Conn.: Yale University Press, 2010.

Abramsky, Sasha. "California Is Fighting Trump for Clean Air." *The Nation*, March 30, 2020. https://www.thenation.com/article/environment /california-trump-clean-air/.

Ackerman, Bruce. "Constitutional Politics/Constitutional Law." *Yale Law Journal* 99, no. 3 (1989): 453–547. https://doi.org/10.2307/796754.

Adler, Jonathan H. "Jurisdictional Mismatch in Environmental Federalism." *New York University Environmental Law Journal* 14, no. 1 (2005): 130–78. https://scholarlycommons.law.case.edu/faculty_publications/185.

Adler, Jonathan H., and Nathaniel Stewart. "Is the Clean Air Act Unconstitutional? Coercion, Cooperative Federalism and Conditional Spending after 'NFIB v. Sebelius.'" *Ecology Law Quarterly* 43, no. 4 (2016): 671–722. https://doi.org/10.15779/Z380V89H45.

Afridi, Farzana. "Child Welfare Programs and Child Nutrition: Evidence from a Mandated School Meal Program in India." *Journal of Development Economics* 92, no. 2 (2010): 152–65. https://doi.org/10.1016/j.jdeveco .2009.02.002.

———. "The Impact of School Meals on School Participation: Evidence from Rural India." *Journal of Development Studies* 47, no. 11 (2011): 1636–56. https://doi.org/10.1080/00220388.2010.514330.

Aiyar, Yamini, and Neelanjan Sircar. "Understanding the Decline of Regional Party Power in the 2019 National Election and Beyond." *Contemporary South Asia* 28, no. 2 (2020): 209–22. https://doi.org /10.1080/09584935.2020.1765989.

Althouse, Ann. "Vanguard States, Laggard States: Federalism and Constitutional Rights." *University of Pennsylvania Law Review* 152, no. 6 (2004): 1745–827.

Amenta, Edwin, Elisabeth S. Clemens, Jefren Olsen, Sunita Parikh, and Theda Skocpol. "The Political Origins of Unemployment Insurance in Five American States." *Studies in American Political Development* 2 (1987): 137–82. https://doi.org/10.1017/S0898588X00001747.

Arora, Balveer. "Autonomy and States' Rights in the Indian Federal Union: Original Intent, Contemporary Content." In *Federalism in India : Towards a Fresh Balance of Power*, edited by Lancy Lobo, Mrutuyanjaya Sahu, and Jayesh Shah, 45–61. Jaipur: Rawat Publications, 2014.

Arora, Balveer, K. K. Kailash, Rekha Saxena, and H. Kham Khan Suan. *Indian Federalism*. Oxford: Oxford University Press, 2013.

Ayyub, Rana. "I've Reported on Modi for over a Decade. His Hindu Nationalist Ideas Will Be Even More Dangerous Now." *Time*, May 24, 2019. https://time.com/5595576/modi-victory-hindu-nationalism/.

Baicker, Katherine, Claudia Goldin, Lawrence F. Katz, Katherine Baicker, and Claudia Goldin. "A Distinctive System: Origins and Impact of U.S. Unemployment Compensation." In *The Defining Moment: The Great Depression and the American Economy in the Twentieth Century*, edited by Michael D. Bordo, Claudia Goldin, and Eugene N. White, 227–64. Chicago: University of Chicago Press, 1998.

Bailey, Thomas A. "The West and Radical Legislation, 1890–1930." *American Journal of Sociology* 38, no. 4 (1933): 603–11. https://doi.org/10.1086 /216182.

Banaszak, Lee Ann. *Why Movements Succeed or Fail : Opportunity, Culture, and the Struggle for Woman Suffrage*. Princeton, N.J.: Princeton University Press, 1996.

Banks, Christopher P., and John C. Blakeman. *The U.S. Supreme Court and New Federalism: From the Rehnquist to the Roberts Court*. Lanham, Md.: Rowman & Littlefield, 2012.

Beida Fabao. "Regulation on Special Economic Zones in Guangdong Province." August 26, 1980. https://www.wto.org/english/thewto_e/acc_e /chn_e/wtaccchn46_leg_8.pdf.

Belge, Ceren. "Friends of the Court: The Republican Alliance and Selective Activism of the Constitutional Court of Turkey." *Law & Society*

Review 40, no. 3 (2006): 653–92. https://doi.org/10.1111/j.1540-5893
.2006.00276.x.

Berenschot, Ward. "The Spatial Distribution of Riots: Patronage and
the Instigation of Communal Violence in Gujarat, India." *World Development* 39, no. 2 (2011): 221–30. https://doi.org/10.1016/j.worlddev.2009
.11.029.

Bhattacharya, D. P. "After Heated Speeches Praveen Togadia Tries to Regain
Lost Ground in Gujarat." *The Economic Times*, April 22, 2014. https://
economictimes.indiatimes.com/news/politics-and-nation/after-heated
-speeches-praveen-togadia-tries-to-regain-lost-ground-in-gujarat/article
show/34067662.cms.

Birchfield, Lauren, and Jessica Corsi. "Between Starvation and Globalization: Realizing the Right to Food in India." *Michigan Journal of International Law* 31, no. 4 (2010): 691–764.

Blaustein, Saul J. *Unemployment Insurance in the United States: The First
Half Century.* Kalamazoo, Mich.: W.E. Upjohn Institute for Employment
Research, 1993.

Bo, Zhiyue. *China's Elite Politics: Political Transition and Power Balancing.*
Hackensack, N.J.: World Scientific, 2007.

Boeckelman, Keith. "The Influence of States on Federal Policy Adoptions."
Policy Studies Journal 20, no. 3 (1992): 365–75. https://doi.org/10.1111/j
.1541-0072.1992.tb00164.x.

Boyd, William, and Ann E. Carlson. "Accidents of Federalism: Ratemaking
and Policy Innovation in Public Utility Law." *UCLA Law Review* 63, no. 4
(2016): 810–93. https://scholar.law.colorado.edu/articles/517.

Brahmanandam, T. "Review of the 73rd Constitutional Amendment: Issues
and Challenges." *Indian Journal of Public Administration* 64, no. 1 (2018):
103–21. https://doi.org/10.1177/0019556117735461.

Brandeis, Elizabeth, and Paul Raushenbush. "Wisconsin Unemployment
Reserves and Compensation Act." *Wisconsin Law Review* 7, no. 3 (1932):
136–45.

Brass, Paul R. "National Power and Local Politics in India: A Twenty-Year
Perspective." *Modern Asian Studies* 18, no. 1 (1984): 89–118. https://doi
.org/10.1017/S0026749X00011239.

Bulman-Pozen, Jessica. "Partisan Federalism." *Harvard Law Review* 127,
no. 4 (2014): 1077–146.

Bureau of Economic Analysis. "National Income and Product Accounts."
Accessed May 19, 2023. https://apps.bea.gov/iTable/?reqid=19&step=2
&isuri=1&categories=survey.

Bussell, Jennifer. *Clients and Constituents: Political Responsiveness in
Patronage Democracies.* New York: Oxford University Press, 2019.

Buzbee, William W. "Clean Air Act Dynamism and Disappointments: Lessons for Climate Legislation to Prompt Innovation and Discourage Inertia." *Washington University Journal of Law & Policy* 32 (2010): 33–77. https://openscholarship.wustl.edu/law_journal_law_policy /vol32/iss1/3.

———. "Contextual Environmental Federalism." *New York University Environmental Law Journal* 14, no. 1 (2005): 108–29.

Cai, Hongbin, and Daniel Treisman. "Did Government Decentralization Cause China's Economic Miracle?" *World Politics* 58, no. 4 (2006): 505–35. https://www.jstor.org/stable/40060148.

California Air Resources Board. "Low-Emission Vehicle Program." Accessed July 2, 2020. https://ww2.arb.ca.gov/our-work/programs/low -emission-vehicle-program/about.

Cameron, David, and Richard Simeon. "Intergovernmental Relations in Canada: The Emergence of Collaborative Federalism." *Publius* 32, no. 2 (2002): 49–72. https://doi.org/10.1093/oxfordjournals.pubjof.a004947.

Carlson, Ann E. "Iterative Federalism and Climate Change." *Northwestern University Law Review* 103, no. 3 (2009): 1097–161. https://escholarship. org/uc/item/7pc2n5qc.

Catt, Carrie Chapman, and Nettie Rogers Shuler. *Woman Suffrage and Politics: The Inner Story of the Suffrage Movement.* Seattle: University of Washington Press, 1969.

Center for American Women and Politics. "Women's Suffrage in the U.S. by State." 2014. https://tag.rutgers.edu/wp-content/uploads/2014/05 /suffrage-by-state.pdf.

Chandra, Kanchan. *Why Ethnic Parties Succeed: Patronage and Ethnic Head Counts in India.* New York: Cambridge University Press, 2004.

Chang, Gene Hsin, and Guanzhong James Wen. "Communal Dining and the Chinese Famine of 1958–1961." *Economic Development and Cultural Change* 46, no. 1 (1997): 1–34. https://doi.org/10.1086/452319.

Chang, Wen-Chen, and David S. Law. "Constitutional Dissonance in China." In *Comparative Constitutional Theory*, edited by Gary Jacobsohn and Miguel Schor, 476–514. Cheltenham: Edward Elgar, 2018.

Chattopadhyay, Raghabendra, and Esther Duflo. "Impact of Reservation in Panchayati Raj: Evidence from a Nationwide Randomised Experiment." *Economic and Political Weekly* 39, no. 9 (2004): 979–86.

Chaudhuri, Shubham. "What Difference Does a Constitutional Amendment Make? The 1994 Panchayati Raj Act and the Attempt to Revitalize Rural Local Government in India." In *Decentralization and Local Governance in Developing Countries: A Comparative Perspective*, edited by

Pranab Bardhan and Dilip Mookherjee, vi–vi. Cambridge, Mass.: MIT Press, 2006.

Chawla, Prabhu. "MGR's Midday Nutritious Meal Scheme: A Shrewd Political Move?" *India Today*, November 15, 1982. https://www.indiatoday.in /magazine/special-report/story/19821115-mgr-midday-nutritious-meal -scheme-a-shrewd-political-move-772378-2013-08-01.

Chay, Kenneth, and Michael Greenstone. "Air Quality, Infant Mortality, and the Clean Air Act of 1970." National Bureau of Economic Research, Working Paper no, 10053, 2003. https://doi.org/10.3386/w10053.

Chen, Xuelian. "A U-Turn or Just Pendulum Swing? Tides of Bottom-Up and Top-Down Reforms in Contemporary China." *Journal of Chinese Political Science* 22, no. 4 (2017): 651–73.

Cheng, Li. "Leadership Transition in the CPC: Promising Progress and Potential Problems." *China: An International Journal* 10, no. 2 (2012): 23–33. https://doi.org/10.1353/chn.2012.0027.

Chhibber, Pradeep, and Rahul Verma. "The Rise of the Second Dominant Party System in India: BJP's New Social Coalition in 2019." *Studies in Indian Politics* 7, no. 2 (2019): 131–48. https://doi.org/10.1177/2321023019874628.

China Information News. "14 Ge Yanhai Chengshi Shoupi Kaifang 20 Nian Chengjiu Huihuang" [The Glorious Achievements of the 14 Cities That Opened First]. August 19, 2008. http://phtv.ifeng.com/program/tfzg /200808/0819_2950_732252.shtml.

Choi, Eun Kyong. "Patronage and Performance: Factors in the Political Mobility of Provincial Leaders in Post-Deng China." *The China Quarterly* 212 (2012): 965–81. https://doi.org/10.1017/S030574101200118X.

Chowdhury, Shreya Roy. "BJP Government in Rajasthan Rewrote School Textbooks to Mirror the Hindutva Worldview." *Scroll.in*, November 14, 2018. https://scroll.in/article/901001/bjps-major-achievement-in-rajasthan -rewriting-schools-textbooks-in-the-rss-worldview.

Chung, Jae Ho. *Central Control and Local Discretion in China: Leadership and Implementation during Post-Mao Decollectivization.* Oxford: Oxford University Press, 2000.

Chutani, Alka Mohan. "School Lunch Program in India: Background, Objectives and Components." *Asia Pacific Journal of Clinical Nutrition* 21, no. 1 (2012): 151–54. https://doi.org/10.6133/apjcn.2012.21.1.21.

Clark, Brietta R. "Safeguarding Federalism by Saving Health Reform: Implications of National Federation of Independent Business v. Sebelius." *Loyola of Los Angeles Law Review* 46, no. 2 (2013): 541–627. https://digital commons.lmu.edu/llr/vol46/iss2/24.

Cole, Judith K. "A Wide Field for Usefulness: Women's Civil Status and the Evolution of Women's Suffrage on the Montana Frontier, 1864–1914."

American Journal of Legal History 34, no. 3 (1990): 262–94. https://doi
.org/10.2307/845887

Commonwealth Fund. "Status of Medicaid Expansion and Work Requirement Waivers." 2020. https://www.commonwealthfund.org/publications
/maps-and-interactives/2020/jul/status-medicaid-expansion-and-work
-requirement-waivers.

"Constituent Assembly of India Debates 4th November 1948." Constituent
Assembly Debates, vol. 7, 1948. https://www.constitutionofindia.net/con
stitution_assembly_debates/volume/7/1948-11-04.

"Constitution of the Communist Party of China." *Xinhua News*, October
24, 2017. http://www.xinhuanet.com//english/download/Constitution_
of_the_Communist_Party_of_China.pdf.

Cross, Frank B. "Realism about Federalism." *New York University Law Review* 74, no. 5 (1999): 1304–35.

Cushman, Barry. "Federalism." In *The Cambridge Companion to the United
States Constitution*, edited by Karen Orren and John W. Compton, 185–
223. Cambridge: Cambridge University Press, 2018.

———. "Rethinking the New Deal Court." *Virginia Law Review* 80, no. 1
(1994): 201–61. https://doi.org/10.2307/1073597.

———. "Some Varieties and Vicissitudes of Lochnerism." *Boston University Law Review* 85, no. 3 (2005): 881–1000.

Das, Upasak, and Diego Maiorano. "Post-Clientelistic Initiatives in a
Patronage Democracy: The Distributive Politics of India's MGNREGA."
World Development 117 (May 1, 2019): 239–52. https://doi.org/10.1016/j
.worlddev.2019.01.011.

DeParle, Nancy-Ann. "The Affordable Care Act Helps America's Uninsured."
The White House, September 16, 2010. https://obamawhitehouse.archives
.gov/blog/2010/09/16/affordable-care-act-helps-america-s-uninsured.

Deshpande, Rajeshwari, K. K. Kailash, and Louise Tillin. "States as Laboratories: The Politics of Social Welfare Policies in India." *India Review* 16,
no. 1 (2017): 85–105. https://doi.org/10.1080/14736489.2017.1279928.

Deutsche Welle. "Chuchuang Xiu Haishi Dongzhenge—Hu Jintao De
Zhenggaige Yiyuan You Duoqiang?" [Window-Dressing or Real Action:
How Strong Is Hu Jintao's Willingness towards Political Reforms?]. September 24, 2004. https://www.dw.com/zh/橱窗秀还是动真格胡锦涛的
政改革意愿有多强/a-1337086-0.

Dhattiwala, Raheel, and Michael Biggs. "The Political Logic of Ethnic Violence: The Anti-Muslim Pogrom in Gujarat, 2002." *Politics & Society* 40,
no. 4 (2012): 483–516. https://doi.org/10.1177/0032329212461125.

Dilger, Robert Jay. "Federal Grants to State and Local Governments: A Historical Perspective on Contemporary Issues." Congressional Research Service, 2019. https://crsreports.congress.gov/product/pdf/R/R40638/29.

Dinan, John J. "The Rehnquist Court's Federalism Decisions in Perspective." *Journal of Law & Politics* 15, no. 2 (1999): 127–94.

Ding, Yi. "Contract-Based Governance under Hierarchy: Rethinking 'Two Initiatives' under the Chinese Constitution." *Peking University Law Journal* 29, no. 4 (2017): 860–90.

Doonan, Michael, and Katharine Tull. "Health Care Reform in Massachusetts: Implementation of Coverage Expansions and a Health Insurance Mandate." *Milbank Quarterly* 88, no. 1 (March 1, 2010): 54–80. https://doi.org/10.1111/j.1468-0009.2010.00589.x.

Doremus, Holly, and W. Michael Hanemann. "Of Babies and Bathwater: Why the Clean Air Act's Cooperative Federalism Framework Is Useful for Addressing Global Warming." *Arizona Law Review* 50, no. 3 (2008): 799–834.

Dorf, Michael C., and Charles F. Sabel. "A Constitution of Democratic Experimentalism." *Columbia Law Review* 98, no. 2 (1998): 267–473. https://scholarship.law.cornell.edu/facpub/120.

Dorn, Stan. "The COVID-19 Pandemic and Resulting Economic Crash Have Caused the Greatest Health Insurance Losses in American History." *Families USA*, July 13, 2020. https://familiesusa.org/resources/the-covid-19-pandemic-and-resulting-economic-crash-have-caused-the-greatest-health-insurance-losses-in-american-history.

Drèze, Jean. "Future of Mid-Day Meals." *Economic and Political Weekly* 38, no. 44 (2003): 4673–83. https://mpra.ub.uni-muenchen.de/17386/.

DuBois, Ellen Carol. *Woman Suffrage and Women's Rights*. New York: New York University Press, 1998.

DW News. "Tackling Coronavirus Pandemic: Is the Kerala Model in India Really Working?" August 5, 2020. https://www.dw.com/en/tackling-coronavirus-pandemic-is-the-kerala-model-in-india-really-working/a-54444978.

Dwyer, John. "The Practice of Federalism under the Clean Air Act." *Maryland Law Review* 54, no. 4 (1995): 1183–225. http://digitalcommons.law.umaryland.edu/mlr/vol54/iss4/4.

Dwyer, Rachel, Gita Dharampal-Frick, Monika Kirloskar-Steinbach, and Jahnavi Phalkey. "Panchayati Raj." In *Key Concepts in Modern Indian Studies*, edited by Gita Dharampal-Frick, Monika Kirloskar-Steinbach, Rachel Dwyer, and Jahnavi Phalkey, 197–98. New York: New York University Press, 2015.

Economic Times. "Muslim Vote: How BJP Trumped Congress." March 27, 2019. https://economictimes.indiatimes.com/news/elections/lok-sabha/muslim-vote-how-bjp-trumped-congress/articleshow/68592698.cms?from=mdr.

———. "Yogi Adityanath Drives BJP Hindutva Campaign in Eastern Uttar Pradesh." March 2, 2017. https://economictimes.indiatimes.com/news/politics-and-nation/yogi-adityanath-drives-bjp-hindutva-campaign-in-eastern-uttar-pradesh/articleshow/57426899.cms.

Election Commission of India. "Election Results." Accessed December 25, 2020. https://eci.gov.in/statistical-report/statistical-reports/.

Engel, Kirsten H. "Harnessing the Benefits of Dynamic Federalism in Environmental Law." *Emory Law Journal* 56, no. 1 (2006): 159–88.

EPA. "The Benefits and Costs of the Clean Air Act 1970 to 1990." 1997. https://www.epa.gov/sites/production/files/2017-09/documents/ee-0295_all.pdf.

———. "The Benefits and Costs of the Clean Air Act from 1990 to 2020: Summary Report." 2011. http://www.epa.gov/oar/sect812/prospective2.html.

Epstein, Lee, and Jack Knight. *The Choices Justices Make.* Washington, D.C.: CQ Press, 1998.

Eskridge, William N. Jr., and John Ferejohn. "The Elastic Commerce Clause: A Political Theory of American Federalism." *Vanderbilt Law Review* 47, no. 5 (1994): 1355–400. https://scholarship.law.vanderbilt.edu/vlr/vol47/iss5/5.

Esty, Daniel C. "Revitalizing Environmental Federalism." *Michigan Law Review* 95, no. 3 (1996): 570–653. https://doi.org/10.2307/1290162.

Fewsmith, Joseph. *China since Tiananmen: From Deng Xiaoping to Hu Jintao.* 2nd ed. Cambridge: Cambridge University Press, 2008.

———. *Elite Politics in Contemporary China.* Armonk, N.Y.: M. E. Sharpe, 2001.

Field, Martha A. "The Differing Federalisms of Canada and the United States." *Law and Contemporary Problems* 55, no. 1 (1992): 107–20. https://doi.org/10.2307/1191759.

Finegold, Kenneth. "The United States: Federalism and Its Counterfactuals." In *Federalism and the Welfare State: New World and European Experiences,* edited by Herbert Obinger, Stephan Leibfried, and Francis G. Castles, 138–78. Cambridge: Cambridge University Press, 2005.

Finnegan, Margaret Mary. *Selling Suffrage: Consumer Culture & Votes for Women.* New York: Columbia University Press, 1999.

Fleisher, Richard, and John Bond. "The Shrinking Middle in the US Congress." *British Journal of Political Science* 34, no. 3 (2004): 429–51. https://doi.org/10.1017/S0007123404000122.

Flexner, Eleanor. *Century of Struggle: The Woman's Rights Movement in the United States.* Cambridge, Mass.: Belknap Press, 1996.

Florini, Ann, Hairong Lai, and Yeling Tan. *China Experiments: From Local Innovations to National Reform.* Washington, D.C.: Brookings Institution Press, 2012.

Forrester, Duncan. "Factions and Filmstars: Tamil Nadu Politics since 1971." *Asian Survey* 16, no. 3 (1976): 283–96. https://doi.org/10.2307/2643545

Franke, Richard W. "Local Planning: The Kerala Experiment." In *Real Utopia: Participatory Society for the 21st Century,* edited by Chris Spannos, 130–35. Chico, Calif.: AK Press, 2008.

Fu, Diana. "Fragmented Control: Governing Contentious Labor Organizations in China." *Governance* 30, no. 3 (2017): 445–62. https://doi.org/10.1111/gove.12248.

Fu, Diana, and Greg Distelhorst. "Grassroots Participation and Repression under Hu Jintao and Xi Jinping." *The China Journal* 79, no. 1 (2018): 100–122. https://hdl.handle.net/1721.1/122353.

Galle, Brian, and Joseph Leahy. "Laboratories of Democracy? Policy Innovation in Decentralized Governments." *Emory Law Journal* 58, no. 6 (2009): 1333–400.

Garfield, Rachel, Kendal Orgera, and Anthony Damico. "The Coverage Gap: Uninsured Poor Adults in States that Do Not Expand Medicaid." Kaiser Family Foundation, March 31, 2020. https://www.kff.org/medicaid/issue-brief/the-coverage-gap-uninsured-poor-adults-in-states-that-do-not-expand-medicaid/.

Ghassem-Fachandi, Parvis. *Pogrom in Gujarat: Hindu Nationalism and Anti-Muslim Violence in India.* Princeton, N.J.: Princeton University Press, 2012.

Ginsburg, Tom, and Tamir Moustafa. "Introduction: The Functions of Courts in Authoritarian Politics." In *Rule by Law: The Politics of Courts in Authoritarian Regimes,* edited by Tamir Moustafa and Tom Ginsburg, 1–22. Cambridge: Cambridge University Press, 2008.

Ginsburg, Tom, and Alberto Simpser. "Introduction: Constitution in Authoritarian Regimes." In *Constitutions in Authoritarian Regimes,* edited by Tom Ginsburg and Alberto Simpser, 1–18. New York: Cambridge University Press, 2013.

Graves, John A., and Katherine Swartz. "Understanding State Variation in Health Insurance Dynamics Can Help Tailor Enrollment Strategies for

ACA Expansion." *Health Affairs* 32, no. 10 (October 2, 2013): 1832–40. https://doi.org/10.1377/hlthaff.2013.0327.

Greenstone, Michael. "The Impacts of Environmental Regulations on Industrial Activity: Evidence from the 1970 and 1977 Clean Air Act Amendments and the Census of Manufactures." *Journal of Political Economy* 110, no. 6 (2002): 1175–219. https://doi.org/10.1086/342808.

Grogan, Colleen M., Phillip M. Singer, and David K. Jones. "Rhetoric and Reform in Waiver States." *Journal of Health Politics, Policy and Law* 42, no. 2 (2017): 247–84. https://doi.org/10.1215/03616878-3766719.

Guangzhou Daily. "Wang Yang: Fan Shehui Zuzhi 'Jiedezhu, Guandehao' De Shi, Dou Jiaogei Tamen" [Wang Yang: Any Governmental Function That Social Organizations Can Perform Well, Just Give To Them]. November 23, 2011. https://m.sohu.com/n/326568029/.

Gupta, Kamlesh. "Gram Sabha: A Step Towards Self Governance: A Study of Madhya Pradesh." *The Indian Journal of Political Science* 70, no. 1 (2009): 209–14.

Halberstam, Daniel, and Roderick M. Hills Jr. "State Autonomy in Germany and the United States." *Annals of the American Academy of Political and Social Science* 574, no. 1 (2001): 173–84. https://www.jstor.org/stable/1049063.

Harriss, Barbara. "Meals and Noon Meals in South India: Paradoxes of Targeting." *Public Administration and Development* 6, no. 4 (1986): 401–10. https://doi.org/10.1002/pad.4230060408.

Hayes, Susan L., Akeiisa Coleman, Sara R. Collins, and Rachel Nuzum. "The Fiscal Case for Medicaid Expansion." The Commonwealth Fund, 2019. https://www.commonwealthfund.org/blog/2019/fiscal-case-medicaid-expansion.

He, Baogang, and Mark Warren. "Authoritarian Deliberation: The Deliberative Turn in Chinese Political Development." *Perspectives on Politics* 9, no. 2 (2011): 269–89. https://doi.org/10.1017/S1537592711000892.

He, Xin. "Maintaining Stability by Law: Protest-Supported Housing Demolition Litigation and Social Change in China." *Law & Social Inquiry* 39, no. 4 (2014): 849–73. https://www.jstor.org/stable/24545764.

———. "The Party's Leadership as a Living Constitution in China." In *Constitutions in Authoritarian Regimes*, edited by Tom Ginsburg and Alberto Simpser, 245–64. New York: Cambridge University Press, 2014.

Heath, Oliver. "Communal Realignment and Support for the BJP, 2009–2019." *Contemporary South Asia* 28, no. 2 (2020): 195–208. https://doi.org/10.1080/09584935.2020.1765986.

Heilmann, Sebastian. "From Local Experiments to National Policy: The Origins of China's Distinctive Policy Process." *China Journal*, no. 59 (2008): 1–30. https://doi.org/10.1086/tcj.59.20066378.

———. "Policy Experimentation in China's Economic Rise." *Studies in Comparative International Development* 43, no. 1 (2008): 1–26. https://doi.org/10.1007/s12116-007-9014-4.

———. "Policy-Making through Experimentation: The Formation of a Distinctive Policy Process." In *Mao's Invisible Hand: The Political Foundations of Adaptive Governance in China*, edited by Sebastian Heilmann and Elizabeth J. Perry, 62–101. Cambridge, Mass.: Harvard University Asia Center, 2011.

———. *Red Swan: How Unorthodox Policy-Making Facilitated China's Rise.* Hong Kong: Chinese University of Hong Kong Press, 2018.

Heilmann, Sebastian, and Elizabeth J. Perry. "Embracing Uncertainty: Guerrilla Policy Style and Adaptive Governance in China." In *Mao's Invisible Hand: The Political Foundations of Adaptive Governance in China*, edited by Elizabeth J. Perry and Sebastian Heilmann, 1–29. Cambridge, Mass.: Harvard University Asia Center, 2011.

Heller, Patrick, K. N. Harilal, and Shubham Chaudhuri. "Building Local Democracy: Evaluating the Impact of Decentralization in Kerala, India." *World Development* 35, no. 4 (2007): 626–48. https://doi.org/10.1016/j.worlddev.2006.07.001.

Hertel, Shareen. "A New Route to Norms Evolution: Insights from India's Right to Food Campaign." *Social Movement Studies* 15, no. 6 (2016): 610–21. https://doi.org/10.1080/14742837.2016.1213161

"Highway Fund Sanctions for Clean Air Act Violations." EveryCRS Report.com, 1997. https://www.everycrsreport.com/reports/97-959 ENR.html.

Hindustan Times. "Gujarat Experiment to Be Repeated in Delhi: Togadia." December 16, 2002. https://www.hindustantimes.com/india/gujarat-experiment-to-be-repeated-in-delhi-togadia/story-KKIkXFDOLZMKA3 GmiJnaWM.html.

Hirschl, Ran. "The Question of Case Selection in Comparative Constitutional Law." *American Journal of Comparative Law* 53, no. 1 (2005): 125–55. https://doi.org/10.1093/ajcl/53.1.125

Hollingsworth, Julia, and Manveena Suri. "India Coronavirus: The Way These States Handled the Virus Shows the Country's Vast Divide." *CNN*, May 12, 2020. https://www.cnn.com/2020/05/12/asia/india-coronavirus-kerala-flatten-curve-intl-hnk/index.html.

Hopkins, June. "The New York State Temporary Emergency Relief Administration: October 1, 1931." VCU Libraries Social Welfare History Project.

Accessed December 8, 2020. https://socialwelfare.library.vcu.edu/eras
/great-depression/temporary-emergency-relief-administration/.

Horwitz, Morton J. "Republicanism and Liberalism in American Constitutional Thought." *William & Mary Law Review* 29, no. 1 (1987): 57–74.
https://scholarship.law.wm.edu/wmlr/vol29/iss1/8.

Hu, Angang. *Zhongguo Jiti Lingdao Tizhi [China's Collective Leadership]*.
Beijing: Zhongguo ren min da xue chu ban she, 2015.

Hu Jintao. "Full Text of Hu Jintao's Report at 17th Party Congress." Government of China, 2007. http://www.gov.cn/english/2007-10/24/content
_785505.htm.

Hu, Xiaoli, and Xixin Wang. "Infrastructure Power and the Optimization
of 'Vertical Governing Structure.'" *Political Science and Law*, no. 3 (2016):
54–65. https://doi.org/10.15984/j.cnki.1005-9512.2016.03.006.

Human Rights Watch. "World Report 2012: China." 2012. https://www.hrw
.org/world-report/2012/country-chapters/china-and-tibet.

"India Election Updates 2020." Elections.in. Accessed December 26, 2020.
https://www.elections.in/.

India Today. "BJP Manifesto 2019: No to Article 370 and Article 35A."
April 8, 2019. https://www.indiatoday.in/elections/lok-sabha-2019
/story/bjp-manifesto-2019-no-article-370-article-35a-1496655-2019
-04-08.

Iqbal, Mohammed. "Rajasthan to Purge 'Distortions' in Textbooks."
The Hindu, May 16, 2019. https://www.thehindu.com/news/national
/other-states/rajasthan-to-purge-distortions-in-textbooks/article
27142840.ece.

Isaac, Thomas, and Richard W. Franke. *Local Democracy and Development:
The Kerala People's Campaign for Decentralized Planning*. Lanham, Md.:
Rowman & Littlefield, 2002.

Jackson, Vicki C., and Mark Tushnet. *Comparative Constitutional Law*. 3rd
ed. St. Paul, Minn.: Foundation Press, 2014.

Jacobsohn, Gary Jeffrey. *The Wheel of Law: India's Secularism in Comparative Constitutional Context*. Princeton, N.J.: Princeton University Press,
2003.

Jaffrelot, Christophe. "India's Democracy at 70: Toward a Hindu State?"
Journal of Democracy 28, no. 3 (2017): 52–63. https://doi.org/10.1353/jod
.2017.0044.

Jaros, Kyle A., and Yeling Tan. "Provincial Power in a Centralizing China:
The Politics of Domestic and International 'Development Space.'" *The
China Journal* 83, no. 1 (2020): 79–104. https://doi.org/10.1086/706256.

Jayaraman, Rajshri, and Dora Simroth. "The Impact of School Lunches on Primary School Enrollment: Evidence from India's Midday Meal Scheme." *Scandinavian Journal of Economics* 117, no. 4 (2015): 1176–203. https://doi.org/10.1111/sjoe.12116.

Jia, Mark. "China's Constitutional Entrepreneurs." *The American Journal of Comparative Law* 64, no. 3 (2016): 619–76. https://www.jstor.org/stable /26425466.

Jia, Ruixue, Masayuki Kudamatsu, and David Seim. "Political Selection in China: The Complementary Roles of Connections and Performance." *Journal of the European Economic Association* 13, no. 4 (2015): 631–68. https://doi.org/10.1111/jeea.12124.

Jiang, Shigong. "Written and Unwritten Constitutions: A New Approach to the Study of Constitutional Government in China." *Modern China* 36, no. 1 (2010): 12–46. https://doi.org/10.1177/0097700409349703.

Jiang, Zemin. "Full Text of Jiang Zemin's Report at 16th Party Congress on Nov 8, 2002." *China Daily*, November 26, 2013. http://language.china daily.com.cn/news/2013-11/26/content_17132209_7.htm.

Johnson, Thomas R. "Regulatory Dynamism of Environmental Mobilization in Urban China." *Regulation & Governance* 10, no. 1 (2016): 14–28. https://doi.org/10.1111/rego.12068.

Jolish, Taly L. "Negotiating the Smog Away." *Virginia Environmental Law Journal* 18, no. 3 (1999): 305–73. https://www.jstor.org/stable/24785976.

Kaiser Commission on Key Facts. "Five Key Questions and Answers About Section 1115 Medicaid Demonstration Waivers." 2011. https://www.kff .org/wp-content/uploads/2013/01/8196.pdf.

Kaiser Family Foundation. "Status of State Medicaid Expansion Decisions: Interactive Map." 2020. https://www.kff.org/medicaid/issue-brief/status -of-state-medicaid-expansion-decisions-interactive-map/.

Kamieniecki, Sheldon, and Michael R. Ferrall. "Intergovernmental Relations and Clean-Air Policy in Southern California." *Publius* 21, no. 3 (1991): 143–54. https://www.jstor.org/stable/3330519.

Karch, Andrew. *Democratic Laboratories: Policy Diffusion among the American States*. Ann Arbor: University of Michigan Press, 2007.

Kashyap, Subhash. "Intergovernmental Relations Revisited: Towards a Fresh Balance of Power." In *Federalism in India: Towards a Fresh Balance of Power*, edited by Lancy Lobo, Mrutuyanjaya Sahu, and Jayesh Shah, 20–29. Jaipur: Rawat Publications, 2014.

Kattumuri, Ruth. "Food Security and the Targeted Public Distribution System in India." London School of Economics, Working Paper 38, 2011. https://eprints.lse.ac.uk/38365/.

Khosla, Madhav. *India's Founding Moment: The Constitution of a Most Surprising Democracy*. Cambridge, Mass.: Harvard University Press, 2020.

———. *The Indian Constitution*. New Delhi: Oxford University Press, 2012.

Klarman, Michael. "Rethinking the Civil Rights and Civil Liberties Revolutions." *Virginia Law Review* 82, no. 1 (1996): 1–67. https://doi.org/10.2307/1073565.

Kommers, Donald P., and Russell A. Miller. *Constitutional Jurisprudence of the Federal Republic of Germany*. 3rd ed. Durham, N.C.: Duke University Press, 2012.

Kostka, Genia. "Command without Control: The Case of China's Environmental Target System." *Regulation & Governance* 10, no. 1 (2016): 58–74. https://doi.org/10.1111/rego.12082.

Kostka, Genia, and Jonas Nahm. "Central-Local Relations: Recentralization and Environmental Governance in China." *The China Quarterly* 231 (2017): 567–82. https://doi.org/10.1017/S0305741017001011.

Kramer, Larry. "Putting the Politics Back into the Political Safeguards of Federalism." *Columbia Law Review* 100, no. 1 (2000): 215–93. https://doi.org/10.2307/1123559.

———. "Understanding Federalism." *Vanderbilt Law Review* 47, no. 5 (1994): 1485–561. https://scholarship.law.vanderbilt.edu/vlr/vol47/iss5/8.

Kuchay, Bilal. "Many Indian States 'Will Not Implement' Modi's Citizenship Law." *Al Jazeera*, January 4, 2020. https://www.aljazeera.com/news/2020/01/indian-states-implement-modi-citizenship-law-200104094411324.html.

Landau, David. "Abusive Constitutionalism." *U.C. Davis Law Review* 47, no. 1 (2013): 189–260.

Landry, Pierre F., Xiaobo Lü, and Haiyan Duan. "Does Performance Matter? Evaluating Political Selection along the Chinese Administrative Ladder." *Comparative Political Studies* 51, no. 8 (2018): 1074–105. https://doi.org/10.1177/0010414017730078.

Larson, Arthur, and Merrill G. Murray. "The Development of Unemployment Insurance in the United States." *Vanderbilt Law Review* 8, no. 2 (1954): 181–217. https://scholarship.law.vanderbilt.edu/vlr/vol8/iss2/2.

Lee, Sangkuk. "An Institutional Analysis of Xi Jinping's Centralization of Power." *Journal of Contemporary China* 26, no. 105 (2017): 325–36. https://doi.org/10.15984/j.cnki.1005-9512.2016.03.006.

Leonard, Kimberly. "Opposing Medicaid Expansion." *U.S. News & World Report*, December 4, 2015. https://www.usnews.com/news/the-report/articles/2015/12/04/opposing-medicaid-expansion.

Li, Cheng. *China's Leaders: The New Generation*. Lanham, Md.: Rowman & Littlefield, 2001.

———. *Chinese Politics in the Xi Jinping Era: Reassessing Collective Leadership*. Washington, D.C.: Brookings Institution Press, 2016.

Li, Hongbin, and Li-An Zhou. "Political Turnover and Economic Performance: The Incentive Role of Personnel Control in China." *Journal of Public Economics* 89, no. 9 (2005): 1743–62. https://doi.org/10.1016/j.jpubeco.2004.06.009.

Li, Lianjiang. "The Politics of Introducing Direct Township Elections in China." *The China Quarterly* 171 (2002): 704–23. https://doi.org/10.1017/S0009443902000438.

Li, Yuanchao. "Li Yuanchao: Tuijin Dangnei Minzhu Jianshe, Zengqiang Dang De Tuanjie Tongyi" [Li Yuanchao: Push for Intra-Party Democratic Development, Enhancing Party Unification]. Government of China, 2007. http://www.gov.cn/ztzl/17da/content_792867_2.htm.

"Li Yuanchao Dui Jiangsusheng 20 Ming Gongxuan Xin Renzhi Ganbu Tichu Wudian Xiwang" [Li Yuanchao Raised Five Expectations to 20 Newly Publically Elected Officials]. Government of China, 2007. http://www.gov.cn/gzdt/2007-07/15/content_684941.htm.

Lieberthal, Kenneth, and Michel Oksenberg. *Policy Making in China: Leaders, Structures, and Processes*. Princeton, N.J.: Princeton University Press, 1988.

Lieu, Sue. "Regional Impacts of Air Quality Regulation: Applying an Economic Model." *Contemporary Policy Issues* 9, no. 3 (1991): 24–34. https://doi.org/10.1111/j.1465-7287.1991.tb00338.x.

Lin, Justin Yifu. "Collectivization and China's Agricultural Crisis in 1959–1961." *Journal of Political Economy* 98, no. 6 (1990): 1228–52. https://doi.org/10.1086/261732.

———."Institutional Reforms and Dynamics of Agricultural Growth in China." *Food Policy* 22, no. 3 (1997): 201–12. https://doi.org/10.1016/S0306-9192(97)00009-2.

Lin, Minshu. "History and Future of New China's Economic Growth Models in the Past 60 Years." *Henan Social Sciences* 17, no. 4 (2009): 12–15. https://doi.org/10.3969/j.issn.1007-905X.2009.04.003.

Lin, Yan. "Constitutional Evolution through Legislation: The Quiet Transformation of China's Constitution." *International Journal of Constitutional Law* 13, no. 1 (2015): 61–89. https://doi.org/10.1093/icon/mov001.

———. "Cooperative Federalism: Law Enforcement Oversight Shapes Center-Local Relations." *Peking University Law Journal* 29, no. 4 (2017): 845–59.

List, John A., Daniel L. Millimet, and Warren McHone. "The Unintended Disincentive in the Clean Air Act." *The B.E. Journal of Economic Analysis & Policy* 4, no. 2 (2004): 2–26. https://doi.org/10.2202/1538-0637.1204.

Liu, Qifang, and Zhong Fang. "Chen Yun Zai Zhonggong Lishi Shang De Shida Gongxian" [The Ten Major Contributions of Chen Yun to the CCP History]. *People's Daily Online*, March 22, 2013. http://dangshi.people .com.cn/n/2013/0322/c85037-20884383-9.html.

Livermore, Michael. "The Perils of Experimentation." *Yale Law Journal* 126 (2017): 636–894.

Long, Sharon K., Karen Stockley, and Kate Willrich Nordahl. "Coverage, Access, and Affordability under Health Reform: Learning from the Massachusetts Model." *Inquiry* 49, no. 4 (2012): 303–16. https://doi .org/10.5034/inquiryjrnl_49.04.03.

Lowry, William R. *The Dimensions of Federalism: State Governments and Pollution Control Policies*. Durham, N.C.: Duke University Press, 1992.

Lu, Xi. "Xi Jinping Chairs the 35th Meeting of the Central Leading Group for Comprehensively Deepening Reforms." Government of China, 2017. http://www.gov.cn/xinwen/2017-05/23/content_5196189.htm.

Ma, Deyong, and M. Rosemary Pang. "The Rise and Fall of Electoral Democracy: A Social Evolutionary Approach to Direct Election Experiments in Local China." *Journal of Chinese Political Science* 22, no. 4 (2017): 601–24. https://doi.org/10.1007/s11366-017-9510-y.

Ma, Deyong, and Zhengxu Wang. "Governance Innovations and Citizens' Trust in Local Government: Electoral Impacts in China's Townships." *Japanese Journal of Political Science* 15, no. 3 (2014): 373–95. https://doi .org/10.1017/S1468109914000152.

Madison, James. "Federalist Papers: No. 10." November 23, 1787. https:// avalon.law.yale.edu/18th_century/fed10.asp.

Mahajan, Megan. "Trump Revoking California Emissions Waiver Will Cost Billions, Fracture U.S. Auto Market." *Forbes*, September 19, 2019. https://www.forbes.com/isites/energyinnovation/2019/09/19/trump -revoking-california-emissions-waiver-will-cost-billions-fracture -us-auto-market/#10c2d5684467.

Mainwaring, Scott, Fernando Bizzarro, and Ana Petrova. "Party System Institutionalization, Decay, and Collapse." In *Party Systems in Latin America: Institutionalization, Decay, and Collapse*, edited by Scott Mainwaring, 17–33. Cambridge: Cambridge University Press, 2018.

Mainwaring, Scott, and Timothy Scully. *Building Democratic Institutions: Party Systems in Latin America*. Stanford, Calif.: Stanford University Press, 1995.

Majeed, Akhtar. "India: A Model of Cooperative Federalism." In *The Ashgate Research Companion to Federalism*, edited by Ann Ward and Lee Ward, 503–16. Farnham: Ashgate, 2009.

Malik, Yogendra K. "Indira Gandhi: Personality, Political Power and Party Politics." *Journal of Asian and African Studies* 22, nos. 3–4 (1987): 141–55. http://dx.doi.org/10.1177/002190968702200302.

Maneesh, P. "Mid Day Meals and Food Security among Children: Assuring Nutritional Security of Tamil Nadu." *Indian Journal of Economics and Development* 3, no. 9 (2015): 1–5.

Manor, James. "COVID-19 and a Valuable Lesson from Grassroots India, Ignored." *The Wire*, May 14, 2020. https://thewire.in/government/covid-19-panchayat-grassroots-india.

———. "Democratic Decentralisation in Two Indian States: Past and Present." *Indian Journal of Political Science* 63, no. 1 (2002): 51–71. https://www.jstor.org/stable/42743574.

———. "India Defies the Odds: Making Federalism Work." *Journal of Democracy* 9, no. 3 (1998): 21–35. https://doi.org/10.1353/jod.1998.0047.

———. "India's States: The Struggle to Govern." *Studies in Indian Politics* 4, no. 1 (2016): 8–21. https://doi.org/10.1177/2321023016634909.

———. "Politics and Experimentation in India—The Contrast with China." *China Analysis*, no. 74 (2009): 2–29.

Mansoor, Sanya. "What Kerala's Challenge to Indian Citizenship Law Signals." *Time*, January 20, 2020. https://time.com/5765954/kerala-citizenship-law-supreme-court/.

Mao Zedong. "On the Ten Major Relationships." 1956. https://www.marxists.org/reference/archive/mao/selected-works/volume-5/mswv5_51.htm.

Mate, Manoj. "The Rise of Judicial Governance in the Supreme Court of India." *Boston University International Law Journal* 33 (2015): 169–222.

Mathur, Kuldeep. *Panchayati Raj*. New Delhi: Oxford University Press, 2013.

Mazur, Allan, and Eric W. Welch. "The Geography of American Environmentalism." *Environmental Science & Policy* 2, no. 4 (1999): 389–96. https://doi.org/10.1016/S1462-9011(99)00033-7.

McCammon, Holly J. "'Out of the Parlors and into the Streets': The Changing Tactical Repertoire of the U.S. Women's Suffrage Movements." *Social Forces* 81, no. 3 (2003): 787–818. https://www.jstor.org/stable/3598176.

McCammon, Holly J., and Karen E. Campbell. "Winning the Vote in the West: The Political Successes of the Women's Suffrage Movements, 1866–1919." *Gender and Society* 15, no. 1 (2001): 55–82. https://doi.org/10.1177/089124301015001004.

McCammon, Holly J., Karen E. Campbell, Ellen M. Granberg, and Christine Mowery. "How Movements Win: Gendered Opportunity Structures and U.S. Women's Suffrage Movements, 1866 to 1919." *American Socio-logical Review* 66, no. 1 (2001): 49–70. https://doi.org/10.2307/2657393.

McConnaughy, Corrine M. *The Woman Suffrage Movement in America: A Reassessment.* New York: Cambridge University Press, 2013.

McCurdy, Charles W. "American Law and the Marketing Structure of the Large Corporation, 1875–1890." *The Journal of Economic History* 38, no. 3 (1978): 631–49. https://doi.org/10.1017/S0022050700082590.

McDonough, John E., Brian Rosman, Fawn Phelps, and Melissa Shannon. "The Third Wave of Massachusetts Health Care Access Reform." *Health Affairs* 25, no. 6 (2006): 420–31. https://doi.org/10.1377/hlthaff.25 .w420.

McMillen, Sally. *Seneca Falls and the Origins of the Women's Rights Move-ment.* Oxford: Oxford University Press, 2009.

Mead, Rebecca J. "The Woman Suffrage Movement in the United States." In *The Oxford Research Encyclopedia of American History.* 2018. https://doi .org/10.1093/acrefore/9780199329175.013.17.

Mehta, Pratap Bhanu. "The Indian Supreme Court and the Art of Demo-cratic Positioning." In *Unstable Constitutionalism*, edited by Mark Tush-net and Madhav Khosla, 233–60. Cambridge: Cambridge University Press, 2015.

Mertha, Andrew. "China's 'Soft' Centralization: Shifting Tiao/Kuai Authority Relations." *The China Quarterly* 184 (2005): 791–810. https:// doi.org/10.1017/S0305741005000500.

———. "'Fragmented Authoritarianism 2.0': Political Pluralization in the Chinese Policy Process." *The China Quarterly* 200 (2009): 995–1012. https://doi.org/10.1017/S0305741009990592.

Meyer, Robinson. "Why Trump Wants to Revoke California's Clean-Air Waiver." *The Atlantic*, March 6, 2017. https://www.theatlantic.com/science /archive/2017/03/trump-california-clean-air-act-waiver-climate-change /518649/.

Ministry of Education of People's Republic of China. "Jiaoyubu Guanyu Zai Guojia Xianfari Shenru Kaizhan Xianfa Xuexi Xuanchuan Jiaoyu Huodong De Tongzhi" [Ministry of Education Requires Launching Edu-cation Campaign Regarding Constitutional Law during National Consti-tution Day]. 2014. http://www.moe.gov.cn/srcsite/A02/s7049/201411 /t20141121_178775.html.

Ministry of Human Resource Development. "National Programme of Nutritional Support to Primary Education Guidelines." Government of India, 2004. http://14.139.60.153/bitstream/123456789/2667/1/NATIONAL %20PROGRAMME%20OF%20NUTRITIONAL%20SUPPORT%20TO %20PRIMARY%20EDUCATION-2004-D12757.pdf.

Mishra, Pankaj. "The Gujarat Massacre: New India's Blood Rite." *The Guardian*, March 14, 2012. https://www.theguardian.com/commentisfree /2012/mar/14/new-india-gujarat-massacre.

Mitchell, Alison, and Sara Bencic. "Overview of the ACA Medicaid Expansion." Congressional Research Service, 2018. https://fas.org/sgp/crs/misc /IF10399.pdf.

Mohanty, Chittaranjan. "Decision Making Process on Policy of Liberalisation in Indian State." *Indian Journal of Political Science* 72, no. 2 (2011): 511–22.

Montinola, Gabriella, Yingyi Qian, and Barry R. Weingast. "Federalism, Chinese Style: The Political Basis for Economic Success in China." *World Politics* 48, no. 1 (1995): 50–81. https://www.jstor.org/stable/25053952.

Moog, Robert. "Activism on the Indian Supreme Court." *Judicature* 82, no. 3 (1998): 124–32.

Moulton, H. Geoffrey, Jr. "The Quixotic Search for a Judicially Enforceable Federalism." *Minnesota Law Review* 83, no. 4 (1999): 849. https://scholar ship.law.umn.edu/mlr/1407.

Moustafa, Tamir. "Law and Courts in Authoritarian Regimes." *Annual Review of Law and Social Science* 10 (2014): 281–99. https://doi.org/10.1146 /annurev-lawsocsci-110413-030532

———. *The Struggle for Constitutional Power: Law, Politics, and Economic Development in Egypt*. Cambridge: Cambridge University Press, 2007.

Mulvad, Andreas. "Competing Hegemonic Projects within China's Variegated Capitalism: 'Liberal' Guangdong vs. 'Statist' Chongqing." *New Political Economy* 20, no. 2 (2015): 199–227. https://doi.org/10.1080 /13563467.2014.914160.

Muringatheri, Mini. "Other States to Emulate Kerala Model of Decentralisation." *The Hindu*, July 12, 2015. https://www.thehindu.com/news/na tional/kerala/other-states-to-emulate-kerala-model-of-decentralisation /article7413015.ece.

Murphy, Bruce Allen. *The Brandeis/Frankfurter Connection: The Secret Political Activities of Two Supreme Court Justices*. New York: Oxford University Press, 1982.

Nadkarni, M. V., N. Sivanna, and Lavanya Suresh. *Decentralised Democracy in India: Gandhi's Vision and Reality*. London: Routledge, 2018. https:// doi.org/10.4324/9781315105345.

Nathan, Andrew. "A Factionalism Model for CCP Politics." *The China Quarterly* 53 (1973): 34–66. https://doi.org/10.1017/S0305741000500022.

———. "Authoritarian Resilience: China's Changing of the Guard." *Journal of Democracy* 14, no. 1 (2003): 6–17. https://doi.org/10.1353/jod.2003.0019.

National Bureau of Statistics of China. "Central and Local Fiscal Income and Percentage." National Data. Accessed September 10, 2019. http://data .stats.gov.cn/.

National Research Council. *State and Federal Standards for Mobile-Source Emissions.* Washington, D.C.: National Academies Press, 2006. https:// doi.org/10.17226/11586.

Ng, Kwai Hang, and Xin He. *Embedded Courts: Judicial Decision-Making in China.* New York: Cambridge University Press, 2017.

Niu, Xiaoxue. "'Songbang' Hou De Guangdong Minjian Zuzhi Zhuce Zhuangkuang Diaocha" [Investigation on the Registration Status of Guangdong Civil Organizations after "Untying Hands"]. China Development Brief, 2012. http://www.chinadevelopmentbrief.org.cn /news-5415.html.

Oates, Wallace E. "A Reconsideration of Environmental Federalism." In *Recent Advances in Environmental Economics*, edited by John List and Aart de Zeeuw, 1–32. Cheltenham: Edward Elgar, 2002.

———. "On the Evolution of Fiscal Federalism: Theory and Institutions." *National Tax Journal* 61, no. 2 (2008): 313–34. https://doi.org/10.17310/ntj .2008.2.08.

OECD. "OECD Fiscal Decentralisation Database." Accessed September 22, 2020. https://www.oecd.org/ctp/federalism/fiscal-decentralisation-data base.htm#C_3.

Organizational Department of Chinese Communist Party Sichuan Provin-cial Committee. "Guanyu Gongxuan/Zhixuan Xiangzhen Lingdao Ganbu Yu Dang De Lingdao Wenti De Diaocha Yu Sikao" [Investigation and Thoughts on the Question of Open Nomination/Direct Election and Party Leadership]. 2004. http://www.chinareform.org.cn/gov/governance /Forward/201006/t20100617_27364.htm.

Panda, Manoj, Purnamita Dasgupta, and William Joe. "Resource Sharing between Centre and States and Allocation across States: Some Issues in Balancing Equity and Efficiency." Institute of Economic Growth, Oc-tober 10, 2019. https://policycommons.net/artifacts/2074508/resource-sharing-between-centre-and-states-and-allocation-across-states /2829806/.

Pandian, M. S. S. *The Image Trap: M. G. Ramachandran in Film and Poli-tics.* New Delhi: Sage Publications.

Parayil, Govindan. "The 'Kerala Model' of Development: Development and Sustainability in the Third World." *Third World Quarterly* 17, no. 5 (1996): 941–58. https://www.jstor.org/stable/3993238.

Parikh, Sunita, and Barry R. Weingast. "A Comparative Theory of Federalism: India." *Virginia Law Review* 83, no. 7 (1997): 1593–615. https://doi.org/10.2307/1073770.

Parrish, Michael E. "The Great Depression, the New Deal, and the American Legal Order." *Washington Law Review* 59 (1983): 723–50. https://digitalcommons.law.uw.edu/wlr/vol59/iss4/3.

People's Daily Online. "Li Yuanchao Tongzhi Jianli" [Resume of Comrade Li Yuanchao]. March 2013. http://politics.people.com.cn/n/2012/1115/c351134-19594905.html.

———. "Lishi Xuanze Le Deng Xiaoping" [History Has Chosen Deng Xiaoping]. July 3, 2018. http://cpc.people.com.cn/n1/2018/0703/c69113-30107101.html.

Peterson, Paul E. *The Price of Federalism.* Washington, D.C.: Brookings Institution Press, 1995.

Peterson, Todd D. "Controlling the Federal Courts through the Appropriations Process." *Wisconsin Law Review* 1998, no. 4 (1998): 993–1050.

Pildes, Richard H. "Why the Center Does Not Hold: The Causes of Hyperpolarized Democracy in America." *California Law Review* 99, no. 2 (2011): 273–333.

Pillai, K. Raman, and R. K. Suresh Kumar. *Panchayati Raj Experience in India.* Lanham, Md.: Kalpaz Publications, 2016.

Press Information Bureau. "Mid Day Meal." Government of India. Accessed May 31, 2020. http://pibmumbai.gov.in/English/PDF/E0000_H12.PDF.

Prosterman, Roy L., Tim Hanstad, and Li Ping. "Can China Feed Itself?" *Scientific American* 275, no. 5 (1996): 90. https://doi.org/10.1038/scientificamerican1196-90.

Punj, Shweta. "Planning Commission's Disbandment Will Boost Fiscal Federalism." *Business Today*, September 14, 2014. https://www.businesstoday.in/magazine/focus/planning-commission-narendra-modi-right-to-education-act/story/209566.html.

Qian, Yingyi, and Barry R. Weingast. "Federalism as a Commitment to Preserving Market Incentives." *Journal of Economic Perspectives* 11, no. 4 (1997): 83–92. https://doi.org/10.1257/jep.11.4.83.

Qian, Yingyi, and Chenggang Xu. "Why China's Economic Reforms Differ: The M-Form Hierarchy and Entry/Expansion of the Non-State Sector." *Economics of Transition* 1, no. 2 (1993): 135–70. https://doi.org/10.7551/mitpress/9780262534246.003.0011.

Qiang, Gang. "'Dangnei Minzhu': Gaide De Qierudian?" ["Intraparty Democracy": Entry Point of Reform?]. *The New York Times*, September 24, 2012. https://cn.nytimes.com/china/20120924/cc24qiangang6/.

———. "'Gongmin Shehui': Shehui Zai Nali?" ["Civil Society": Where Is the Society?]. *The New York Times*, September 26, 2012. https://cn .nytimes.com/china/20120926/cc26qiangang8/.

Quadagno, Jill S. "Welfare Capitalism and the Social Security Act of 1935." *American Sociological Review* 49, no. 5 (1984): 632–47. https://doi.org /10.2307/2095421.

Raghunandan, T. R. "Responding to COVID-19 at the Grassroots." *The Hindu*, May 11, 2020. https://www.thehindu.com/opinion/op-ed /responding-to-covid-19-at-the-grassroots/article31552359.ece.

Rajashekara, H. M. "The Nature of Indian Federalism: A Critique." *Asian Survey* 37, no. 3 (1997): 245–53. https://doi.org/10.1525/as.1997.37.3.01p0229r.

Ramachandran, Srinivasan. "Mid-Day Meals: High Noon of Welfare." *The Times of India*, March 14, 2016. https://blogs.timesofindia.indiatimes .com/tracking-indian-communities/mid-day-meals-high-noon-of -welfare-2/.

Rao, M. Govinda. "Incentivizing Fiscal Transfers in the Indian Federation." *Publius* 33, no. 4 (2003): 43–62. https://doi.org/10.1093/oxfordjournals .pubjof.a005012.

Ray, Amal, and John Kincaid. "Politics, Economic Development, and Second-Generation Strain in India's Federal System." *Publius* 18, no. 2 (1988): 147–67. https://doi.org/10.1093/oxfordjournals.pubjof.a037706.

"Regulation on Registration and Administration of Social Organizations." 1998. http://www.lawinfochina.com/display.aspx?lib=law&id=5613&CGid=.

"Report of the Task Force on Panchayati Raj Institutions." Planning Commission, December 2001. https://casi.sas.upenn.edu/sites/default/files/iit /Report of Task Force on PRIs.pdf.

Revesz, Richard L. "Federalism and Environmental Regulation: A Public Choice Analysis." *Harvard Law Review* 115, no. 2 (2001): 553–641. https:// doi.org/10.2307/1342673.

———. "Federalism and Interstate Environmental Externalities." *University of Pennsylvania Law Review* 144, no. 6 (1996): 2341–416. https://doi .org/10.2307/3312672.

———. "Rehabilitating Interstate Competition: Rethinking the 'Race-to-the-Bottom' Rationale for Federal Environmental Regulation." *New York University Law Review* 67, no. 6 (1992): 1210–54.

Riker, William H. *Federalism: Origin, Operation, Significance.* Boston: Little, Brown, 1964.

Riker, William H., and Ronald Schaps. "Disharmony in Federal Government." *Behavioral Science* 2, no. 4 (1957): 276–90. https://doi.org/10.1002 /bs.3830020405.

Robertson, David Brian. "The Bias of American Federalism: The Limits of Welfare-State Development in the Progressive Era." *Journal of Policy History* 1, no. 3 (1989): 261–91. https://doi.org/10.1017/S0898030600003523.

Rose-Ackerman, Susan. "Risk Taking and Reelection: Does Federalism Promote Innovation?" *The Journal of Legal Studies* 9, no. 3 (1980): 593–616. https://doi.org/10.1086/467654.

Rosen, Jeffrey. *Louis D. Brandeis: American Prophet.* New Haven, Conn.: Yale University Press, 2016.

Rosenberg, Gerald N. *The Hollow Hope: Can Courts Bring about Social Change?* 2nd ed. Chicago: University of Chicago Press, 2008.

Roy, Avik. "How Mitt Romney's Health-Care Experts Helped Design Obamacare." *Forbes*, October 11, 2011. https://www.forbes.com/sites/aroy/2011/10/11/how-mitt-romneys-health-care-experts-helped-design-obamacare.

Rubinow, I. M. "The Ohio Idea: Unemployment Insurance." *The Annals of the American Academy of Political and Social Science* 170, no. 1 (1933): 76–87. https://doi.org/10.1177/000271623317000110.

Rudolph, Lloyd I., and Susanne Hoeber Rudolph. "The Old and New Federalism in Independent India." In *The Routledge Handbook of South Asian Politics*, edited by Paul Brass, 147–61. London: Routledge, 2010.

Ryan, Erin. "Federalism and the Tug of War Within: Seeking Checks and Balance in the Interjurisdictional Gray Area." *Maryland Law Review* 66, no. 3 (2007): 503–667. http://digitalcommons.law.umaryland.edu/mlr/vol66/iss3/3.

Sabel, Charles F., and William H. Simon. "Minimalism and Experimentalism in the Administrative State." *Georgetown Law Journal* 100, no. 1 (2011): 53–94. https://scholarship.law.columbia.edu/faculty_scholarship/735.

Safi, Michael. "Cow Slaughter to Be Punishable by Life Sentence in Gujarat." *The Guardian*, March 14, 2017. https://www.theguardian.com/world/2017/mar/14/indian-state-government-life-sentence-cow-slaughter.

Sardesai, Shreyas. "The Religious Divide in Voting Preferences and Attitudes in the 2019 Election." *Studies in Indian Politics* 7, no. 2 (2019): 161–75. https://doi.org/10.1177/2321023019874892.

Sarma, Atul, and Debabani Chakravarty. *Integrating the Third Tier in the Indian Federal System: Two Decades of Rural Local Governance.* Singapore: Springer, 2018.

Sarratt, Reed. *The Ordeal of Desegregation.* New York: Harper & Row, 1966.

Saxena, Rekha, and Mahendra P. Singh. "The Role of the Federal Judiciary in Union-State Relations in India." In *New Directions in Federalism*

Studies, edited by Jan Erk and Wilfried Swenden, 50–67. London: Routledge, 2010.

Schapiro, Robert A. "From Dualist Federalism to Interactive Federalism." *Emory Law Journal* 56, no. 1 (2006): 1–18.

Schapiro, Robert A., and William W. Buzbee. "Unidimensional Federalism: Power and Perspective in Commerce Clause Adjudication." *Cornell Law Review* 88, no. 5 (2003): 1199–277. https://doi.org/10.2139/ssrn.346481.

Scheiber, Harry N. "American Federalism and the Diffusion of Power: Historical and Contemporary Perspectives." *University of Toledo Law Review* 9 (1977): 619–80.

Schwartz, Jonathan. "Environmental NGOs in China: Roles and Limits." *Pacific Affairs* 77, no. 1 (2004): 28–49. https://www.jstor.org/stable/40022273.

Sen, Ronojoy. "India's Democracy at 70: The Disputed Role of the Courts." *Journal of Democracy* 28, no. 3 (2017): 96–105. https://doi.org/10.1353/jod.2017.0048.

Shambayati, Hootan. "Courts in Semi-Democratic/Authoritarian Regimes: The Judicialization of Turkish (and Iranian) Politics." In *Rule by Law: The Politics of Courts in Authoritarian Regimes*, edited by Tamir Moustafa and Tom Ginsburg, 283–303. Cambridge: Cambridge University Press, 2008.

Shamdasani, Ravina. "The Gujarat Riots of 2002: Primordialism or Democratic Politics?" *The International Journal of Human Rights* 13, no. 4 (2009): 544–51. https://doi.org/10.1080/13642980802532879.

Sharma, B. M. *Panchayati Raj and Reservation Policy: Study of Impact of Reservation Policy on the Marginalised Sections of the Society.* Jaipur: Rawat Publications, 2018.

Shashidhar, Ajita. "The Great Branding Campaign that Made PM Modi the Winner." *Business Today*, May 28, 2019. https://www.businesstoday.in/buzztop/buzztop-feature/lok-sabha-eelction-results-2019-pm-narendra-modi-bjp-victory-pm-modi-brand-namo/story/351239.html.

Shastri, Amita, and A. Jeyaratnam Wilson. "Economic Crisis, Momentary Autonomy and Policy Reform: Liberalisation in India 1991–95." In *The Post-Colonial States of South Asia: Democracy, Development, and Identity*, edited by Amita Shastri and A. J. Wilson, 226–51. London: Curzon Press, 2001.

Shenzhen Bureau of Statistics. "1979 Nian Yilai Shenzhen Jingji Shehui Fazhan De Juda Bianhua" [Huge Social and Economic Change in Shenzhen Since 1979]. December 13, 2018. https://www.sohu.com/a/281686154_675420

Shepardson, David. "Nevada to Join Other States in Adopting California Zero Emission Vehicle Rules." *Reuters*. June 22, 2020. https://www.reuters.com/article/us-autos-emissions-usa/nevada-to-join-other-states-in-adopting-california-zero-emission-vehicle-rules-idUSKBN 23U005.

Shih, Victor C. *Factions and Finance in China: Elite Conflict and Inflation.* Cambridge: Cambridge University Press, 2008.

Shih, Victor, Christopher Adolph, and Mingxing Liu. "Getting Ahead in the Communist Party: Explaining the Advancement of Central Committee Members in China." *American Political Science Review* 106, no. 1 (2012): 166–87. https://doi.org/10.1017/S0003055411000566.

Siddiqui, Zeba, Krishna N. Das, Tommy Wilkes, and Tom Lasseter. "In Modi's India, Cow Vigilantes Deny Muslim Farmers Their Livelihood." *Reuters*, November 6, 2017. https://www.reuters.com/investigates/special -report/india-politics-religion-cows/.

Siegel, Reva B. "She the People: The Nineteenth Amendment, Sex Equality, Federalism, and the Family." *Harvard Law Review* 115, no. 4 (2002): 947–1046. https://doi.org/10.2307/1342628.

Siegel, Stephen. "Lochner Era Jurisprudence and the American Constitutional Tradition." *North Carolina Law Review* 70, no. 1 (1991): 1–111. http:// scholarship.law.unc.edu/nclr/vol70/iss1/9

Simon, Karla W. *Civil Society in China: The Legal Framework from Ancient Times to the New Reform Era.* New York: Oxford University Press, 2013.

Sina News. "Qiu He Ceng Zai Suqian Shoutui Ganbu Renyong Gongtui Gongxuan Zhidu" [Qiu He Was the First to Introduce Public Nomination and Public Election System in Suqian]. March 19, 2008. http://news .sina.com.cn/c/2008-03-19/151615181586.shtml.

———. "Wang Yang: Jianshe Da Shehui, Hao Shehui, Xiao Zhengfu, Qiang Zhengfu" [Wang Yang: Building Big Society, Good Society, Small Government, Stong Government]. February 28, 2012. http://news.sina .com.cn/c/2012-02-28/063924018287.shtml.

———. "Wen Jiabao: Gongong Fuwu Ke Shidang Jiao Shehui Zuzhi Chengdan" [Wen Jiabao: Public Service Functions Can Be Partially Transferred To Social Organizations]. March 19, 2012. http://news.sina .com.cn/c/2012-03-19/194224139578.shtml.

Singh, Abhijeet, Albert Park, and Stefan Dercon. "School Meals as a Safety Net: An Evaluation of the Midday Meal Scheme in India." *Economic Development and Cultural Change* 62, no. 2 (2014): 275–306. https://doi .org/10.1086/674097.

Singh, Mahendra Pal. "The Federal Scheme." In *The Oxford Handbook of the Indian Constitution*, edited by Sujit Choudhry, Madhav Khosla, and Pratap Bhanu Mehta, 451–65. Oxford: Oxford University Press, 2016.

Singh, Nirvikar. "Fiscal Federalism." In *The Oxford Handbook of the Indian Constitution*, edited by Sujit Choudhry, Madhav Khosla, and Pratap Bhanu Mehta, 521–39. Oxford: Oxford University Press, 2016.

Singh, Prerna. *How Solidarity Works for Welfare: Subnationalism and Social Development in India*. New York: Cambridge University Press, 2015.

Sinha, Aseema. "The Changing Political Economy of Federalism in India: A Historical Institutionalist Approach." *India Review* 3, no. 1 (January 1, 2004): 25–63. https://doi.org/10.1080/14736480490443085.

Sisodia, Yatindra Singh. *Experiment of Direct Democracy: Gram Swaraj in Madhya Pradesh*. Jaipur: Rawat Publications, 2007.

Sivaram, Anuradha. "Why Citizen Suits against States Would Ensure the Legitimacy of Cooperative Federalism under the Clean Air Act." *Ecology Law Quarterly* 40, no. 2 (2013): 443–82. https://doi.org/10.15779/Z38R85Q.

Sodhi, J. S., and M. S. Ramanujam. "Panchayati Raj System: A Study in Five States of India." *Indian Journal of Industrial Relations* 42, no. 1 (2006): 1–41. https://www.jstor.org/stable/27768050.

Sommers, Benjamin D., Meredith Roberts Tomasi, Katherine Swartz, and Arnold M. Epstein. "Reasons for the Wide Variation in Medicaid Participation Rates among States Hold Lessons for Coverage Expansion in 2014." *Health Affairs* 31, no. 5 (May 2, 2012): 909–19. https://doi.org/10.1377/hlthaff.2011.0977.

South China Morning Post. "Disgraced Officials Zhou Yongkang and Bo Xilai Formed 'Clique' to Challenge Leaders: State Media." January 15, 2015. https://www.scmp.com/news/china/article/1679889/disgraced-officials-zhou-and-bo-formed-clique-challenge-leaders-says.

Southern Metropolis Daily. "Zhengfu Fangquan Gaige, Zainan Yeyao 'Pengyipeng'" [Government Decentralization Reform, Must Try Despite Hardships]. Editorial, December 12, 2012. http://www.shundecity.com/view-53450-1.html.

Spodek, Howard. "In the Hindutva Laboratory: Pogroms and Politics in Gujarat, 2002." *Modern Asian Studies* 44, no. 2 (2010): 349–99. https://doi.org/10.1017/S0026749X08003612.

Srinivasan, Vivek, and Sudha Narayanan. "Food Policy and Social Movements: Reflections on the Right to Food Campaign in India." In *Case Studies in Food Policy for Developing Countries: Policies for Health, Nutrition, Food Consumption, and Poverty*, edited by Per Pinstrup-Andersen and Fuzhi Cheng, 247–59. Ithaca, N.Y.: Cornell University Press, 2019.

Steiner, E. E. "A Progressive Creed: The Experimental Federalism of Justice Brandeis." *Yale Law & Policy Review* 2, no. 1 (1983): 1–48. https://www.jstor.org/stable/40239152.

Stern, Rachel, and Kevin O'Brien. "Politics at the Boundary: Mixed Signals and the Chinese State." *Modern China* 38, no. 2 (2012): 174–98. https://www.jstor.org/stable/23217439.

Strumpf, Koleman S. "Does Government Decentralization Increase Policy Innovation?" *Journal of Public Economic Theory* 4, no. 2 (2002): 207–41. https://doi.org/10.1111/1467-9779.00096.

Sud, Nikita. "The 'Laboratory of Hindutva' Began Experimenting during Vajpayee's Reign." *The Wire*, August 18, 2018. https://thewire.in/communalism/the-laboratory-of-hindutva-began-experimenting-during-vajpayees-reign.

Swaminathan, Padmini. "Tamil Nadu's Midday Meal Scheme: Where Assumed Benefits Score over Hard Data." *Economic and Political Weekly* 39, no. 44 (2004): 4811–21.

Tarr, G. Alan. "Laboratories of Democracy? Brandeis, Federalism, and Scientific Management." *Publius* 31, no. 1 (2001): 37–46. https://doi.org/10.1093/oxfordjournals.pubjof.a004880.

Teele, Dawn Langan. "How the West Was Won: Competition, Mobilization, and Women's Enfranchisement in the United States." *The Journal of Politics* 80, no. 2 (2018): 442–61. https://doi.org/10.1086/696621.

Teets, Jessica C. *Civil Society under Authoritarianism: The China Model.* New York: Cambridge University Press, 2014.

———. "The Evolution of Civil Society in Yunnan Province: Contending Models of Civil Society Management in China." *Journal of Contemporary China* 24, no. 91 (2014): 1–18. https://doi.org/10.1080/10670564.2014.918417.

———. "Let Many Civil Societies Bloom: The Rise of Consultative Authoritarianism in China." *The China Quarterly* 213 (2013): 19–38. https://doi.org/10.1017/S0305741012001269.

Teets, Jessica C., and Reza Hasmath. "The Evolution of Policy Experimentation in China." *Journal of Asian Public Policy* 13, no. 1 (2020): 49–59. https://doi.org/10.1080/10670564.2014.918417.

Teets, Jessica C., and William Hurst. *Local Governance Innovation in China: Experimentation, Diffusion, and Defiance.* London: Routledge, 2014.

Thakur, Ramesh. "The Politics of India's Economic Liberalisation Agenda." *Agenda* 3, no. 2 (1996): 207–17. https://doi.org/10.22459/AG.03.02.1996.08.

"The Declaration of Causes of Seceding States." American Battlefield Trust. Accessed January 8, 2021. https://www.battlefields.org/learn/primary-sources/declaration-causes-seceding-states#lincoln.

"The End of Reconstruction." U.S. History I (AY Collection). Accessed December 8, 2020. https://courses.lumenlearning.com/suny-ushistory1ay/chapter/the-end-of-reconstruction-2/.

"The Pure Food and Drug Act." U.S. House of Representatives: History, Art & Archives. Accessed December 8, 2020. https://history.house.gov/Historical-Highlights/1901-1950/Pure-Food-and-Drug-Act/.

Thomas, Clarence. "Why Federalism Matters." *Drake Law Review* 48, no. 2 (2000): 231–38.

Tillin, Louise. "India's Democracy at 70: The Federalist Compromise." *Journal of Democracy* 28, no. 3 (2017): 64–75. https://doi.org/10.1353/jodx.2017.0045.

———. *Indian Federalism.* Oxford: Oxford University Press, 2019.

Tillin, Louise, Rajeshwari Deshpande, and K. K. Kailash. "Introduction." In *Politics of Welfare: Comparisons across Indian States*, edited by Louise Tillin, Rajeshwari Deshpande, and K. K. Kailash, 1–39. New Delhi: Oxford University Press, 2015.

Tiwari, Nupur. *Panchayati Raj and Women Empowerment: Dependency versus Autonomy.* New Delhi: New Century Publications, 2016.

Tsai, Wen-Hsuan, and Nicola Dean. "Experimentation under Hierarchy in Local Conditions: Cases of Political Reform in Guangdong and Sichuan, China." *The China Quarterly* 218 (2014): 339–58. https://doi.org/10.1017/S0305741014000630.

Tsai, Wen-Hsuan, and Wang Zhou. "Integrated Fragmentation and the Role of Leading Small Groups in Chinese Politics." *The China Journal* 82, no. 1 (2019): 1–22. https://doi.org/10.1086/700670.

Tsai, Wen-Hsuen. "Explaining Political Reform in China's Provinces: A New Perspective from a 'Performance/Faction' Model." *Taiwanese Journal of Political Science*, no. 44 (2010): 105–44.

Tushnet, Mark. "Authoritarian Constitutionalism." *Cornell Law Review* 100, no. 2 (2015): 391–461. http://scholarship.law.cornell.edu/clr/vol100/iss2/3.

UNESCO Institute for Statistics. "Literacy Rate, Adult Total (% of People Ages 15 and above)—India." World Bank. Accessed April 18, 2020. https://data.worldbank.org/indicator/SE.ADT.LITR.ZS?locations=IN.

Van Rooij, B. "The People vs. Pollution: Understanding Citizen Action against Pollution in China." *Journal of Contemporary China* 19, no. 63 (2010): 55–77. https://doi.org/10.1080/10670560903335777.

Varghese, Sanjana. "Why Has Kerala Been So Successful in Tackling Coronavirus?" *The New Statesman*, May 21, 2020. https://www.newstates man.com/world/asia/2020/05/kerala-coronavirus-cases-response-india -KK-Shailaja.

Venkatramani, S. H. "AIADMK Govt in Tamil Nadu Recommends Assembly Dissolution and Simultaneous Polls." *India Today*, December 15, 1984. https://www.indiatoday.in/magazine/indiascope/story/19841215-aiadmk -govt-in-tamil-nadu-recommends-assembly-dissolution-and-simultane ous-polls-803470-1984-12-15.

———. "MGR Banks on Surge of Sympathy for Him to Translate Itself into Votes." *India Today*, December 31, 1984. https://www.indiatoday.in/maga zine/nation/story/19841231-mgr-banks-on-surge-of-sympathy-for-him-to -translate-itself-into-votes-803521-1984-12-31.

Venugopal, Varsha, and Serdar Yilmaz. "Decentralization in Kerala: Panchayat Government Discretion and Accountability." *Public Administration and Development* 29, no. 4 (2009): 316–29. https://doi.org/10.1002 /pad.541.

Verma, Sunny, and P. Vaidyanathan Iyer. "NK Singh: Federalism Desirable for India; Concurrent List, 7th Schedule and Article 282 Require Holistic Review ." *The Indian Express*, September 30, 2020. https:// indianexpress.com/article/business/nk-singh-federalism-desirable-for-india-concurrent-list-7th-schedule-and-article-282-require-holistic -review-6636048/.

Vermont Department of Environmental Conservation. "Zero Emission Vehicles." 2020. https://dec.vermont.gov/air-quality/mobile-sources/zev.

Vogel, Ezra F. *Deng Xiaoping and the Transformation of China*. Cambridge, Mass.: Belknap Press, 2011.

Walker, Jack L. "The Diffusion of Innovations among the American States." *American Political Science Review* 63, no. 3 (1969): 880–99. https://doi .org/10.2307/1954434.

Wang, Alex L., and Jie Gao. "Environmental Courts and the Development of Environmental Public Interest Litigation in China." *Journal of Court Innovation* 3 (2010): 37–50.

Wang, Jin. "The Economic Impact of Special Economic Zones: Evidence from Chinese Municipalities." *Journal of Development Economics* 101, no. 1 (2013): 133–47. https://doi.org/10.1016/j.jdeveco.2012.10.009.

Wang, Peng, and Xia Yan. "Bureaucratic Slack in China: The Anti-Corruption Campaign and the Decline of Patronage Networks in Developing Local Economies." *The China Quarterly* 243 (2020): 611–34. https:// www.cambridge.org/core/article/bureaucratic-slack-in-china-the

-anticorruption-campaign-and-the-decline-of-patronage-networks
-in-developing-local-economies/8CBF5E3B2DEF19012ED980C2F62
FDDFE.

Wang, Shaoguang. "Adapting by Learning: The Evolution of China's Rural Health Care Financing." *Modern China* 35, no. 4 (2009): 370–404. https://doi.org/10.1177/0097700409335381.

Wang, Xuejin. "NGO Zhucenan De Xianzhuang Haiyao Chixu Duojiu" [How Long Will the Difficulty in NGO Registration Last]. *China Youth Daily*, December 15, 2010. http://zqb.cyol.com/content/2010-12/15/content_3463301.htm.

Wang, Yueduan. "'Detaching' Courts from Local Politics? Assessing Judicial Centralization Reforms in China." *The China Quarterly* 246 (2021): 545–64.

Wang, Yueduan, and Sijie Hou. "Breaking the Cycle? China's Recent Attempt to Institutionalize Centralization." *Journal of Contemporary China* 31, no. 138 (2022): 882–97. https://doi.org/10.1080/10670564.2022.2030996.

Wang, Zhengxu, and Deyong Ma. "Participation and Competition: Innovations in Cadre Election and Selection in China's Townships." *Journal of Contemporary China* 24, no. 92 (2014): 298–314. https://doi.org/10.1080/10670564.2014.932164.

Weiner, Myron. "The Regionalization of Indian Politics and Its Implications for Economic Reform." *The Journal of Policy Reform* 2, no. 4 (1998): 337–67. https://doi.org/10.1080/13841289808523389.

Welch, Susan, and Kay Thompson. "The Impact of Federal Incentives on State Policy Innovation." *American Journal of Political Science* 24, no. 4 (1980): 715–29. https://doi.org/10.2307/2110955.

Wheare, K. C. *Federal Government.* 4th ed. New York: Oxford University Press, 1964.

Wilkinson, Steven. *Votes and Violence: Electoral Competition and Ethnic Riots in India.* Cambridge: Cambridge University Press, 2004.

Williams, Norman R. "The Commerce Clause and the Myth of Dual Federalism." *UCLA Law Review* 54, no. 6 (2007): 1847–930.

Winerman, Marc. "The Origins of the FTC: Concentration, Cooperation, Control, and Competition." *Antitrust Law Journal* 71, no. 1 (2003): 1–97.

Wiseman, Hannah J., and Dave Owen. "Federal Laboratories of Democracy." *U.C. Davis Law Review* 52, no. 2 (2018): 1119–91. https://www.jstor.org/stable/40843580.

Witte, Edwin E. "Development of Unemployment Compensation." *The Yale Law Journal* 55, no. 1 (1945): 21–52. https://doi.org/10.2307/792816.

Wong, Christine P. W. "Central-Local Relations Revisited: The 1994 Tax-Sharing Reform and Public Expenditure Management in China." *China Perspectives* 31 (2000): 52–63.

World Bank. "Overview of Rural Decentralization in India." Vol. 1, 2000. http://documents.worldbank.org/curated/en/382081468751537287/pdf/280140v1100INoRuralodecentralization.pdf.

———. "Overview of Rural Decentralization in India." Vol. 2, 2000. http://documents.worldbank.org/curated/en/816981468749991223/pdf/280140v120INoRuralodecentralization.pdf.

Wu, Yuenong. "Xi Zhongxun Yu Woguo Jingji Tequ De Chuangjian" [Xi Zhongxun and the Establishment of SEZs]. *People's Daily Online*, December 27, 2017. http://dangshi.people.com.cn/n1/2017/1227/c85037-29731092.html.

Xinhua News. "1984 Nian Guowuyuan Queding Kaifang 14 Ge Yanhai Gangkou Chengshi" [The State Council Confirmed the Opening of 14 Coastal Port Cities in 1984]. October 7, 2008. http://news.cctv.com/science/20081007/105674.shtml.

———. "Xi Jinping Kaocha Xiaogangcun, Chongwen Zhongguo Gaige Licheng." April 25, 2016. http://www.xinhuanet.com//politics/2016-04/25/c_1118732259.htm.

Xu, Chenggang. "The Fundamental Institutions of China's Reforms and Development." *Journal of Economic Literature* 49, no. 4 (2011): 1076–151. https://www.jstor.org/stable/23071664.

Xu, Qingquan, and Mingming Du. "Baochandaohu Tichu Guocheng Zhong De Gaoceng Zhenglun" [Debates among Top Leaders on the Introduction of Household Responsibility System]. *Yanhuang Chunqiu*, October 9, 2015. http://inews.ifeng.com/yidian/44802306/news.shtml?ch=ref_zbs_ydzx_news.

Yao, Yuerong. "Guanyu Zhongguo Xianfa Yuanyuan De Zairenshi" [Re-Understanding the Source of Constitutional Law in China]. *Legal Science* 9 (2010): 122–31.

Yin, Deyong. "China's Attitude toward Foreign NGOS." *Washington University Global Studies Law Review* 8, no. 3 (2009): 521–43. https://openscholarship.wustl.edu/law_globalstudies/vol8/iss3/4.

Young, Ernest A. "Just Blowing Smoke? Politics, Doctrine, and the Federalist Revival after Gonzales v Raich." *The Supreme Court Review* 2005, no. 1 (2006): 1–50. https://doi.org/10.1086/655193.

Zhang, Guifeng. "Fazhi Ribao: Shehui Zuzhi Guangli Shifang Chu Liangxing Xinhao" [Legal Daily: Social Organization Management Releasing Benign Signals]. *People's Daily Online*, November 25, 2011. http://www .chinanews.com/gn/2011/11-25/3485554.shtml.

Zhang, Taisu, and Tom Ginsburg. "China's Turn toward Law." *Virginia Journal of International Law* 59, no. 2 (2019): 306–89.

Zhang, Weibin. "Nongcun Gaige Qi Damu" [Unveiling Rural Reform]. *Nongmin Ribao*, December 7, 2018. http://www.npc.gov.cn/zgrdw/npc /lfzt/rlyw/2018-12/28/content_2069479.htm.

Zhao, Zhirong Jerry. "Fiscal Decentralization and Provincial-Level Fiscal Disparities in China: A Sino-U.S. Comparative Perspective." *Public Administration Review* 69, no. S1 (2009): S67–74. https://doi.org/10.1111/j .1540-6210.2009.02091.x.

Zhao Ziyang. *Prisoner of the State: The Secret Journal of Zhao Ziyang*. Edited by Pu Bao, Renee Chiang, Adi Ignatius, and Roderick MacFarquhar. New York: Simon & Schuster, 2009.

Zheng, Yongnian. "Explaining the Sources of De Facto Federalism in Reform China: Intergovernmental Decentralization, Globalization, and Central-Local Relations." *Japanese Journal of Political Science* 7, no. 2 (2006): 101–26. https://doi.org/10.1017/S1468109906002222.

"Zhengzhiju Jiu Caishui Tizhi Gaige Jinxing Jiti Xuexi Hu Jintao Zhuchi" [Hu Jintao Hosts Politburo Collective Study on Fiscal and Taxation Reforms]. Government of China, 2010. http://www.gov.cn/ldhd/2010 -01/09/content_1506799.htm.

Zhou, Benshun. "Zou Zhongguo Tese Shehui Guanli Chuangxin Zhilu" [Walk the Path of Social Management Innovation With Chinese Characteristics]. *Qiu Shi* 10 (2011): 37–38.

Zhou, Yongkang. "Jiaqiang He Chuangxin Shehui Guanli, Jianli Jianquan Zhongguo Tese Shehuizhuyi Shehui Guanli Tixi" [Strengthen and Innovate Social Management, Establish and Consolidate Social Management System With Chinese Characteristics]. *Qiu Shi* 9 (2011): 5–11.

Zhu, Suli. "The Division of Power between the Central and Local Governments in Contemporary China: Reinterpretation of Chapter Five of 'On the Ten Prominent Relations' by Mao Zedong." *Social Sciences in China*, no. 2 (2004): 42–55.

———. "Federalism in Contemporary China —A Reflection on the Allocation of Power between Central and Local Government." *Singapore Journal of International & Comparative Law* 7 (2003): 1–14.

Zhu, Xufeng. "Mandate versus Championship: Vertical Government Intervention and Diffusion of Innovation in Public Services in Authoritarian

China." *Public Management Review* 16, no. 1 (2014): 117–39. https://doi.org /10.1080/14719037.2013.798028.

Court Cases

United States

A. L. A. Schechter Poultry Corporation v. United States, 295 U.S. 495 (1935).
Arizona v. Evans, 514 U.S. 1 (1995).
Benton v. Maryland, 395 U.S. 784 (1969).
Boy Scouts of Am. v. Dale, 530 U.S. 640 (2000).
Brown v. Board of Education, 347 U.S. 483 (1954).
Cantwell v. Connecticut, 310 U.S. 296 (1940).
Carter v. Carter Coal Company, 298 U.S. 238 (1936).
Chandler v. Florida, 449 U.S. 560 (1981).
Chicago, Burlington and Quincy Railroad v. City of Chicago, 166 U.S. 226 (1897).
DeJonge v. Oregon, 299 U.S. 353 (1937).
District of Columbia v. Train, 521 F.2d 971 (D.C. Cir. 1).
Fay v. New York, 332 U.S. 261 (1947).
Garcia v. San Antonio Metropolitan Transit Authority, 469 U.S. 528 (1985).
Giles v. Harris, 189 U.S. 475 (1903).
Gitlow v. New York, 268 U.S. 652 (1925).
Gonzales v. Raich, 545 U.S. 1 (2005).
Hammer v. Dagenhart, 247 U.S. 251 (1918).
Helvering v. Davis, 301 U.S. 619 (1937).
Hipolite Egg Co. v. United States, 220 U.S. 45 (1911).
Hoke v. United States, 227 U.S. 308 (1913).
Humphrey's Executor v. United States, 295 U.S. 602 (1935).
Lochner v. New York, 198 U.S. 45 (1905).
Lottery Case, 188 U.S. 321 (1903).
Louisville Joint Stock Land Bank v. Radford, 295 U.S. 555 (1935).
Mapp v. Ohio, 367 U.S. 643 (1961).
Massachusetts v. Environmental Protection Agency, 549 U.S. 497 (2007).
McCulloch v. Maryland, 17 U.S. 316 (1819).
Minor v. Happersett, 88 U.S. 162 (1875).
Miranda v. Arizona, 384 U.S. 436 (1966).
Murphy v. National Collegiate Athletic Association, 138 S. Ct. 1461 (2018).
National Federation of Independent Business v. Sebelius, 567 U.S. 519 (2012).

National League of Cities v. Usery, 426 U.S. 833 (1976).
Near v. Minnesota, 283 U.S. 697 (1931).
New State Ice Co. v. Liebmann, 285 U.S. 262 (1932).
New York v. United States, 505 U.S. 144 (1992).
NFIB v. Sebelius, 567 U.S. 519 (2012).
NLRB v. Jones & Laughlin Steel Corp., 301 U.S. 1 (1937).
Oregon v. Ice, 555 U.S. 160 (2009).
Plessy v. Ferguson, 163 U.S. 537 (1896).
Printz v. United States, 521 U.S. 898 (1997).
Reed v. Reed, 404 U.S. 71 (1971).
Reeves v. Stake, 447 U.S. 429 (1980).
Roe v. Wade, 410 U.S. 113 (1973).
San Antonio Indep. Sch. Dist. v. Rodriguez, 411 U.S. 1 (1973).
South Dakota v. Dole, 483 U.S. 203 (1987).
Steward Machine Co. v. Davis, 301 U.S. 548 (1937).
Stromberg v. California, 283 U.S. 359 (1931).
United States v. Butler, 297 U.S. 1 (1936).
United States v. Darby Lumber Co., 312 U.S. 100 (1941).
United States v. Lopez, 514 U.S. 549 (1995).
United States v. Morrison, 529 U.S. 598 (2000).
Welton v. Missouri, 91 U.S. 275 (1876).
West Coast Hotel Co. v. Parrish, 300 U.S. 379 (1937).
Whalen v. Roe, 429 U.S. 589 (1977).
Wickard v. Filburn, 317 U.S. 111 (1942).
Williams v. Mississippi, 170 U.S. 213 (1898).

India

Bhim Singh v. Union of India (2010) 5 SCC 538 [56].
PUCL v. Union of India and others (Writ Petition [Civil] No. 196 of 2001).
S.R. Bommai v. Union of India, (1994) 2 S.C.R. 644.

Index

Harvard East Asian Monographs
(most recent titles)